THE EAST-WEST CENTER—officially known as the Center for Cultural and Technical Interchange Between East and West—is a national educational institution established in Hawaii by the U.S. Congress in 1960 to promote better relations and understanding between the United States and the nations of Asia and the Pacific through cooperative study, training, and research. The Center is administered by a public, nonprofit corporation whose international Board of Governors consists of distinguished scholars, business leaders, and public servants.

Each year more than 1,500 men and women from many nations and cultures participate in Center programs that seek cooperative solutions to problems of mutual consequence to East and West. Working with the Center's multidisciplinary and multicultural staff, participants include visiting scholars and researchers; leaders and professionals from the academic, government, and business communities; and graduate degree students, most of whom are enrolled at the University of Hawaii. For each Center participant from the United States, two participants are sought from the Asian and Pacific area.

Center programs are conducted by institutes addressing problems of communication, culture learning, environment and policy, population, and resource systems. A limited number of "open" grants are available to degree scholars and research fellows whose academic interests are not encompassed by institute programs.

The U.S. Congress provides basic funding for Center programs and a variety of awards to participants. Because of the cooperative nature of Center programs, financial support and cost-sharing are also provided by Asian and Pacific governments, regional agencies, private enterprise and foundations. The Center is on land adjacent to and provided by the University of Hawaii.

East-West Center Books are published by The University Press of Hawaii to further the Center's aims and programs.

*Japanese Patterns
of Behavior*

Japanese Patterns of Behavior

Takie Sugiyama Lebra

AN EAST-WEST CENTER BOOK
The University Press of Hawaii
Honolulu

First printing 1976
Second printing 1979

Book design by Roger J. Eggers
Cover design by A. O. K. Hammond

Library of Congress Cataloging in Publication Data

Lebra, Takie Sugiyama, 1930-
  Japanese patterns of behavior.

  "An East-West Center book."
  Bibliography: p.
  Includes index.
  1. National characteristics, Japanese.
2. Japan—Social life and customs. I. Title.
DS821.L346   301.29'52   76-10392
ISBN 0-8248-0396-5
ISBN 0-8248-0460-0 pbk.

To Bill

Contents

Preface ix

Introduction xiii

1. Social Relativism as the Japanese Ethos:
   A Postulate 1

2. Belongingness 22

3. Empathy 38

4. Dependency 50

5. Occupying the Proper Place 67

6. Reciprocity 90

7. The Three Domains of Situational Interaction 110

8. Early Socialization 137

9. Selfhood 156

10. Organized Delinquency:
    Yakuza as a Cultural Example 169

11. Suicide 190

12. Culturally Based Moral Rehabilitation:
    The Naikan Method 201

13. *Shinkeishitsu* and Morita Therapy   215

14. Spirit Possession: The "Salvation Cult"   232

15. Conclusion   248

    Appendix   259

    Bibliography   271

    Index   289

Preface

Over the years, I have taught Japanese culture and behavior at the University of Hawaii. Confronted with the challenge of communicating in English (not my native tongue) with a large number of multiethnic students, including many Japanese Americans, I found myself in a perpetual search for a way of organizing and presenting lectures that would lower cultural thresholds and maximize receptivity. This effort to achieve intercultural communication has resulted in this book.

The Japanese have been studied and reported about so often and by so many people of all backgrounds that it might appear that there is little left to say about them. Nevertheless, we continue to encounter the amazement, fascination, or exasperation expressed by foreigners—be they newspaper correspondents, travelers in Japan, observers of Japanese tourists abroad, or TV watchers. In many respects the Japanese still do "strange," "surprising," "hilarious" things, or their behavior simply makes "no sense." I hope to dispel such puzzlement about the Japanese by explaining why they behave as they do. If the reader begins to make sense out of what used to perplex him about Japanese behavior, I would feel my goal achieved.

I have drawn upon several sources of information. I have consulted part of the enormous amount of literature available on the Japanese, including scientific and nonscientific, professional and popular publications. While Western and other non-

Japanese writers are not ignored, I have paid as much attention to what the Japanese have said and written about themselves. The insider's self-conceptualization may illuminate something that no outsider can hope to grasp, whereas the outsider can spot the insider's culture blindness. Although historical materials are referred to now and then, the focus is on information regarding contemporary Japan. This does not contradict my belief that historical continuity is a defining criterion of culture. My aim is to delineate those aspects of culture and behavior that are both observable in contemporary scenes and that are considered to have persisted roughly over the last one hundred years. What is happening today, dramatic or routine, will be interpreted in light of historically based cultural regularity. The "present," where I stand writing this book, refers to the time span of 1972 to 1973.

A second source of information is the fund of personal experiences I have accumulated during many years of "naïve" participation in Japanese culture. Instead of being inhibited by the scientific norm prescribing full public accessibility to the source of information, I shall take advantage of the private availability of a native's memory. The only methodology conceivable here is what might be called introspection.

A third source of information also involves my own experiences, but as a critical observer, not as a naïve participant. I visited Japan four summers in a row from 1968 to 1971, and made two more short trips in 1972 and 1973, to do fieldwork in a provincial city, which I have chosen to call Eastern City, not very far from Tokyo. Whether the residents of Eastern City represent average Japanese remains to be determined. I have no reason not to believe, however, that Eastern City is representative of the rapidly urbanizing, tourist-oriented provincial cities of today's Japan. My fieldwork centered on two topics, occupation and religion. In studying occupation, I conducted open-ended interviews with individuals of different occupations ranging from priest to gardener to cook. The informants were asked to recall the experiences of their occupational lives. In studying religion, I selected the local branches of a sect that I have designated the Salvation Cult. Fieldwork included interviews with local members and attendance at branch meetings. Some of those findings are given in chapter 14.

What I saw and heard in my contacts with all these informants was most enlightening for my understanding of the Japanese and myself. Descriptions of the Japanese in this book reflect this field experience, whether or not specific reference is made to a given informant.

Along with the study of occupation and religion, I investigated the state of moral values held by Japanese as revealed in projective tests. To this end, I first administered a Japanese version of the Thematic Apperception Test to residents of Eastern City ranging in age from junior high school children to adults. Second, I designed and administered a sentence-completion test to two groups of residents, high school students and middle-aged adults, representing postwar and prewar generations, respectively. This was intended to elicit responses indicative of moral expectations and sensitivity and to reveal any generation gap in this respect (Lebra 1971*b*). The findings were so illuminating of Japanese culture and behavior that I have included some of them in tabular form as an appendix to this volume. The reader will occasionally be referred to the Appendix, which shows where the younger generation differs from or accords with the older generation on cultural values.

Finally, I have lived long enough in Hawaii to have studied the characteristics of Japanese Americans, especially the Issei (first-generation immigrants), Nisei (immigrants' children), and Sansei (immigrants' grandchildren). Japanese Americans in Hawaii cannot be lumped with the Japanese in Japan as bearers of the same culture, and I have no intention of using this source of information directly. However, contact with Japanese Americans has given me new insight into the Japanese, inasmuch as Japanese American behavior manifests the overinternalization and compulsive retention of some aspects of classical Japanese culture. Even the way many Japanese Americans reject anything Japanese has been informative about Japanese culture.

It might sound trite to say that teaching is the best way of learning, but this is very true with me. Both the students who have responded to my presentations enthusiastically and those who have dismissed them as boring or incomprehensible have stimulated me to work toward greater clarity of analysis. William P. Lebra, my husband and colleague, has contributed to this work with insightful and often witty comments, warm companionship, and shared housework. The competent staff and student assistants at the Social Science Research Institute, University of Hawaii, have rendered indispensable assistance in the completion of the manuscript. Christine D'Arc Sakaguchi has demonstrated her editorial expertise in improving my writing.

I also wish to acknowledge the financial support of the National Institute of Mental Health (Grant MH09243), which has enabled me to do research in culture and mental health and thus has contributed to this book directly and indirectly.

Introduction

This volume is an endeavor to shed light upon what the Japanese are like, with a focus upon their behavior in the cultural context. I hope the reader will gain a better understanding of the behavior patterns as manifested within a culture that has been generated and accumulated, taught and learned, carried and circulated, believed in and acted out by the Japanese. Before launching into the subject, I propose to spell out the general lines of orientation and the commitment of this book. The reader is requested to indulge my compulsion for getting involved in a somewhat pedagogical discourse, but the following are the theoretical and methodological foundations of the rest of the book.

ETHNOGRAPHIC BOUNDARY

The Japanese are, in countless ways, similar to other nationals, and it goes without saying that their behavior, however extraordinary it might often appear, does not go beyond the limit of humanly possible variation. It is equally important to assume that studying the Japanese should lead to a deeper understanding of human culture and behavior. It would be legitimate to observe Japanese behavior as a sample of the behavior of Homo sapiens. Let this stress upon universality be called a nomothetic point of view.

The nomothetic point of view in its extreme form has its pitfalls and weaknesses, however. I am not confident of the extent to which we know human universals with regard to culture and behavior. I am afraid that an observer tends to confuse his own culture with universal culture and thus tends to impose his ethnocentric interpretation upon the culture he is observing. And when he encounters something that does not appear universal at all, he might well dismiss it as nothing more than a random error. Furthermore what can be identified as definitely universal tends to be too obvious to deserve special attention. The nomothetic extreme is thus apt either to encourage the observer to commit an ethnocentric sin or to result in the generation of little information.

This book, following the ethnographic tradition, is committed to drawing a boundary of Japanese culture under the assumption that no other culture shares completely the same boundary. In this limited sense, my bias is more toward an idiographic point of view. Positively, I believe this is a more efficient approach to the area-bound culture of a national society; negatively, I am too agnostic about human culture to claim the universality of the Japanese at the outset. To be sure, it is more risky to say that the Japanese are different from the Chinese or Americans than to stress cross-cultural similarities. But I am willing to take that risk.

The concept of area-bound cultures calls our attention, furthermore, to the phenomenon of culture borrowing from other areas, particularly from neighboring cultures. It is only natural, because of such diffusion and resultant acculturation, that Japanese differ from Koreans and Chinese less than from Africans and Europeans. In addition, the Japanese are known for their eagerness to borrow indiscriminately. Despite the fact that such borrowing is likely to obliterate cultural differences, it is also known that the Japanese have maintained their identity, and that nothing has been borrowed without becoming Japanized to some degree. This provides historical justification for considering Japanese culture unique.

This idiographic commitment is not without qualifications. First, even a unique system cannot be understood unless it is viewed against general concepts and propositions. Thus, universally applicable concepts and theories derived from social science will be freely imposed in order to locate Japan uniquely in a universal map. Logically, we should start from a universal statement and proceed to a statement that identifies particular instances of Japanese culture and behavior; the latter statement, in turn, is expected to contribute to the understanding of human culture and behavior in general. Second, the claimed uniqueness of Japanese culture holds for its system as a whole, but not for all the specific sectors thereof. Taken out of the systemic context, there may well be many elements that are shared by Japanese and others alike. Unless we keep this qualification in mind, we may be tempted to read "peculiarly Japanese" into everything a Japanese does. Overexaggeration of uniqueness is another version of ethnocentrism, which allows no cross-cultural comparison. The ideological implication of "culture relativism," I believe, joins with ethnocentrism rather than opposes it as is often claimed. How, then, can we reconcile an idiographic viewpoint with cross-cultural comparability? I claim that two cultures are not comparable if taken as wholes but are comparable as far as some properly selected parts of each culture are concerned.

The argument above partially overlaps with the emic-etic controversy, the controversy over the priority of either the subjective standpoint held by cultural insiders or the objective judgment by an outsider. I think that it goes right against the anthropological principle to regard the two as opposed to each other, to pit etic against emic. "Emic description requires etics, and by trying to do emic descriptions we add to our etic conceptual resources for subsequent description" (Goodenough 1968:112).

Culture and Behavior

Culture is manifested in various forms. Social anthropologists study culture as it is manifested in social institutions, such as kin groups, economic organizations, power structures, and so on. Mythology, art, literature, language, and other symbolic representations are another form. This book approaches Japanese culture from the point of view of the behavior of participants in that culture. It attempts to throw light upon the area where culture and behavior intersect. Reference to social institutions and symbolic representations may also be made, but only to illuminate Japanese behavior.

We must begin by clarifying both culture and behavior and their relationship to each other. In line with the viewpoints of Keesing and Keesing (1971), I suggest that culture is a set of general, abstract, or ideational symbols, whereas behavior is a series of observable, specific, muscular, organism-attached motions or postures. Behavior is a manifestation of, or a vehicle for conveying, culture. Two analytically distinct functions of culture may be suggested in relation to behavior. First, culture provides a meaning, explanation, or interpretation for an observed behavior. Culture is, then, a set of cognitive codes whereby the otherwise meaningless behavior is made meaningful. A certain behavior of a Japanese may make no sense to a foreigner until he becomes aware of that sector of Japanese culture that explains it. Second, culture gives a set of alternative directions for behavior. Involved here are a destination of behavior, namely, the goal or end to which behavior is oriented, pathways or means to reach the destination, and norms and rules controlling behavior toward that destination.

Two Dimensions of Value

In short, this book attempts to delineate a set of culturally meaningful, culturally standardized behaviors—but not all such behaviors. The Japanese person beckons to someone by a gesture similar to one that would mean goodbye among Americans; he refers to himself by pointing to his nose with his index finger, while the American tends to indicate the same by touching his chest with his thumb. These certainly represent culturally meaningful and guided behavior, but they are not relevant to my objective. I want to locate what is essential to the ordinary Japanese, to identify what their life goals are, what elates them or upsets them, what makes them happy or unhappy, pleased or angry—what "turns the Japanese on." In other words, I am interested in those aspects of cultural behavior that are "value-charged."

What is value and how does it relate to behavior? Drawing upon theoretical contributions by Parsons and his associates (Parsons 1951; Parsons and Shils 1951), I suggest two dimensions of value, each of which is conceptualized in a dichotomy. One dimension refers to (1) the obligatory-desirable dichotomy. A value as an obligatory standard is inhibitive, and may be perceived as a constraint or burden. A value as a desirable attribute, on the other hand, corresponds with the affective aspect of behavior; it is something that carries emotional attachment, is voluntarily sought. The one is a more or less objective criterion for choice, whereas the other is embedded in the subjective realm. This distinction may be difficult to draw, as in the case of a well-internalized moral standard. Nonetheless, precisely because of value-internalization, this distinction seems necessary as a means of appraising the possible range of fluctuation of a given value. A value may become manifest as a desirable in one situation, and as an obligatory or even prohibitory rule of conduct in another situation.

The other dimension of value refers to (2) the expressive-instrumental dichotomy. A value is expressive if it is exalted as an end in itself, whereas a value is instrumental if it is considered a useful means to an end. A certain status or power position may be desired or glorified as an expressive value by some people, while others may seek it instrumentally as a means of acquiring yet another value. Even religious belief can be instrumental as well as expressive, as suggested by the Marxian label "opiate." Such variation implies the complementarity of the two aspects of value. A value cannot be instrumentally desirable unless it is expressively valuable. Using the above example, a status would have no instrumental value to one person unless it were regarded as an end value by another person. Conversely, unless the status had some instrumental utility, its expressive value would eventually decline.

CONFLICT AND ALTERNATIVES

Once culture is defined as a repertoire of values or a hierarchy of values, it becomes apparent that no culture is conflict-free because value presupposes scarcity and involves choice. A valued object or attribute, such as wealth, status, or power, generates conflict and competition among seekers for that value because of its scarcity. One person's success in obtaining a valued object reduces or eliminates another person's accessibility to it. Furthermore, value compels the actor to make choices, decisions, and commitments. Choice of one value necessitates giving up another, perhaps equally desirable, value because "he who runs after two hares will catch neither," or "one cannot eat one's cake and have it too." Once a decision is made and the "Plan" (Miller, Galanter, and Pribram 1960) is executed, one must follow a more or less fixed course of action; one's decision becomes one's "vested interest." Both scarcity and the need for choice thus constrain action and generate conflict and ambivalence, which ultimately obstruct the channels for articulating, transmitting, or regularizing the value system.

This logically conceivable conflict within a culture necessitates a recognition of alternative values side-by-side with dominant values. American culture, for example, juxtaposes individualism and egalitarianism. Japanese culture places emphasis upon achievement and striving for success, but at the same time preaches the virtue of resignation and serenity. In a pioneering study of Japanese culture and personality, Ruth Benedict encountered "the most fantastic series of 'but also's' ever used for any nation of the world." The Japanese were found to be extremely polite "but also insolent and overbearing"; rigid but also innovative; submissive but not amenable to control; loyal but spiteful, and so on (1946:1-2). Japanese authors, too, have pointed out such dichotomies in Japanese culture as the samurai vs. the peasant tradition and repression vs. naturalism (Kawashima 1949; Sofue 1972). The two sets of values appear logically contradictory but seem functionally complementary or necessary. I am tempted to state a priori that Benedict's "but also's" apply not only to Japanese but to all other cultures.

INTERACTION

The foregoing discussion on values indicates my approach to this entire work. My objective is to set forth the dynamic, conflict-ridden interplay of the components of culture in conjunction with individual behavior. This further relates to the importance attached throughout this volume to social interaction between individuals or groups as the key linkage between culture and behavior. The reader might detect my intellectual debt to such interaction-oriented social scientists as Simmel, G. H. Mead, Goffman, and Bateson. The interaction focus should provide another explanation for variation and contrast, as well as uniformity and redundancy, in behavior from individual to individual within a culture. I will leave the task of elaborating this point to the rest of this volume. The same issue will be tackled theoretically in the concluding chapter.

CHAPTER 1

Social Relativism as the Japanese Ethos: A Postulate

CULTURE LABELING

Let us begin our delineation of Japanese culture and behavior by singling out the chief characteristic of the Japanese ethos. The term "ethos" may belong in an anthropological museum, but I am reviving it here to convey both the thematic distinctiveness and entirety of the Japanese cultural matrix. This chapter is an attempt to attach a proper label to the Japanese ethos.

Admittedly it is presumptuous and dangerous to label a culture, and the history of anthropology contains ample warnings against it. Witness the severe criticism Benedict incurred from both Japanese and non-Japanese for her labeling of Japanese culture as "shame culture" (1946). Nonetheless, I believe that labeling is a necessary initial step in understanding anything at all. The question What is X? can begin to be answered by giving a name to X.

What should be indicted is not the label or stereotype per se but the value judgment or prejudice often attached to it. I have no evidence that Benedict consciously used "shame culture" as a pejorative. But many Japanese readers reacted against it, not only because they believed it to be untrue but apparently because they felt insulted. If the label conveyed a Western prejudice, the Japanese native had to defend his culture against it. This is a warning against the temptation to rely upon another culture as the ideal reference point and to find one's own culture deficient simply because it deviates from that ideal. Some Japanese writers themselves have been trapped in the temptation to take Western culture as the universal standard and to describe the Japanese with such negative adjectives as "immature" and "backward." On the other hand, the same Japanese would show no resistance to more flattering labels such as industrious, achievement-oriented, and intelligent, and would willingly believe in the superior quality of the Japanese race.

When I propose a label for Japanese culture, I intend it to be as value-free as possible, neither insulting nor flattering. To be sure, labeling involves hunches and speculation on my part. Throughout this chapter I try to set forth my assumptions and rationale so that the reader may better verify the postulate presented here in the chapters to come.

Social Preoccupation

The overwhelming impression from the literature, as well as from my personal observations, is that the Japanese are extremely sensitive to and concerned about social interaction and relationships. Among the different kinds of things people can relate to, the Japanese seem most sensitized to "social" objects, namely, other human beings, *hito* in Japanese (*hito* means both "person[s]" and "other person[s]"). When the individual experiences inner pleasure or pain, joy or suffering, hope or despair, he tends to be preoccupied with his relationship to some *hito*. I shall call this orientation "social preoccupation."

Let us agree on some other terms. Social interaction or relationships can best be analyzed by singling out the central actor and then identifying his social object. I shall call the central actor "Ego" and his social object "Alter," both terms being capitalized to signify their social emphasis as distinct from their psychological implications. The Japanese speaker would differentiate Ego and Alter as *Jibun* and *Hito*.

Alter, who is the main object of preoccupation for the Japanese Ego, may be in regular contact with Ego or may be inaccessible except on special occasions and thus only recalled from memory. Alter may be a single person or a group; Alter and Ego may be of equal standing or hierarchically graded; their relationship may be lifelong or only transient, a desirable one Ego wants to maintain or an undesirable one from which Ego wishes to extricate himself. We can think of many other variations, yet they are all identical with respect to social preoccupation. Because of the variety of relationships involved, "social preoccupation" differs from David Riesman's (1955) "other-directed," which is used in a much narrower sense.

If the social preoccupation of the Japanese is to be taken as a hypothesis, there should be a ground whereupon it can be refuted. What orientations other than social preoccupation are conceivable, then? This question boils down to What objects are there other than social? Following the Parsonian scheme (Parsons 1951; Parsons and Shils 1951), we can place all possible objects of behavior in one of three categories: social, physical, and symbolic. Let us consider, first, preoccupation with physical objects. Physical objects include both what exists in nature and what is produced by human energy and technology. They constitute the physical environment that interests Ego as the object of adaptation and accommodation, subjugation and exploitation, scientific cognition and esthetic appreciation, or faith and fear. Ego may be preoccupied with producing, owning and accumulating, or consuming and enjoying a physical object that may or may not be convertible into money.

How do the Japanese react to this world of physical things? Take their esthetic attitude toward nature, for instance. It is widely believed by foreigners and Japanese alike that the Japanese are nature lovers (see, for example, Haga 1968:251-256). Closer observation reveals that when a Japanese turns to the beauty of nature he seems to do so either as a temporary escape from the trouble-ridden social world or as a very expression of his social preoccupation. Even the prescribed reference to the season in haiku poetry is most often a subtle means of conveying a message to someone or as a metaphor of a social relationship.

The more familiar category, food, offers another example. The Japanese like food as much as other peoples do, but for the Japanese eating and drinking are inseparable from social interactions and gatherings. The husband comes home drunk late at night with the excuse that he was compelled by friendship to go drinking with his colleagues. Even the most distrustful, unforgiving wife understands, if not tolerates, the irresistibility of social drinking. The sociologist Ikutaro Shimizu has pointed out that

Japanese plays on television are filled with scenes of eating and drinking. He attributes it to the fact that the Japanese do not know how to enjoy conversation as a social technique; they use their mouths primarily for eating instead of speaking (1968:204-205). I think, rather, that the Japanese converse with one another *by* eating and drinking together.

The same is true of production and possession of wealth. The Japanese are indeed proud of being, in the free world, second only to the United States in Gross National Product, and no one would deny their diligence and productivity. Their ultimate objective, however, seems to be a socially motivated one in that they want to be second, and eventually first, primarily to have that status in the eyes of the world. The Japanese may appear more materialistic than any other people if one only looks at the compulsive way they covet or acquire the newest model of every product, whether an automobile or a vacuum cleaner. But here again I believe that their motivation is less materialistic than it is social—that they are motivated by the fear of being left out or behind, or by the wish to be a little ahead, of others. The same orientation, then, is likely to make them responsive to the presently heard world outcry for ecological conservation.

I do not mean that establishment of a desirable social relationship is always an end, and that everything else, such as acquisition of wealth, is only a means to that end; the very opposite may well be true. The point is that in order to attain an end—whether social or nonsocial—the creation, maintenance, or manipulation of a relevant social relationship is a foremost and indispensable means. Hence, elaborate co-drinking and co-dining, funded by the "expense account," precede a business transaction.

These examples suggest that social preoccupation overwhelms the Japanese Ego, even when he is acting upon a physical object. Let us turn to the other nonsocial object, that is, the symbolic object. The symbolic object refers to a set of meanings, concepts, or values that are expressed in language or other equivalent symbols and signs. Beliefs, ideologies, information—all these are included in this category.

Of course, the exchange of symbols presupposes social actors: information sent by Ego must be received by Alter; the scholar who discovers and records meanings must find his readers; the creative artist needs an appreciative audience; the prophet hopes his doctrine will be heard and accepted. It is also true that the world of symbols is not totally dependent upon the social relations of its users but is governed by its own logic. Without the independence of the symbolic from the social world, it would be difficult to understand why one can enjoy reading a novel without knowing its author; why an able sociologist can be like a child in handling actual social situations; why a man, when committed to a revolutionary cause, can transcend his social ties and obligations.

In dealing with symbols, too, the Japanese seem socially oriented. The truthfulness or value of a given symbolic system is likely to be judged by the personality of its producer or sender, or by the kind of relationship obtaining between its sender and receiver. An extreme example is found among the *yakuza*, members of the Japanese underworld, where whatever the boss says is to be taken by his subordinate as true, "even if he says white is black." Here a particular social bond, loyalty, determines the truthfulness of a statement. This might be dismissed as a deviant case, too remote from the average Japanese. However, a similar social influence is recognizable even in the academic world, where truth is supposedly pursued for its own sake. A professor and his subordinate (of professorial or lower rank) in the same department can be so linked by obligation that the latter will rarely challenge even a professional paper by the former.

The Japanese press publishes, week by week, month after month, an enormous amount of what might be called biographical essays on certain individuals. This alone indicates the prevalence of an intense curiosity among the Japanese as to what other people are like. More significant is the fact that few of these essays lead the reader to a better knowledge of the subject. The writer is more likely to reveal a particular relationship between himself and the subject, friendly or hostile, than to provide objective information on the person. A friend will emerge as an impeccable personality, whereas an enemy will be described as grievously flawed. Both are worthless as far as information goes.

Social preoccupation also seems responsible for the Japanese style of humanism, or better, anthropocentrism. It is my hunch that people who are socially preoccupied tend to reduce even nonsocial objects, whether symbolic or physical, to human size. This inhibits curiosity about the unreal world of extravagance and gigantism. As anthropocentrism in this sense will be touched upon later, suffice it here to note what Isaiah BenDasan said about the Japanese in comparison with the Jews. For the Japanese, *ningensei* ("humanity" or "human-beingness") takes precedence over everything else. *Ningensei*, in other words, comprises the primary reality, whereas symbolic representations like law, words, and reason remain only secondary; the Japanese thus are cognizant and respectful of "law behind law," "words behind words," and "reason behind reason" (1970:55-85). By contrast, says BenDasan, the Jews take law, words, and reason literally and seriously.

I have taken a roundabout way in my efforts to characterize the Japanese in terms of social preoccupation, trying to rule out other possibilities. I have attempted to provide a clue to the question of why the Japanese invest so much sensitivity, compulsiveness, circumspection, and refinement to the creation or maintenance of smooth and pleasant social relationships. They distinguish themselves by doing so not for the sake of a marital or family relationship but for other social relationships, even at the expense of the former. In this respect the Japanese are different from the Chinese and Koreans, not to mention Americans or Israelis. It may be that these East Asians outside Japan have had to be more concerned than have the Japanese with survival needs and therefore with physical well-being; if so, BenDasan is right in describing the Japanese as a bunch of suffering-free, "well-protected boys" who take for granted the free availability of "water and safety" (1970:9-25). Perhaps the conditions of their societies have made it more difficult for the Koreans or Chinese than for the Japanese to establish solidarity and mutual trust over and beyond those founded upon kinship. Francis L. K. Hsu remarked in a personal conversation that the Chinese do not feel as much affinity with people outside the kin group as do the Japanese. It is also possible that the Chinese and Koreans have internalized Confucian teachings more intensely or compulsively than have the Japanese, so that the symbolic system of Confucianism directs their behavior and stands in the way of their social sensitization.

INTERACTIONAL RELATIVISM

We must now consider the characteristics of the action or actor influenced by social preoccupation. What are the main differences between the socially preoccupied action and the action determined by preoccupation with symbols or physical objects? If the object of action is symbolic or physical, the actor is likely to single out what might be called the prime mover. The prime mover may be located on the side of either the actor or the object. To the extent the actor feels that physical or symbolic objects are to be created, manipulated, exploited, or controlled, the prime mover exists within the actor and may be identified as his wish, goal, or power. If, conversely, these objects are taken as the ultimate reality or irresistible force that demands reverence and submission, the prime mover exists on the side of the object world. The prime mover may be identified variously as the cause, origin, purpose, initiator, or controller of the behavior of elements of the universe. Influence flows unilaterally from center to periphery. I call this orientation "unilateral determinism."

One might think that I have a monotheistic religion in mind; indeed, monotheism fits here, with an absolute god as the prime mover. But the prime mover may take various forms: a "spirit," as in Hegelian metaphysics; and "idea," as in Platonic realism; the so-called natural law; or from the point of view of historicism, "history." Nor does it have to be of such lofty quality. The prime mover could be an individual human being, either superhuman, such as a dictator or a savior, or an ordinary citizen, as in sanctified individualism. Or, as in the tradition of metaphysical materialism, it may be "matter" that determines every phenomenon. Running through all these is the ethos of unilateral determinism.

If the actor is primarily concerned with a social object, as the Japanese are, his actions will be governed by something far removed from unilateral determinism. The Japanese Ego acts upon or toward Alter with the awareness or anticipation of Alter's response, and Alter in turn, by responding according to or against Ego's expectation, influences Ego's further action. If Ego talks, Alter is likely to talk back, and thus they will alternate in a chain of interaction until a conversational trajectory is felt completed. Activation of the chain cannot be attributed to either Ego or Alter exclusively but to both or to the relationship between the two. The actor is unable to locate the prime mover and is likely to be indifferent to its existence. Instead, he is more aware of influence flowing both ways between himself and his object. I call this orientation "interactional relativism."

In interactional relativism, an actor acts in a certain way not because he is forced to do so by an external prime mover such as an environmental force, nor because he is driven by an internal prime mover such as an irresistible passion or desire; his behavior is, rather, a result of interaction and mutual influence between himself and his object. In a culture dominated by interactional relativism, even a supernatural actor, not to mention a human actor, may become involved in a reciprocal deal with other beings, supernatural, human, or subhuman. Even a dictator, when viewed as a social subject or object rather than in light of the political ideology for which he stands or of the physical power behind him, does not appear unilaterally influential but bound by mutual influence. I might add that a culture permeated by interactional relativism is not prone to produce a dictator, a topic to which I will return later in this chapter.

Unilateral determinism seems to entail epistemological and ideological compulsions to differentiate or separate one element from another: subject from object, one object from another object, the supernatural from the natural, human from infrahuman species, mind from matter, infinite from finite, true from false, right from wrong, white from black, winning from losing, yes from no, and so on. Interactional relativism, by contrast, tends to suppress such distinctions and, rather, tends to connect things that appear discrete. For this reason, interactional relativism may be said to be accompanied by an imperative of interlocking and fusion, whereas unilateral determinism is accompanied by an imperative of differentiation and separation.

Where unilateral determinism prevails, the behavior of a certain actor tends to be explainable clearly and simply: "That's what I wanted," "So-and-so ordered him to do it," "It is so written in the Bible," and the like. Explaining actions governed by interactional relativism involves situational variability and complexity and consideration of the overall balance among relevant factors. The whole thing "depends."

The two types depicted here are ideal types that cannot be found in any existing culture. However, it seems safe to say that the Japanese ethos has more affinity with interactional relativism than with unilateral determinism, whereas traditional Western culture comes closer to the latter than the former. Whether other cultures such as the Chinese or Fijian can also be characterized by their relative distance from these types remains to be seen, although I have a hunch that Chinese culture, for example, is less distant from unilateral determinism than is Japanese culture.

SOCIAL RELATIVISM

My assumption is that social preoccupation and interactional relativism imply each other, the one being conducive to the other, and that the two together characterize the Japanese ethos. "Social relativism" is the term for this combination.

Because of the primacy of social interaction and relationships in Japan, I have called Japanese culture a "sociocult" in the sense that society is the object of deification (Lebra 1971a). However, this label may be misleading to the extent that it implies unidirectional influence or control by society over individual actors. It is the "interaction" or "relationship," not society as an entity, that is deified. The weakness of "sociocult" as a label is rectified, I believe, by the term "social relativism." What I mean by social relativism is far from Durkheimean sociologism expounded in *The Elementary Forms of the Religious Life* (Durkheim 1961), in which "Society" looms as the prime mover. Durkheim's social philosophy belongs definitely to unilateral determinism.

Social relativism as the Japanese ethos is what this book is all about, and detailed analyses of its components will be made in the following chapters. But let us here take a brief overview as an introduction.

Cosmology

Drawing upon two well-known chronicles of antiquity, the *Kojiki* and *Nihongi*, Pelzel (1970) describes Japanese myths as reflective of an earth-bound cosmology. The myth-makers do not seem to have had imagination beyond this earth, especially the earth "the Japanese knew" (p. 41). This does not mean that the Japanese had no concept of the supernatural. Rather, supernatural beings were brought down to human status, sharing the earthly dwelling and a this-worldly way of life with their human counterparts.

Japanese indifference to the transcendental realm has also been pointed out by Yaichi Haga (1968), a well-known scholar who was influential in prewar school education. The Japanese remained this-worldly even after the importation of Buddhism, which introduced another world of prior and future existences.

Not only have the Japanese used Buddhism to insure their this-worldly welfare, but they have never been sympathetic to the Buddhistic alienation from this life. Instead, says Haga, the Japanese often make fun of Buddhism by sacrilegious references to *hotoke* ("Buddhas") in proverbs, folk sayings, and comedies. Supernatural beings, particularly those borrowed from foreign countries, are subject to ridicule, whether they are Buddhas or Seven Gods of Fortune. This does not imply arrogance on the part of the Japanese but the lack of a clear differentiation in the Japanese mind between this world and the other world, man and Buddha, life and death (pp. 246-251, 260). I might add that Haga did not consider this characteristic of the Japanese undesirable or regrettable at all.

Similarly, for the Japanese, man has no claim to superiority over other animals; even inanimate things behave like humans. Japan's unique contribution to the study of primates has been attributed by a Japanese anthropologist to a Japanese sense of intimacy between man and monkeys (E. Ishida et al. 1971:18). Imbued with a sense of harmony and affinity between the supernatural and natural, and between man and other forms of life, the ancient Japanese seem to have been indifferent to ontological speculation on the universe and human existence. Japanese culture has since been exposed to foreign cultures, such as Chinese, Buddhist, and, later, European. But the Japanese have not changed fundamentally in this respect, as Pelzel observed. This cosmological "humanism," Japanese style, may be said to accord with social relativism in that social relativism demands that all elements of the universe be related horizontally and mutually, that they share the same "human" status, rather than being hierarchically controlled with the ultimate keeper of the order at the top.

The affinity between humans and lower forms of life that characterizes Japanese cosmology is not shared by Chinese, let alone Judeo-Christian, cosmology. According to Pelzel:

> In the Chinese myths, physical nature is pictured as only a passive entity. It is troublesome for man because he still, at that early date, lacked the cultural artifact to exploit its inertness for his own benefit. The continental heroes were therefore inventors of artifacts and customs—of ditches to drain the swamps, or plows to tear the grass-matted soil, thus techniques for growing grain. The

Chinese view thus assumed an absolute gulf of nature between man and even beasts, let alone the "lower" order of life. Man adores man, and only man. (1970:47)

In this passage we can find a suggestion of unilateral determinism, with Man, instead of God, as the keeper of universal order. In contrast, "the task of the [Japanese] culture heroes was to make nature civil, removing from it the troublesome qualities of speech, mobility, and violence" (p. 47).

Morality

An earthly cosmology is further reflected in the sphere of morality. The clear-cut dualism of good and bad, right and wrong that is characteristic of unilateral determinism is not congenial to the Japanese sense of morality. For the Japanese, goodness or badness is a relative matter, relative to social situation and impact, whose complexity may often be beyond any judge's comprehension. The Japanese are used to sayings like: "Even a thief may be 30 percent right"; "To hold a grudge against others is not good, but to do something that arouses a grudge in others is just as bad." The Japanese tend to hold everyone involved in a conflict responsible for it. The Anglo-American compulsion for a court trial that determines one party to be guilty and the other innocent is in remarkable contrast to the Japanese ideal that mutual apology and compromise be attained between the parties before the conflict attracts public attention. If in the Western case the verdict is "recorded" once and for all in the collective as well as individual memory, the Japanese solution lies in the consignment of what has happened to oblivion. While the culture that has internalized the moral authority of a Jehovah reveals "inhuman" intolerance against rule-breakers because of the conviction of man's moral impeccability, Japanese morality stresses recognition of man's frailty and the necessity of compassion and tolerance.[1] Nor are the Japanese, who consider morality socially relative, keen on systematizing moral doctrines as independent entities.

---

1. An American student of mine, during her field work in Japan in 1974, discovered to her surprise that most of the Japanese who referred to the Watergate scandal were sympathetic toward Nixon and unable to understand how Americans could be so harshly punitive. But, of course, if Nixon had been a Japanese prime minister he would have resigned voluntarily at a much earlier time.

Pelzel again offers a contrast between the Japanese and Chinese in stating that the Japanese have "no sense . . . of that massive concentration of 'evil' at one point and time, and of 'good' at another, which is so characteristic of Chinese thought and of the theory of the dynastic cycle on the continent" (1970:45-46).

That social relativism underlines the Japanese idea of morality finds analytical expression in a classical work on ethics by philosopher Tetsuro Watsuji:

> The problem of ethics does not lie in the consciousness of an isolated individual but in *the relationship between man and man*. It would be impossible to reach a real understanding of what distinguishes a good from a bad action, or what comprises a duty, responsibility, or virtue, unless considered as a problem of the relationship between man and man. (1962:12; Watsuji's italics)[2]

Sincerity, for instance, does not come into existence as an ethical value from the one-track-minded persistence of a mental attitude alone. Sincerity emerges as an ethical issue only after one person has expressed his attitude toward another person in a manner that arouses in the latter a certian expectation about the former's future conduct (Watsuji 1962:293-294). The novelty of this position can be realized by contrasting it with the Western notion of morality, which is associated with an "absolute" standard and the individual's "inner" conviction.

The Japanese sense of morality may be further inferred from patterns of self-imposed negative sanction, especially of guilt feelings. In Western ethics, guilt is viewed as internal sanction against the violation of an absolute moral standard. Based on this definition of guilt, Benedict saw the Japanese as devoid of guilt and, instead, as inundated with shame. It was George DeVos who pointed up the blindness of Western observers to the strong sense of guilt among Japanese, and he attributed this blindness to the fact that they "tend to look for guilt, as it is symbolically expressed, in reference to a possible transgression of limits imposed by a generalized ideology or religious system circumscribing sexual and aggressive impulses" (1960:288). He saw the source of Japanese guilt primarily in the mother's self-sacrifice, which arouses in the child the obligation to make recompense for

---

2. This is my translation, as are all the quotations cited in this text from works originally published in Japanese.

it. For Japanese, guilt seems to stem at least in part from one's empathetic feelings for the pain and sacrifice suffered by another person. It is intensified, I might add, when another person's suffering is understood as due to one's action or as intended to benefit one.

Another interpretation of Japanese guilt has been offered by Doi: "Guilt takes the sharpest form for Japanese when it is generated from the awareness that one might possibly betray the social group one belongs to" (1971:49). When the individual feels he has done something wrong against the group in spite of the trust it holds for him, Doi argues, guilt reaches its maximum. Both DeVos' and Doi's interpretations, though distinct from each other, emphasize that Japanese guilt is inseparable from social relationships. Doi himself states succinctly, "guilt feelings are a function of human relationships" (p. 50). Many other possible manifestations of guilt are explored in the following chapters, but they all reflect the social anchorage of morality.

Morality based on social relativism involves what has become widely known as "situationalism" or "situation ethic." Hamaguchi (1966, 1970), among others, characterized the Japanese normative orientation as "particularism-situationalism." Even universalistic ideas like *bachi* ("heaven's punishment") or *innen* ("karma") seem, according to Kato (quoted by Hamaguchi 1970:147-148), to be particularistic when applied in Japan. *Bachi*, presupposing "the causal law applying to a particular group (e.g., the family)," refers to the punishment of members of a group that once produced a rule-breaker. Typically, deviance by an ancestor results in the misfortune of a descendant, and wrongdoing by a parent leads to, for example, the deformity of a child.

The situation ethic was manifested in dramatic form by Japanese war prisoners in World War II. Benedict reports, "Some men asked to be killed, 'but if your customs do not permit this, I will be a model prisoner.' " They turned out to be most cooperative in the American war effort, locating ammunition dumps and even guiding pilots to military targets (1946:41). The same situation ethic has contributed to the adaptability and progressivism with which the Japanese are often credited and which have smoothed Japan's remarkably rapid modernization.

Whether the situation ethic is regarded as good or bad, the overall impression of Japanese behavior patterns, viewed in light of this ethic, is their changeability. To Western observers this may appear synonymous with inscrutability or unreliability. To me, situationalism is only one side of social morality. Social relativism is more than a here-and-now orientation: once social bonds and obligations are fixed and internalized, the actor is likely to show enormous persistence and rigidity regardless of situational fluctuation. I might add that the autonomous actor with free will may find it easier to change his mind as the situation changes. Side by side with situationally attuned Japanese, we find as many Japanese who are characteristically stubborn, refuse to change their minds, stick to their initial commitment, and are looked upon as reliable. Indeed *shinyō* ("trustworthiness") is at the center of the Japanese moral vocabulary. The behavior of war prisoners, as observed by Benedict, is striking precisely because of its contrast with this side of social morality, equally prevalent among Japanese, the deep commitment to obligations. The reader may recall the recent discovery of Sgt. Shoichi Yokoi, who had been hiding in a cave on Guam for as long as twenty-eight years (since World War II) (*Asahi Shimbun* special correspondents 1972). It may be speculated that he did so either because he could not conceive of surrendering or because he could not face the Japanese who might accuse him of not having fought to the death.

AUTHORITY

Alien to interactional relativism is the idea of a single godlike figure who monopolizes authority over the whole society. The image of a divine king, absolute ruler, or despot who serves as prime mover in secular society is a product of unilateral determinism rather than of interactional relativism.

Congenial to the Japanese ethos is the authority figure who plays his limited role in emotional as well as functional interdependence with his subjects, much as between an indulgent parent and obedient children. The authority holder is no more autonomous than those subject to him. In fact, the higher up one goes along the hierarchy of authority, the higher the price one seems to pay in freedom and autonomy, partly because of taboos surrounding authority but mainly because of the higher concentration of social obligations in the person of the authority figure. The emperor is no exception. Even the Imperial constitution, which was framed in the late nineteenth century to foster national unity and patriotism, did not dispense with this relativistic structure of authority, despite its formal establishment of the "absolute" sovereignty of the emperor. Though sacred and "inviolable," the emperor needed help and support from his subjects, it appeared, as much as the subjects depended upon his *ōmikokoro* ("great august benevolence"). Mutuality of influence was idealized, here too, in the analogy of the parent-child attachment. Moreover, the emperor was considered too sacrosanct to be involved in the actual administration of the state, which made him totally dependent on those closest to him. The result was that the emperor's "supreme" authority was apparently devoid of power and he was reduced to an apolitical, cultural symbol.

The emperor being politically impotent, authority and power were distributed among those below the sovereign but were exercised in his name. If the emperor was not free, his agents appeared no more free since their authority derived ultimately from the emperor, or, as stressed by political theorist Masao Maruyama, from "the awareness of relative proximity to the emperor" (1956:16). Assumed delegation by the emperor was the sole justification for the exercise of power. Such an authority relationship does not require an independent ideology, moral system, or law as the ultimate standard for legitimation. Legitimacy is measured in "relatedness" to the sovereign, yet the sovereign is far from being a free, independent actor. Authority in Japanese culture, especially in prewar times, is a good example of the lack of a prime mover in social relativism. The emperor was a god but not a monotheistic god; all other Japanese were also gods, though of lesser stature. In Maruyama's words, there were too many *shōtennō* ("lesser emperors") all over the country.

Maruyama finds the same cultural propensity responsible for the difference between German and Japanese fascists. In contrast to the audacity, fearless determination, and self-assertion demonstrated by Nazi leaders even after the war, Japanese fascists, particularly war criminals, turned out to be disappointingly weak when deprived of their borrowed authority (1956:16). Social relativism seems both to inhibit the ideological demand for moral perfection on the part of the authority holder and to suppress the despotic assertion of naked power. Hence, everything ends up being "dwarfed" (p. 15).

All this is dynamically related to the political anarchy that Japan has suffered, which Maruyama calls "the gigantic system of irresponsibility" in which everyone moves not by his own decision but under pressure from someone else. When the chain of pressure goes downward, it takes the form of *yokuatsu ijō* ("transference of repression"), whereby pressure from one's superior is simply transferred to one's inferior all the way down the line. When, conversely, pressure goes upward, which also has been a common phenomenon in Japanese political life, it is called *gekokujō* ("control of superiors by inferiors") or, a phrase Maruyama coined, *tōsaku demokurashii* ("topsy-turvy democracy"). Imbedded in the same structure is the proclivity toward factionalism.

Maruyama's view of Japanese political structure and behavior is thus pessimistic. One can argue, however, that the socially sensitive orientations in Japanese politics have also been mobilized for the quick termination of chaos and achievement of unity and efficiency. Among the nations of the world, Japan has distinguished itself by its successful retention of national unity and identity. We should not forget the bipolar functionality of social relativism.

BenDasan has given a positive evaluation of Japanese politics. In contrast to the political naïveté of the Jews, bound by their obsession with Mosaic law, he calls the Japanese "political geniuses." Political crises throughout Japanese history have been surmounted, he says, by "restoration of mutual trust between man and man," not by reliance upon a fixed law or upon a dictator. He praises the dual political system under feudalism, where authority was divided between the imperial court and the warrior government, as a remarkable invention stemming from this native talent of the Japanese (1970:55-74).

EMOTIONS

Cosmology, morality, and authority pertain to the superstructure of an ethos. Now let us turn to a more elementary aspect of it, the emotional life of individuals. From the point of view of social relativism, an emotion, too, is unable to claim autonomy. One's affect can and must be controlled, subdued, circumscribed, or diluted because it is the social relationship, not one's own emotions, that counts. Eiichiro Ishida (1961) points out the sharp contrast between this aspect of Japanese culture and that of Western civilization as represented by a Hitler, God, or Christ. Emotions in the West are characterized by "thoroughgoing loves and hates." While "gentle pathos" is the Japanese ideal of emotion, Western love is "intense and full-blooded." Japanese inclinations for compromise, tolerance, and pliability are diametrically opposed to the implacable severity and intolerance of Western emotions. The Westerner pursues his love tirelessly until he gets it, but the Japanese lover is resigned to the evanescence of human emotions. Traditional popular songs in Japan lament *hakanai koi* ("fleeting love"). The awareness of such evanescence may also account for the desire for maximal intensification of love during the short period of time it flourishes.

Ishida offers an ecological explanation for this difference. It is worth quoting because this viewpoint is still shared by many students of Japanese culture, although I am not among them. The passionate disposition of the Westerner is derived, he suggests, from nomadic pastoralism, as against the sedentary, wet agriculture of the East. The Westerners, under this ecological condition, "slaughtered large numbers of domestic animals, tanned their hides, spun their fur, made dairy products of every kind and even blood sausages, and cut and ate their meat with knives and forks, while their dress was derived from the horseman's trousers and narrow-sleeved jacket." The religious expression of this is the jealous male god. Japanese emotions are a product of wet-rice agriculture, conditioned further by Buddhism, which is "the gospel of the tropics, the doctrine of vegetable growth" (Keyerling, quoted by Ishida, 1961).

Although Pelzel stresses the importance of love in the Japanese myths, what he describes as love is quite different from Ishida's love. Even sexual emotions somewhat lack heat or rage.

> There is no suggestion of brutal initiatives, of sadism or rape, of neurosis, and if a person refuses it is simply because he finds the other unattractive. The myth even makes it clear that it is improper to deny a person who proposes love his or her pleasure merely because the attraction is not reciprocated. (1970:51)

That accepting a sexual proposal should be taken as a social obligation is an eloquent demonstration of social relativism.

The weakness of sexual obsession or passion has also been pointed out by Haga.

> The Japanese give it up rather readily. In the literature that has appeared since olden days we find few stories which bring insanity or suicide to the person who lost love.

> It is considered manly to be free from a lingering attachment so that one does not hesitate for a second to kick one's wife out, demanding divorce once something is found wrong with her.
>
> [The Japanese male] would not remain attached to a woman who does not like him, or unmarried all his life because no other woman is acceptable. (1968:258)[3]

Even double suicide (or triple suicide in the case of a triangular relationship) takes place not so much out of love as of obligation (p. 258).

Paradoxically, Western emotions, particularly sexual desires and passions, must be subjected to stern asceticism. If love and hate are strong and irresistible, they must be controlled by the religious sense of sin. Supremacy of the mind over the flesh is the Western theme of morality. It is no coincidence that Freudian theory, based on the premise of sexual aggression and repression, grew in European soil. On the other hand, the Japanese, whose emotions tend toward "gentle pathos" and soft feelings, find the Western guilt associated with desire of the flesh unnatural, inhuman, or tiresome. Nature is nature, Japanese would say, and whatever exists in nature, including sexual desire, cannot be denied. The Japanese themselves have labeled this attitude toward nature and desire *yokubō shizenshugi* ("desire-naturalism"). It is not that the Japanese have known no inhibition in sex; Confucian-based prewar education, in fact, prescribed sexual segregation even for primary school children. For this reason it is believed that a duality has arisen in the Japanese sexual attitude—laxity and austerity (Sofue 1972). I contend that these two attitudes are compatible since the emotion is socially circumscribed. The open acceptance of sexuality is compatible only with balanced, tamed emotions and would be dangerous in a culture where emotions are "full-blooded." Whereas Westerners split a person into mind and body, or into godly half and beastly half, and try to subjugate the one to the other, the Japanese do not recognize such a split and rather accept man's whole existence as a balanced, natural unity. Westerners' fluctuation from untamed, godless aggression to guilt-ridden pious prostration seems either exhausting or senseless to Japanese.

---

3. Haga presents a male's point of view in total disregard of a female's attitude toward love. I should point out that there is some asymmetry between sexes in that a woman tends to show more tenacity including a readiness to commit suicide for lost love.

Related to the foregoing is the exalted status of rationality in Western intellectual history. The development of Western civilization may be said to be a process of increasing rationalization whereby man has attained freedom from emotional irrationality. Compulsive rationality and suppression of emotional involvement seem to be another paradoxical outcome of the recognition of irresistible passions. In Japan, rationality has not enjoyed such status; nor has emotionality been degraded as being irrational. Within this limited sense of emotionality, I agree with Reischauer that "the Japanese are an emotional people" (1965:117). Rationality and emotionality do not appear to the Japanese mind to be mutually exclusive. This difference is likely to have much to do with a difference in the concept of selfhood. Since that subject occupies the whole of chapter 9, let me here merely mention a view presented by Hayao Kawai (1972). Ego function for the Japanese, he speculates, is based upon the dynamic interplay between intuition and sensation, whereas that for Westerners is built upon the dynamic interrelation between thought and emotion (p. 195).

Esthetic Sensibility

In esthetic matters, cultural uniformity is most difficult to establish, for esthetic taste is legitimately idiosyncratic from the point of view of both producer and consumer. Nonetheless, one cannot help recognizing a peculiarly Japanese pattern of esthetic sensibility. My hunch is that interactional or social relativism does not tolerate autonomous esthetic expression but encourages that artistic creation or appreciation be attuned to the rest of the environment, particularly to social situations. In the first place, artificial appearance should be avoided and naturalness should be sought. Secondly, ostentatious, conspicuous creativity is to be disdained as being in bad taste, while simplicity, modesty, and refinement are to be esteemed as true signs of esthetic sophistication. Hasegawa (1966) contrasts the Japanese taste for plainness, austerity, and delicacy with the continental or Western prejudice for grandiloquence, overcomplexity, and overstimulating effects. The Japanese thus, he finds, tend to lavish their sensibility on small details and to seek small-scale perfection; architecture, for instance, is appreciated not so much with reference to overall design and structure as to such details as the smoothness of a pillar (pp. 113-122).

Japanese words expressing esthetic properties are typically diffuse and undefinable. *Shibui* is an example. Kawakita (1961) tries to define it in terms of mutual opposites: *shibui* can refer to *jimi*, "plain, quiet, restrained and introvert," but does not exclude its opposite, *hade*, "gay, showy." Further, *shibui* is a combination of *iki*, "stylish, urbane, polished, sophisticated," and its opposite, *yabo*, "awkward, naïve, uncouth, rustically artless." In short:

> The concept of *shibui* implies an outlook which is practical, devoid of frills, and unassuming, one which acts as circumstances require, simply and without fuss. In baseball, neither the spectacular home-run batter nor the brilliant infielder can really become valuable players unless they acquire this *shibui* quality. Unless the spectacular and the brilliant include in themselves this element of the *shibui*, the technique can never really be called mature. The ever-available ability to go concisely and simply to the heart of what is required . . . the pursuit of high efficiency, shorn of excessive individual technique, neither flashy nor yet dull. . . . It is in such qualities that one finds the *shibui*. (pp. 35-36)

Such diffuseness or complexity surrounding esthetic taste seems to stem from the importance that the Japanese attach to the feelings flowing between the artistic creator or performer and his audience. In the traditional tea cult, "the host and guest joined to produce for that occasion the utmost beatitude of the mundane. The tearoom was an oasis in the dreary waste of existence where weary travellers could meet to drink from the common spring of art appreciation" (Okakura 1923:43). The Noh drama is thought to have no appeal unless the audience joins its feeling with the player's in vicariously participating in the world of illusion, which is portrayed but not displayed on the stage, and in capturing the player's emotional intensity, which is veiled by the Noh mask.

The importance of feeling in tune with the atmosphere is apparent even in the culinary art. Japanese cookery, which appeals more to the eye than to the gustatory sensibility, is known for its visual effect, derived from the harmony of colors or the beauty of the serving plates and bowls, which creates a proper setting for an occasion.

It is understandable, then, that for Japanese real "taste" derives less from perfectionism in conforming to a single standard of artistic creation or performance (as in flawless accuracy in rhythm or intonation in music) than from a slight deviation from the standard in tune with the situational variation. This type of tastefulness is called *iki*, implying a sophisticated, urbane, some-what sensuous kind of artistic sensibility.

Japanese esthetics is not something that transcends daily life; it is *in* daily life. Artistic creativity and sensibility are not set apart from but penetrate the ordinary person's routine. This means that almost everyone is a minor artist and that the level of artistry must be brought down to a size manageable for ordinary persons. The lack of class distinction in this respect was recognized by Reischauer:

> From the top to the bottom of their society, [the Japanese] exhibit a high artistic appreciation for what is in their own tradition and uniformly good taste in a myriad of intimate details of their daily life. There is relatively little of the dichotomy we find in our own culture between the self-conscious good taste of the self-appointed artistic minority and the bad taste and artistic vulgarity which they so deplore in others. (1965:121)

No wonder Japanese art tends to be miniature with an emphasis upon refinement in details. This explains the seemingly con-tradictory attitude of the Japanese toward nature: on the one hand they extol harmony with nature, but on the other they bring it down (or up) to their own level and confine it "unnaturally" in miniature boxed gardens and bonsai. Such miniaturization of nature is an important part of Japanese esthetics. Japanese "naturalism," then, is far from either the recognition of nature as independent of human beings, or belief in the subjection of humans to the power of nature. Rather, the essence of Japanese naturalism seems to lie in an appreciation of the interaction and affinity between humans and nature.

CHAPTER 2

Belongingness

Social relativism finds direct expression in the elaboration and refinement of Japanese culture in the area of social interaction and relationships. This and the following five chapters will investigate normative patterns of social interaction. Let us begin with belongingness.

REFERENCES FOR BELONGINGNESS

An analysis of belongingness must first answer the question, Belong where? In Japan, references for belonging are conceived primarily as reference groups. The reference group varies widely from small to large, intimate to impersonal, formal to informal. It may be one's household, residential area, village or town, the company or factory where one works, the nation, and so forth. Reference is found not only in the gemeinschaft based on *ketsuen* ("blood ties") or *chien* ("geographical ties") but, more importantly, in *shaen* ("company ties") (H. Kato et al. 1971). Such a reference group is what Nakane refers to as *ba*, "frame," as distinct from "attribute." She argues that in identifying himself, the Japanese person stresses his position in a social frame rather than his individual attributes (1970:1-8).

Belongingness usually refers to a frame existing here and now, such as the company where one currently works. But, it is also common to refer to a frame one previously belonged to, such as one's birthplace, the house in which one was reared, the school from which one has graduated. Belonging by memory thus cannot be overlooked. Japanese identify themselves by both their *shozoku* ("current belonging") and *shusshin* ("origin").

Belonging by memory makes us aware of the symbolic, as well as the social and physical, nature of the frame for belonging. The reference group or place for belonging does not have to be a tangible social group in which Ego interacts with Alters, or a physically sensible place such as a hometown; it can be purely symbolic, such as the house registry where one's "name" belongs. Japanese further indulge in the sense of belonging to a certain historical period, as when they describe themselves as belonging to the Meiji era, Shōwa era, or the prewar or postwar era. A keen sense of generation gap, held widely by Japanese today, is expressed, for example, when people identify themselves as "one-digit" or "two-digit" Shōwa generation. (The first year of Shōwa era was A.D. 1926, so people born from 1926 to 1934 are in the "one-digit" generation, and those born after 1934 are in the "two-digit" generation.) To indicate total belongingness, Japanese sometimes use the term of filiation, calling themselves *Edokko* (child of old Tokyo), *Asakusakko* (Asakusa-child), *Shōwakko* (child of the Shōwa era), as if the place (Edo, Asakusa) or era (Shōwa) assumed a parental position.

MANIFESTATIONS OF THE CONCERN FOR BELONGING

Establishment of Identity

Ego tries to establish the identity of an Alter whom he meets for the first time primarily by where Alter came from or where he belongs. The first question Ego would ask, after the introduction, is *"Dochira desuka?"* "Where is it (that you work or belong)?" If Alter is young enough to still be in school, he should answer that question by naming his school. Students derive their primary identity from the school they attend. If Alter is older, the question implies the name of his company. As Nakane points out, without persistent questioning it is often difficult is find out what work Alter actually does, though he immediately volunteers the name of his company. This would be demonstrated in a questionnaire in which the respondent is asked to give his occupational identity; many would simply write *kaishain* ("company member") or give the name of the company for which they work. This is particularly true when the company happens to be a prestigious one and the worker holds a position of relatively low status in it. In such a case, self-identification by the "frame" constitutes a sort of social euphemism that is nonetheless perfectly acceptable to Japanese.

While Ego is curious about Alter's identity in terms of belongingness, he, too, tries to exhibit his identity by belongingness because he wants recognition from Alter, because he feels obliged to satisfy Alter's curiosity, or because he wants to dispel any suspicions about his identity. In addition to oral self-introduction, the Japanese rely heavily on the use of *meishi* ("name cards") to indicate where they belong. A typical *meishi* contains the user's name, place of employment, office or rank, and home address. The *meishi* is so important for self-introduction that one cannot do without it in Japan if one wants to become known or trusted by a group of strangers. There are other visible indicators of belongingness that the Japanese have taken to: school uniforms, badges, caps. When students or laborers conduct a mass demonstration or campaign, they indicate their group identity by uniforms, headbands, ribbons, and so forth; militant students in the late 1960s displayed their faction-belongingness by wearing helmets of a certain color.

Establishing identity by belongingness is further demonstrated by the desire for pure, unambiguous belonging. One is proud of being a "pure Edo child," one who was born and has since lived only in Tokyo. The Japanese in general are frankly proud of belonging to the "pure *Yamato* race." Ambiguity in belonging arouses suspicion or contempt. In daily conversations, one often hears derogatory remarks about someone who is *sujō no shirenai* or *doko no uma no hone ka wakaranai*, both meaning "of obscure origin or belonging," Not only those whose belonging is obscure but those whose belonging is mixed are discredited or mistrusted. Many Japanese feel uncomfortable with people of multicultural backgrounds and are repelled by racially mixed, "hybrid" people (*ainoko*). Such people are popularly classified "of unknown nationality" (*kokuseki fumei*). Many Japanese are naïve enough to readily express their prejudice against mixed races. Read the following passage from an anonymous short essay in the monthly *Sōbun*, entitled "Human Faces," critical of university students:

They shout and yell, but their eyes do not have the sparkle which is a sign of firm conviction. They only stare with suspiciousness. In olden days, Japanese travellers in Paris were mistaken for Annamese, we are told. I am afraid that Japanese are indeed coming to look like Annamese or Mexicans. I do find in today's youth the kind of filthiness unique to the mixed race. (No. 87, November 1969, p. 1)

Japanese are offended at being taken for another race; Japanese who do not "behave like Japanese" are thought deplorable; overseas Japanese such as Japanese Americans are not easily trusted and may be ridiculed because of their apparent ambiguity of identity in terms of belongingness. Such intolerance for mixed identity applies to foreigners as well. Japanese expect foreigners in Japan to retain their foreign identity, even if they are Japanophiles and well versed in Japanese culture. Japanized foreigners, who may be liked by their Japanese friends, to be sure, nevertheless often disturb the sense of belongingness held by most Japanese. Such foreigners may be described as *hen na gaijin*, "odd foreigners," though Japanese declare that this term is not derogatory.

Repulsion or mistrust is not the only reaction to someone whose belongingness is ambiguous. Another reaction is a feeling of mystery mixed with admiration. The striking popularity of *ainoko* actors and singers demonstrates this. The point is that Japanese set such a person apart from themselves, whether they admire or are repelled by him.

Collectivism

The Japanese concern for belonging relates to the tendency toward collectivism, which is expressed by an individual's identification with the collective goal of the group to which he belongs. Collectivism thus involves cooperation and solidarity, and the sentimental desire for the warm feeling of *ittaikan* ("feeling of oneness") with fellow members of one's group is widely shared by Japanese.

What would be strictly a private matter in an individualistic society tends to be a group enterprise in Japan. When guests are invited to a household, neighbors, kin, and others volunteer to help in the preparations. The host fulfills only a portion of the host's responsibility. Collective cooperation is taken so much for granted that a Japanese may not become aware of it until he is displaced from his group or is confronted with another culture. Jun Eto described in his essay *America and I* (1969) his amazement at the load of responsibility an individual has to carry in American society. He was particularly impressed by the role played by the wife as hostess at a party. It was the wife, Eto declared, who took primary responsibility for giving a successful party. The responsibility included not only shopping and preparing dinner but exercising tact in introducing strangers and carrying on interesting and innocuous conversations. Eto felt that in America, where the individual is supposed to discharge his tasks all by himself, he can rely upon no one but his spouse. Thus, the wife plays an indispensable role even at a social gathering including the husband's colleagues. Eto visualized the American household as a soap bubble that would disappear at any moment unless sustained from inside by two pairs of arms. The severity of the struggle for survival in the midst of America's individualistic, competitive society made the wife as well as the husband indispensable (1969:73-87). In Japan, an equivalent party would be a collective task; more likely, the party would be held at a teahouse where professional female service is available. Eto seems to imply that the Japanese household is sustained from outside by a collectivity, which lightens the couple's responsibility.

Collectivism fosters a taste for togetherness, intensive interaction, and gregariousness. Those who share the same belongingness get together often to enjoy intimate interaction, to confirm the mutual solidarity. This is true with belonging by memory too. Kindergarten alumni may continue to have a reunion every year, even after they reach middle age, to refresh the memory of belonging. Retired schoolteachers look forward to being invited to the annual alumni reunions held by their former students. Even Christian ministers were found to share this inclination for gregariousness. Bishop Boutflower discovered while staying in Japan that his "fellow clergy were at their best when *together*."

> No one would say that a clerical meeting was the place to see English parsons at their best: here the commonplace man is often best appreciated when seen at work in his own parish. But I was to learn that quite uninspiring priests and catechists will wake up and give vent to astonishing noble sentiments when happily gathered in Shu-yo-kwai ("refreshment conferences"). It is their more natural state. (1939:8-9)

Gregariousness serves to confirm and reconfirm solidarity and group identification, it is true. But it also indicates the Japanese concern not to be left out of any collective activities. I am quite sure that this tendency contributes to overcrowding in Tokyo's main streets late at night, not to mention during rush hour. Crowds are readily formed by Japanese, who want not to be left out of whatever group action is taking place: the slightest incident on a street attracts eager passersby, and huge crowds rapidly form.

As Shintaro Ryu writes, the Japanese individual seems to feel really alive only when in a group. He wants to go wherever others do; even when he goes to the beach to swim, he avoids an uncrowded place but chooses a spot where people are practically on top of one another as if in a public bath. This proclivity for togetherness, Ryu continues, caused the tragic incident at a famous shrine in Niigata Prefecture in which more than a hundred people were crushed to death by the enormous crowd that had gathered there to celebrate on New Year's Day 1956 (1971:214-216).

The Japanese prefer group tours in domestic as well as overseas travel. People the world over are aware that Japanese tourists not only come and go in a group but stay together while sightseeing. Not a few Japanese I know expressed a preference for traveling by ship because, in contrast to the shortness of plane trips, a ship journey allows many long days in which to interact with other passengers within a limited space and make new friends.

The enthusiasm of the Japanese for togetherness and sharing carries over into their attitude toward supernatural beings, especially deceased kin and ancestors. Dore found, among the various reasons for which Japanese pray and make offerings at the *butsudan* ("Buddist household altar"), the belief that the dead "should not be left out of anything—the doors of the *butsudan* are opened when, for instance, a marriage is celebrated in the house—and they have a right to the first share in all delicacies the family enjoys" (1958:324).

Given their cultural gravitation toward togetherness, it is no wonder that Japanese readily admit to being lonely (*sabishii*) or that lonely persons are likely to receive attention and sympathy. Loneliness is a major theme of popular songs. This may contribute to the fact that Japanese find a type of culture hero in the man who fights for justice all by himself, bravely overcoming loneliness. Popular heroes in movies are often masterless samurai or traveling gangsters, belonging nowhere, drifting from place to place. Precisely because togetherness is so desirable, mild depression engendered by loneliness becomes a culturally articulated style of behavior.

Physical togetherness tends to dispel the need for verbal communication between in-group members. Among the Japanese, "heart-to-heart talk" refers to a nonverbal exchange of emotional feelings with all their subtleties. The desirability of such nonverbal interaction is coupled with the moral belief that silence is a sign of honesty and trustworthiness. The person with a "skilled mouth" (*kuchi ga umai*) is discredited for this reason.

Dependence on physical contact for "real" communication makes correspondence difficult between two persons who are physically apart. Hence, as Nakane (1967:59) has pointed out, "out of sight, out of mind" fits the Japanese scene. This tendency is substantiated by behavior related to traveling. Travel means total separation, however temporary, between the traveler and his in-group, and thus it is initiated by a farewell party and terminated by a welcome-back party, often too extravagant for the scale of the travel. These parties include ritualized speeches by both the traveler and his friends expressing gratitude and good wishes. The number of people who gather at dock or airport in Japan to see off or welcome back traveling friends is an indication of the importance of physical togetherness. But "out of sight, out of mind" does not mean that the absent one will be forgotten forever. Since belonging by memory is at work, that person will be welcomed back and will enjoy revived friendship and togetherness as soon as he returns, provided he has not lost his old group identity.

Conformism

Collectivism, with stress upon harmony and consensus, generates pressures for conformity to group norms, pressure to "be like everybody else." Conspicuous idiosyncracy and dissension are avoided or suppressed, and acquiescence is upheld as a main mechanism for maintaining consensus. Paradoxically, conformism has served as a cultural basis for egalitarian ideology in Japan, an otherwise hierarchically ordered country. This fact was well observed by Agnes Niyekawa when she pointed out that a distinction must be made between two types of authoritarianism, the ideological type and the acquiescent type. The latter can be expressed, she argued, either in authoritarian ideology or in democratic ideology, depending on the source of information. She found that "Japanese were more authoritarian than Americans on authoritarian items (F+ scale), while on democratic items (F− scale) they turned out to be more democratic than Americans" (1966:284). In this sense, the Japanese may legitimately be characterized as "other-directed."

The sense of identity anchored in group belongingness is thus sustained by going along with peers. This goes with the desirability of being accepted by peers, anxiety about being left out, and a competitive urge for always being "in." The overwhelming influence of school education on Japanese children seems to stem not only from the hierarchical pressures of teachers, school administrators, and government, but also from horizontal pressures of schoolmates for conformity, although these two kinds of pressures often work against each other. The amazing speed of cultural diffusion among the Japanese owes to this motivational factor as well as to the widespread, centralized mass media. Faddism does not refer to the rapid diffusion of material culture or gadgetry alone but also of behavioral repertoire, including vocabulary and hobbies. At any one time the whole country seems to be reading, watching, talking about, or doing the same thing. Millions of copies of a best-selling book can be sold at once. Catch phrases appearing in TV commercials are quickly assimilated into popular speech.

Ego's willingness to conform to group norms is coupled with his intolerance for Alter's failure or refusal to conform; the exhibition of idiosyncrasies or expression of dissension is certain to make one unpopular in the group. Internally, such conformism operates as an egalitarian pressure against arrogant, overbearing group members; externally it is mobilized to build a united front, especially when the group faces an external threat.

Pressure for conformity often results in a type of self-restraint called *enryo*, refraining from expressing disagreement with whatever appears to be the majority's opinion. This has been noted by Kerlinger in situations of formal decision-making. He perceived a peculiar method of decision-making in a variety of groups ranging from a PTA to the national Diet (parliament), which he labeled "the *Suisen-Sansei-Iginashi* (Recommendation-Agreement-No Objection) System."

> For example, an organization will need a president. Recommendations (*suisen*) will be made by someone prominent in the organization or in the community. If whoever is in charge of the meeting at which this choice is being made then asks the members their opinion on a certain candidate, they will usually say *Sansei* (agreement), and the particular person recommended at the time is elected. Similarly, if an organization needs to reach a decision on an important matter, seldom is a vote taken. Instead, the chairman may state the matter under consideration. The members will usually say *Iginashi* (no objection). (1950:39)

Particularly interesting is the absence of objection, rather than the presence of agreement, as the basis for reaching a decision. A manipulative chairman would see to it that the silence of participants is taken as an indication of agreement rather than of disagreement. He would ask whether there is any objection instead of asking who and how many agree. This is an example of a cultural value that is held as an expressive value in general and may be used as an instrumental value by a few leaders.[1]

While conformity is thus maintained in socially expressed behavior, the individual's inner self is likely to lack such conformity. This kind of inner autonomy, as one might call it, is taken for granted in Japan, and it is what BenDasan calls "human dialectics." Unlike orthodox Jews, who, he says, bind themselves by laws, the Japanese believe that "no decision binds people by a hundred percent" (1970:81). Herein lies the Japanese version of tolerance for individual inner autonomy and of resistance to totalitarian control. Both conspicuous dissension and dictatorial suppression are alien to social relativism.

This paradox takes dramatic form in a group like the Communist party, to which ideological commitment as well as group conformity are essential. A former leader of the Japan Communist party denounced the party for forcing its members to appear outwardly submissive to party decision while remaining recalcitrant at heart. A party member is "obliged to tell lies con-

---

1. There are occasions where dissension and mutual criticism are encouraged at a formal meeting set up especially for that purpose. Under such circumstances, the Japanese participants are likely to express themselves without reservation.

stantly while knowing the real truth, and to declare the victory of the party in an election while knowing the opposite to be true" (Kasuga 1961:78).

The frustration of the unexpressed nonconforming self can sometimes be released through social interaction without spoiling the united front. Sometimes, however, it builds up so much as to become irreversible. In that case the dissenting member may organize a splinter group or defect from the group entirely. The above-mentioned Communist leader did abandon the party. Asked why he did not express his disagreement at the party congress before his defection, he answered, "The party congress is not so organized that the will of the entire party is truly represented. A minority opinion, even if expressed, will be reduced to nil the moment the congress makes a decision" (p. 75). We can detect in this remark the writer's sensitivity to social pressure for conformity side by side with his ideological commitment.

Total Commitment

The strong sense of belongingness as a stake for self-identity, reinforced by collectivism and conformism, calls for the individual's total commitment and loyalty to his group. It also means that the group is responsible for taking care of all the needs of its members. These mutual obligations of loyalty and total protection are an established practice in the Japanese employment system, particularly in large corporations. To repeat some of the characteristics of that system, which have become cliches through the widely quoted work by Abegglen (1958):

- Lifetime employment.
- Promotion in wage and rank based on length of service.
- Paternalistic relationship between superior and subordinate and between employer and employee.
- Extension of the rights and duties of employer and employee to their family members.
- Provision by the company of most of the employee's basic needs, including housing, dining rooms, medical, educational, and recreational facilities, and so on.

In such a system, the employee not only is obligated to stay on in the same company even when he is offered a more attractive job, but he cannot afford to move. Chances are that he will not be offered a job from the outside. Choice and competition in a relatively free market are made only at the initial stage of one's career. It is not to the taste of Japanese to move wherever and whenever an opportunity for advancement presents itself. Nor is it culturally commendable for an employer to attract (or steal) someone else's employee with a better offer. Compare this with the American occupational market, where mobility and stealing of employees are taken for granted. Not only is the Japanese employer socially prohibited from stealing employees, but he does not want to hire anyone who has already internalized loyalty to another employer or occupational group.

All this reflects the tendency of the Japanese employee to find his identity in belongingness rather than in the cultivation and exhibition of professional expertise. The employer, for his part, is more interested in recruiting a novice who may have no special skill but enough aptitude and motivation to learn a skill after being employed than he is in finding an established expert who could immediately improve productivity. Employment seems to mean, above all, the teaching and learning of the employee's role in relation to the employer and other senior employees, with emphasis upon loyalty and group identification. Through such personal loyalty, the impersonal rules of a bureaucracy are learned and followed. The American employment system, in contrast, seems to necessitate and reinforce a highly rational bureaucracy that lets rules speak for themselves, independently of personnel. Where competition and mobility are in full play, the personnel filling bureaucratic slots must be made as expendable as possible so that replacement will pose no big problem.

Total commitment to a group necessitates the careful screening of groups and a rank-ordering evaluation of groups before a decision to join is made; it also engenders competition among candidates to get into the most desirable group. Everything goes all right for the person who makes a right choice for his career. But one who makes an initial error has a hard time establishing identity by belongingness: he will either be stuck in a small, obscure place of work, or will remain a loner, drifting from one odd job to another. The group, for its part, must carefully screen prospective members since induction implies the offer of total protection. Hence, in education, there is the fierce entrance examination system as described by Vogel (1963:40–67). One must undergo an "infernal" examination, it seems, whenever one's primary-group belongingness shifts—from the family to a school, from elementary school to secondary school, then to a university, then to an occupational group.

Kiefer saw the Japanese examination system as "a series of crisis rites through which the child passes from family-centered to peer-group-centered values" rather than as a mechanism for minimizing competition within a group. Through these crisis rites, comparable to puberty rites in preliterate societies, Kiefer argues, the educational system in Japan serves as a bridge between the family and the bureaucracy, and thus enables the individual in the course of his maturation to transfer the focus of group identity, without inner conflict, from his family to his classroom to his occupational setting (1970:66). The initiation rites are performed not only at the in-between stage, as in an entrance examination, but after entry into a group. New employees, for example, are given orientation courses, or what might be better called "brainwashing," as reported by Rohlen (1971). He witnessed a program of "spiritual education" (*seishin kyōiku*) for new employees of a bank that included a group endurance walk and volunteering to work free for strangers accidentally encountered. (Naturally, the strangers were nonplussed by, and disinclined to accept, such an unexpected offer.) The severity of that training is another indication of the identity change required by entry into a new group.

The total commitment a Japanese makes in belonging to a group is highlighted when he faces the choice of retaining Japanese citizenship or of acquiring a new national identity. As former ambassador Kawasaki relates in his outspoken characterization of Japanese behavior, "there are very few Japanese who settle permanently abroad," while "the Chinese settle wherever there is a chance to make a decent living, even under adverse circumstances" (1969:49).

Use of Shared Belongingness as a Strategy

Insofar as belongingness is a shared value, Ego can manipulate and influence Alter by appealing to this value. Recall the differentiation between expressive and instrumental values made in the Introduction. Ego can persuade Alter to comply with his request by pointing out their shared group identity. Drawing upon an autobiographical essay, "How I Got My Job," Dore describes how a Hōsei University graduate succeeded in getting a good job at a newspaper company by using a chain of connections (abbreviated *kone* in Japanese-English slang) with Hōsei-affiliated men, including alumni. The job-seeker mobilized the sense of belongingness to Hōsei University, shared by graduates who occupied high positions, to get support. Viewed one way, the *sempai* ("senior graduate") was only carrying out his obligation to the *kōhai* ("junior graduate"), though they were unknown to each other. As Dore observed, recruiting through such connections is favored by the employer since the new employee's good behavior is thus guaranteed by his personal obligation to his *sempai* and by the latter's responsibility for his *kōhai*'s conduct (1967:125-127). These factors apparently contribute to the practice common among certain companies of recruiting employees from certain universities only, ruling out a truly universal examination system. Similar but more extreme is the recruitment of faculty in academic establishments from among their own graduates: in spite of a widely felt need for cross-fertilization, the tradition of inbred recruitment appears hard to break.

The *sempai-kōhai* relationship, well described by Nakane (1970), is a mixture of shared belongingness and a hierarchical order that has a pleasant connotation for Japanese. It is thus common to introduce oneself as a *kōhai* of so-and-so, or to introduce someone else as one's *sempai* or *kōhai*. The psychiatrist Akira Kasamatsu has remarked that whenever a patient of his is younger he tells the patient that he is not talking to him as a doctor but as a *sempai* (Morita Ryōhō 1966:723). This makes it sound as if the doctor and patient belonged to the same group and thus seems to expedite psychiatric persuasion.

Priority of Group Goals

Concern for belongingness urges the individual to contribute to the group goal at the expense of his personal interest. Sacrifice for the group or nation is expected even when one is in fact pursuing his self-interest; profit-making businessmen are obliged to justify their actions in the name of a collectivity (Hirschmeier 1970). Yataro Iwasaki, the famous founder of Mitsubishi Zaibatsu (a gigantic combine of finance and industries), is depicted in the movie *Will to Win* as a strong-minded leader who saved Japan from economic crisis; he was portrayed as being dedicated foremost to the country, not to himself, although he was lucky enough to make money while demonstrating his loyalty.

There are dissenters to this widely accepted view of the patriotism of business leaders of samurai background in the Meiji era (1868-1912). Kozo Yamamura (1968), for instance, draws upon biographical data to argue that Meiji businessmen were economically as rational as businessmen in any other country, as much motivated by self-interest and profits. Their personal interests often overrode group interests or national goals, contends Yamamura. Whether or not Yamamura's point of view is valid, and his historical documentation *is* convincing, the fact remains that self-interest had to be pursued in the name of a collectivity. Making money for its own sake simply was not justifiable. True or not, every rich Japanese vowed that he made his money for the sake of *ie* ("house"). Compare this attitude with that of an American businessman like J. C. Penney, who reportedly said, "I just love to sell."

Today, Japanese describe themselves as "economic animals" devoid of ideals and sentiments. Although Japanese in general are more openly economically motivated than they used to be, the raison d'être of their economic interest still remains focused on the group.

Not only in economic enterprises, but in politics and even personal matters like marriage, the group tends to claim priority over the individual. Politicians stress their group identification and their personal sacrifice for the sake of group goals, be they those of the party, constituents, or nation; altruism tends to be a main theme in campaigns for political office. Again, American politicians are a contrast in that, while extolling altruism, they openly admit that they love political games.

If the group interest or goal overrides individual interest, it also overrides the interests of other groups unless a coalition is formed. Under the present capitalist system in Japan, company employees are aware of the keen competition between companies and try to ensure that their own company wins over other companies. This kind of collective egotism flourishes most uninhibitedly in international competition. For Japanese, legitimate egotism includes nation egotism, company egotism, or family egotism, not individual egotism.

Collective Implications of Inner Experience

Group identification is so internalized that even the inner experience of an individual tends to have collective implications.

First, both the pride and the shame of an individual are shared by his group, and in turn the group's pride and shame are shared individually by its members. A glorious solo performance by a group member makes other members proud, while a disgraceful action by another member causes a collective loss of face. Ego, then, tries to enhance the reputation of the group through his distinguished achievement and tries to avoid disgraceful conduct in order not to shame fellow members of the group. No one who causes his group shame is tolerated. Instances of international crime committed by Japanese, an example of which was the random firing by pro-Arab Japanese at an Israeli airport in 1972 that resulted in the murder of twenty-four innocent bystanders, are certain to arouse collective shame in all Japanese. In the example cited, it was because of this shared shame, I believe, that the three murderers were condemned most strongly by their countrymen. It would never occur to their Japanese accusers that these pro-Arab Japanese might have renounced their Japanese identity to join the anti-Israeli movement.

The collective sharing of shame becomes most acute when the dishonorable action by a group member is exposed to outside groups. The worst crime of a group member, then, is to expose the group shame. A famous instance of *mura hachibu* (village ostracism) was occasioned in 1952 when a case of political scandal involving a violation of law in a village election was exposed by a high school girl through her letter to a newspaper editor. She and her family became victims of *mura hachibu*, excluded from social interaction with villagers. Former ambassador Kawasaki's books on the Japanese upset Japanese readers not so much because the author mentioned some undesirable features of the Japanese character as because he exposed them internationally by publishing the book in English. The Japanese audience was particularly offended by Kawasaki's mention of the physical unattractiveness of Japanese in the eyes of foreigners (1969:49). Criticism against him culminated in the government's decision to dismiss him as ambassador.

Not only pride and shame, but also suffering, is collectively shared. The suffering of a group member is vicariously experienced by the other members, arousing guilt feelings in the latter even when they are by no means responsible for the suffering. The nation-wide excitement about the discovery of Sergeant

Yokoi seems compounded by the guilt aroused in many Japanese through their vicarious retroexperience of his deprivation and loneliness. They may also have felt proud of his endurance and unswerving Japanese loyalty.

The collective implications of individual experience are further found in Doi's characterization of the Japanese sense of guilt. As noted in the previous chapter, Doi believes that Japanese guilt is sharpest when a person is afraid that his action may result in betraying his group (1971:49).

CHAPTER 3
Empathy

For the Japanese, empathy (*omoiyari*) ranks high among the virtues considered indispensable for one to be really human, morally mature, and deserving of respect. I am even tempted to call Japanese culture an "*omoiyari* culture."

Omoiyari refers to the ability and willingness to feel what others are feeling, to vicariously experience the pleasure or pain that they are undergoing, and to help them satisfy their wishes. Kindness or benevolence becomes *omoiyari* only if it is derived from such sensitivity to the recipient's feelings. The ideal in *omoiyari* is for Ego to enter into Alter's *kokoro*, "heart," and to absorb all information about Alter's feelings without being told verbally. *Omoiyari* takes several forms.

Maintenance of Consensus

Omoiyari requires suppression of Ego's own ideas or wishes if they are opposed to Alter's. This is manifested in the conventional form of communication where Ego tries not to assert himself unless Alter is found to agree with him. In conversation the speaker does not complete a sentence but leaves it open-ended in such a way that the listener will take it over before the former clearly expresses his will or opinion. This is possible because, in Japanese, the verb expressing the speaker's will comes at the end of the sentence. By letting a sentence trail off before coming to the verb, the speaker can avoid expressing and imposing his ideas before knowing the listener's response. Seidensticker's remark about Japanese speech behavior is interesting in this respect: the Japanese attach importance to nouns and pronouns perhaps because they mistrust the definitiveness of verbs (1970*b*:406).

The fear of deviating from Alter's viewpoint, or the wish to maintain consensus with Alter, is further demonstrated by the frequency with which Ego interjects his speech with the particle *ne* ("isn't it?"), which sounds as if he is soliciting Alter's agreement. Here, not merely external conformity but inner agreement is being demanded. If properly empathetic, Alter assures and reassures Ego of his receptivity, congeniality, or agreement by frequently nodding and exclaiming, "I am listening," "That is so!" or "Yes." This becomes quite noticeable in a telephone conversation, where there are no cues other than vocal ones. The listener constantly breaks his silence to let the speaker know that he is listening with interest and agreement. The speaker, for his part, expects to hear such assuring utterances as signals to go on. Before I became aware of this characteristic of Japanese behavior, I felt abandoned, I must confess, whenever I had a telephone conversation with an American, who would not respond until I had completely finished saying what I wanted to say. I would keep asking, "Are you listening?" Conversely, a Japanese listener in an English conversation is likely to make such assuring interjections in English—"Yes, yes"—which sound too strongly expressive of agreement. This often leads the English speaker to underestimate the Japanese listener's comprehension of English, and to believe, wrongly, that the Japanese agreed before knowing the speaker's proposition. Furthermore, an American speaker, I am told, would take such interjections as a sign of the listener's impatience and demand for a quick completion of the statement.

Empathetic concern for maintaining consensus must be distinguished from conformism derived from belongingness, although the two overlap somewhat. Conformity based on shared belongingness may be easy to maintain and is therefore taken for granted. Consensus-maintenance out of *omoiyari* goes over and beyond shared belongingness and often applies to interaction between strangers as well. Such interaction mobilizes *omoiyari* to the fullest degree precisely because of the expected difficulty of reaching consensus.

Optimization of Alter's Comfort

Empathy is manifested in Ego's readiness to anticipate and accommodate Alter's need. Ego tries to optimize Alter's comfort by providing what Alter needs or likes and by avoiding whatever might cause discomfort for him. Vogel observed this sort of hospitality in the Japanese preference for *ozendate* meaning, literally, "a table set with a full-course dinner." "The Japanese concept of hospitality is to have everything arranged ahead of time, including lodging, food, transportation, and detailed itinerary, rather than waiting to consult with the guest" (1963:235). All this should be done on the basis of an understanding of Alter's feelings without verbal communication.

Contrast that with the situation encountered in the United States. Yuji Aida has pointed out that in family settings on American television one often sees the wife, serving coffee, ask the husband whether he would like to have cream. It would be inconceivable for a Japanese woman not to know what her husband likes after many years of living together (1970:161). This example demonstrates the American belief that each individual knows best what he wants and that no one else can claim better knowledge. In a similar vein, Doi writes about the American host who, before offering anything, asks his guest, first, whether he would like a soft drink or hard liquor. If the guest decides to have liquor, the host then asks whether scotch or bourbon is preferred. And then how would the guest like it—on the rocks, with water, and so forth—and how much? After dinner, the guest is again asked whether he prefers coffee or tea, and whether he wants cream and sugar in it. Having been the recipient of such hospitality, Doi realized that it was an American custom, but at the same time noted, "I could not care less," in reference to the choices offered (1971:3).

Doi's anecdote is a reminder that there are cultural differences in the concept of empathy. In America, empathy is shown by giving Alter freedom to make up his mind, while Japanese empathy refers to anticipating and taking care of Alter's wants. The extreme form of empathy, whether Japanese or American, may be grotesque and far from genuine empathy. Indeed, *omoiyari* often goes far beyond and even against Alter's wishes. A Japanese writer, on returning from the United States, wrote in a weekly magazine that in the United States nothing happens to you unless you yourself initiate action to get what you want, whereas in Japan you experience the reverse. Japanese, he felt, will offer help and will work for you if you remain inactive. You suddenly find yourself caught up by kind, well-meaning friends and neighbors who want to help you find a spouse or buy a house. If you do not want to be helped in this way, you must not just sit but take action (recalled from memory—source untraceable).

At this point, *omoiyari* becomes synonymous with *osekkai* ("meddlesomeness"), which is the antithesis of empathetic understanding. If *omoiyari* is considered a virtue, *osekkai* behavior is considered a vice. But Japanese society is no shorter on *osekkai* than on *omoiyari*. Perhaps *osekkai* must be accepted as the other side of the coin of *omoiyari*. The reader may recall the variation of cultural values discussed in the Introduction: the same value may appear desirable in one situation and an undesirable, obligatory constraint in another.

Alter's comfort is optimized not only by providing pleasure, but by preventing displeasure. One should note how often in speech the Japanese refer to the need not to cause *meiwaku*, "trouble," for another person, not to be in his way, and not to hurt his feelings. In actual behavior, too, they tend to be circumspect and reserved so as not to offend other people. Thus, the virtue of *enryo*, "self-restraint," is exercised not only to respond to group pressure for conformity but to avoid causing displeasure for others, regardless of their group membership.

Analyzing the basic personality of the Japanese, Takizawa singled out their weakness in aggression and immaturity with aggressive mechanisms. He traced this characteristic to the oral fixation of the Japanese, compared with Westerners' anal fixation, and thus to the immaturity and primitiveness of Japanese culture (1972:160-162). This interpretation may be perfectly sound from the standpoint of Freudian psychoanalysis, which is biased toward the Western ideals of individual autonomy and aggressiveness. Lack of aggression, however, can be taken as the very sign of maturity and humanness if considered in the light of empathetic consideration and self-restraint practiced so as not to offend others. Indeed, the Japanese believe that the ability to empathize with others depends upon the amount of hardship and suffering one has gone through. One of the sentence fragments in the sentence-completion test I administered was "Perhaps because I experienced suffering when I was young" (see Appendix, Table 2). Response data showed that 14.9 percent of adults and 5.7 percent of youths responded by expressing empathetic understanding for other people who were suffering (category 5a). For example: "I cannot help offering help when someone is in trouble"; "I do not want my children to suffer." Even in free associations like this the Japanese tend to connect Ego's suffering with his capacity for empathy.

The imposition of self-restraint to avoid hurting Alter's feelings also can reach an extreme that reveals immaturity even to most Japanese. The individual may acquiesce in the face of an intrusion on his rights or autonomy only because he is reluctant to offend another person by claiming his right. The Japanese customer at a shop or restaurant does not examine the bill or count his change, not only because such action may cost him face, but often because he does not want to hurt the feelings of the waiter or cashier by even a hint of mistrust. This is in gross contrast to Chinese behavior. The Chinese seem to take pride in being sharp in monetary matters and consider it foolish to lose even a penny by miscalculation. The Chinese host does not hesitate, in front of his guests, to negotiate with the restaurant manager on the price of the meal, to examine the bill carefully, and protest to the waiter if he finds the slightest overcharge. Bargaining for a discount at various shops and even for metered taxi fares seems generally to be enjoyed by the Chinese.

A few years ago in Japan, a large-scale real estate fraud was brought to public attention by the mass media. One of the victims, who had lost money to a perfidious realtor, was asked in a television interview why he had signed the contract when he was not quite confident, as he said he was not, about the transaction. He replied to the effect that he had been pressed to sign to such a degree that he could no longer resist without hurting the agent's feelings (NHK-TV, 6/4/71).

If this verifies Takizawa's hypothesis of the immaturity of the Japanese ego, the concern for not causing trouble for others may conversely lead to a compulsion for independence. Something that Japanese most insist on avoiding is becoming a nuisance or burden to someone else. Reliance on other people for help even in an emergency is disapproved of if it involves burdening others. One outcome of such thinking is a stubborn insistence on self-help, on the rejection of others' offers of help, and thus on the apparent autonomy of the individual. Japanese individuality, thus conceived, rests not on the imposition of one's will on the social environment but on the refusal to impose oneself on it.

Sentimental Vulnerability

In social interactions, the Japanese experience hurt feelings at the slightest provocation. Their emotions appear to be as fragile as eggshells. This sentimental vulnerability dovetails with empathy in that vulnerability necessitates empathetic care, while the availability of the latter encourages the persistence of the former. There is no way of pinning down which comes first—the very essence of social relativism. Furthermore, if Ego's expectation of empathetic treatment by Alter is culturally imbedded, as in Japan, any deviation by Alter from that expectation is likely to hurt Ego. If the customer counts his change, the cashier is likely to feel offended. In Chinese culture, customers do count and protest if there is any mistake, and the cashier, far from being offended, takes it for granted that this will be done. We can trace the interrelatedness of empathy and vulnerability even further: Alter's disapproval of Ego is a sign of Alter's displeasure, which arouses depression in Ego because Ego is empathetically concerned with Alter's comfort.

Given such vulnerability, one can hurt another's feelings as an effective strategy for social sanction. When Ego wants to punish Alter, all he has to do is to show his or someone else's displeasure, to allude to Alter's misbehavior, or more severely, to embarrass Alter in front of others. Such displayed lack of empathy would not work as an effective sanction in cultures where people are generally tough or "hard-boiled."

Wounded feelings must be healed. Social interaction is the best therapy for sentimental injury. The individual, hurt and depressed, will not be left abandoned but will be picked up by an empathetic colleague or friend. A close co-worker may immediately sense the injury and invite him to a bar after work. As he talks out his feelings to the receptive listener, who responds with consoling remarks, while they empty one glass after another, he finds his injury gradually healed. Without this kind of routinized social therapy, the injured feeling might become stabilized into a neurosis.

When the lack of empathy is shown deliberately and unjustly, the wound is likely to fester, instead of being healed, into an *urami*, "a grudge" or "rancor." Japanese of all classes and levels of sophistication often refer to themselves as either holders or targets of *urami*. Many religious sects, including the Salvation Cult, admonish their followers to transform *urami* into gratitude. This indicates the propensity of a Japanese to hold and accumulate *urami*, instead of fighting back, against someone who has violated the norm of *omoiyari*. Likewise, the Japanese are fearful of and prove vulnerable to an *urami* directed at them. In the Salvation Cult, many of the spirits of the dead, and even gods, were revealed to hold an *urami* against someone, dead or alive, which could be nullified only through an empathetic propitiation by the living. Preoccupation with *urami* seems to reflect the sentimental vulnerability interlaced with empathy that is so common among the Japanese.

Vulnerability is further demonstrated by the masochistic display of wounded feelings. When Alter calls Ego by nasty names like "fool" or "good-for-nothing," Ego may, instead of protesting, accept them in conspicuous masochism by saying, "Yes, as you say, I am a fool." Such a response should be understood as a punishment for Alter's lack of *omoiyari* or as a threat that Ego is indeed going to behave foolishly or hold a grudge against Alter.

A grudge against the person who, lacking *omoiyari*, has hurt Ego may be turned into psychic energy for advancements. Many success stories, actual and fictional alike, reflect the Japanese propensity for thus transforming a revengeful motivation into an achievement motivation. The most effective retaliation, it seems, is to move upward in status—high enough to look down upon the former offender.

The Social Echo Effect

The cultural stress on *omoiyari* is derived from, and in turn conducive to, the sensitivity with which people interact with one another. The social sensitivity of the Japanese often extends to sensitization to interpersonal vibrations, an echo effect whereby Ego and Alter share feelings and thus influence each other. With such sensitization, a social relationship cannot be unilaterally determined. Initially one-sided love will eventually be accepted and returned, or will die down if not reciprocated. It is not that a Japanese never experiences lost or thwarted love but that his suffering in a romantic relationship owes not so much to lack of reciprocation as to intervention by a third party or other social obstacle.

The Japanese believe that if one wants to be trusted, one should first demonstrate trustworthiness; if one has to launch a risky business based on another's sincerity, the best way to begin is by trusting him. Ego's trustfulness will penetrate Alter's receptor, which in turn will rebound trustworthiness upon Ego. If, on the other hand, trust is held back even slightly, Alter will sense it and react in such a way that Ego's suspicions will be verified.

The Japanese emphasis upon sincerity or trueheartedness (*magokoro*) as the ultimate in moral rectitude may be partly explained by this belief in social reverberation. They believe that one's *magokoro* will eventually open another's closed heart and induce a desired reaction; that an event, however tragic or far-reaching, must be evaluated and judged by the presence or absence of *magokoro* in the parties involved.

The logic of social echo compels the suffering individual to look for the cause of his suffering within himself. This masochistic version of reverberation is a major teaching of the Salvation Cult. The cult followers are taught to attribute their experiences of suffering and misfortune to their own actions or dispositions, which, after release into the social environment, return to themselves. This interpretation is applied especially to cases in which suffering, including illness, is associated with interpersonal friction and estrangement, such as between husband and wife, parent and child, employer and employee.

Ego and Alter, in their mutual stimulation and repercussion, serve as a mirror for each other's image. Salvation Cult followers believe that "other people are mirrors reflecting your face" and that "everybody in the world is your teacher." Both expressions mean that Ego can perceive his sins and faults by watching others because their behavior faithfully reflects his own. A similar logic is used in the teachings of many other Japanese sects, including Seichō no Ie and Sōka Gakkai (Lebra 1974*a*).

The last point stresses that Alter does not only reciprocate Ego but comes to replicate Ego, much as a child replicates its parent. If Alter goes wrong, it is Ego's fault too, and Ego must share the blame. (This may explain why Japanese apologize too readily for no obvious reason.) One step further and the boundary between Ego and Alter disappears: social echo ends up in social fusion, where one person joins another in *ittaikan*, "feeling of oneness."

Social fusion seems to underlie the concept of *ninjō*, "human feeling." By *ninjō*, the Japanese mean two attitudes without consciously distinguishing them: (1) indulgence of Ego's natural inclination or desire in disregard of *giri* ("social obligations"), and (2) empathetic understanding and tolerance of Alter's desire, which may go against Ego's. "It is *ninjō*," a Japanese would say, "for a man to wish to marry a girl he has chosen." He would also say, "It is *ninjō* to let him have his way." In the word *ninjō*, self-indulgence seems to merge with empathetic consideration for others. The common usage of this term may facilitate social fusion, where one makes no distinction between his own and another's desire.

Intuitive Communication

Consideration of the echo effect in social interaction, which is apt to result in social fusion, brings us to the priority that the Japanese attach to implicit, nonverbal, intuitive communication over an explicit, verbal, rational exchange of information. Doi alluded to this aspect of Japanese behavior in saying that he "could not help feeling that Americans hate silence, whereas Japanese can sit together comfortably without saying a word to one another" (1972:6).

There may be many reasons for this. One reason was already proposed in the last chapter with reference to gregariousness, and more reasons will be offered in the following chapters. In the context of empathy, we can think of the following reasons. First, the existence of a social sensitivity acute enough to generate a social echo obviates explicit, verbal communication. If Ego is sensitive and responsive enough to what is in Alter's mind, verbal information from Alter will only be redundant or superfluous. And more than to avoid superfluity, the Japanese who stress the value of empathy feel that speech is a poor substitute for an intuitive understanding of what is going on in other people's minds.

Second, the Japanese find esthetic refinement and sophistication in a person who sends nonverbal, indirect, implicit, subtle messages. Such a "sophisticated" form of communication is made possible by the empathy between the sender and receiver of the message. The Japanese believe that only an insensitive uncouth person needs a direct, verbal, complete message. Aida refers to the use of a sign for subtle communication in this sense in an anecdote mentioned by another writer, Shunsuke Tsurumi.

> The husband comes home. He looks at the flowers at the alcove arranged by the wife. There is something disorderly in the way the flowers are put together. He then senses something upsetting his wife and tries to understand what has happened. Even if such arrangement was deliberately made by the wife with the view of letting her husband know her feelings, this, I think, still shows Japanese character. For instance, the wife is in no position to talk against her mother-in-law and yet wants to have her husband understand her trying experience [with the mother-in-law]. This dilemma can be overcome by this means [flower arrangement]. (Aida 1970:95)

Note that an arrangement of flowers would not serve as a symbol of the wife's state of mind unless the husband were empathetic and sensitized to such an implicit message.

Third, among the reasons for the priority of nonverbal communication is that an intuitive, roundabout form of communication based upon empathy is necessary to maintain the Japanese way of life; a verbal, explicit form may disrupt it. As long as people live in houses that are partitioned by unlocked sliding doors made of paper, there is need for a nonvocal way of sending and receiving messages; unthoughtful vocalization would endanger the harmony among those living under the same roof. Furthermore,

> "*Fusuma* [sliding doors] can serve as room-partitioning walls," says Dr. Watsuji, "only if the people using them respect their function as walls." That is not all, however. If there are people behind closed doors, the closure should be understood as a sign to "keep out" in some cases or "signal before entering" in other cases. (Aida 1970:147)

When one must resort to vocal communication, one should be sensitive to what is implied rather than what is expressed. If one wants to enter a closed room but is afraid of intruding upon the privacy of the people in it, one should exercise discretion in signaling his presence nearby and his intention to enter by a self-addressed mumble, such as, "It's cold today." Asking the people behind the door if one may come in would be too crude and unsympathetic (Aida 1970:147). It may be for this reason that Japanese do not hesitate to follow fixed conventions in conversation, and that even in films, as observed by Richie, no attempt is made to avoid cliches, truisms, or boredom. "To be boring, as the Noh play is undoubtedly boring, is merely another way of communicating" (Richie 1971:17). Of course in this case, "boring" is the judgment of an alien observer who is not sensitized to the message behind the message. The message of a conversation is not what was said but what was *not* said; silence is communication. One should further note the importance of *ma*, a silent interval or pause, in Japanese music.

Along the same line, we should consider why many Japanese avoid looking each other in the face while talking to each other. This occurs all the more when they are engaged in serious talk, such as a confession of love. Shimizu points out that actors in a television drama look away from each other. "Even at the essential moment, as in a love scene, when two persons are wholly related to each other, and when they stand close together, the man looks up to the stars, while the woman looks down toward her feet." Shimizu then speculates that his own exhaustion during a trip abroad owed partly to his exposure to the unfamiliar custom of having people look into his eyes while talking (1968:206-207).

Besides speech, the eye is most expressive of one's state of mind. A culture that emphasizes intuitive communication is unlikely to encourage direct eye-to-eye communication. If people are inordinately sensitive receptors of social stimuli, as the Japanese are, the information sent and received by the eyes may be overwhelming. *Omoiyari* thus involves not only a constraint upon verbal expression but also upon ocular expression. Thus, *omoiyari*, while based upon one's ability to enter into another's inner state, also demands the inhibition of that ability in some respects. Intuitive communication involves both sides of *omoiyari*.

Guilt

For Japanese, guilt, while derived from many sources, seems especially sharply felt when empathy is stimulated at the sight of a sufferer. Guilt is thus associated with the feeling of *kawaisō*, "pitiable." It is not so much Ego's own aggression as Alter's pain that makes Ego feel guilty. If Alter's pain is due to Ego's aggression, the guilt will be overwhelming in intensity. Similarly, Ego will feel more guilty if Ego finds Alter suffering vicariously in Ego's behalf. This can be further extended to a group under the pressure of belongingness. In August 1970, twenty-five years after an atomic bomb was dropped over Nagasaki, the mayor of Kitakyūshū, a city north of Nagasaki on the island of Kyūshū, sent a gift of money (¥300,000) to the people of Nagasaki. It was in token of sympathy for "those in Nagasaki who were victimized by an atomic bomb as substitutes for the people of Kokura [the old name for a ward of the present Kitakyūshū]." The mayor's message, printed in the newspaper, explained:

> According to MacArthur's memoirs, the initial target of bombing was Kokura. Because of bad weather, however, the B-29 carrying the atomic bomb could not locate the intended target. After vainly circling the area for 50 minutes, the pilot turned to your city. Even though this may be a quirk of fate, the citizens of Kitakyūshū have felt profound sympathy and a sort of guilty conscience. Please use this money for the victims. (*Seibu Nippon* 8/8/70)

Note that the "guilty conscience" of the Kitakyūshū citizens had nothing to do with their aggression or responsibility. They felt guilty because they felt the pain of the Nagasaki citizens even more keenly when they learned that they had been the intended target.

CHAPTER 4

Dependency

A culture that extols empathy must tolerate or even promote dependency, since an empathetic actor needs a dependent partner and vice versa. Indeed, empathy and dependency stimulate and sustain each other.

The Japanese have a variety of commonly used idiomatic phrases expressing dependency or helplessness. Among them are: *Otanomi shimasu* ("I am asking you," or "I depend upon you"); *Anata dake ga tayori desu* ("I have no one but you to rely upon"); *Issai o omakase shimasu* ("I shall leave everything to you"). When strangers are introduced to each other, they say, *"Yoroshiku onegai shimasu,"* which is equivalent to "How do you do?" but conveys the future dependency of the greeters on each other. Asked "How are you?" a conventionally minded Japanese is likely to answer *"Okagesamade,"* literally meaning "Thanks to your protection (or benevolence)," which may or may not be followed by "I am well."

The Japanese concept of dependency should not be understood as implying unilateral passive reliance upon another without reciprocal exchange. The right to be dependent must be "bought" by acts fulfilling obligations or by making concessions. We are still within the framework of social relativism.

CULTURAL TYPES OF DEPENDENCY

Dependency on Patronage: Symbolic Filiation

When two persons are unequal in status or power, the inferior becomes dependent upon the superior for help and support. The latter is expected to exercise his power in favor of the dependent, thus forming a patron-client tie. This type of dependency is found in the relationships between employer and employee, chief and subordinate, leader and follower, teacher and disciple, *sempai* and *kōhai*, landowner and tenant, a wealthy man and his entourage, main house and branch house, and so forth.

In Japanese tradition, this type of dependency occurs most often as a quasi-familial relationship, where the dependent partner assumes the role of a child toward the supporting partner, who plays the role of a parent. Certain occupational, economic, and political groups, as well as gangsters, use quasi-kinship terms indicating such symbolic filiation. Typical examples are: *oyabun* and *kobun*, *oyakata* and *kokata*, or just *oya* and *ko* (*oya* and *ko* meaning "parent" and "child," respectively, and *bun* and *kata* both meaning "role" or "status"). (For *oyabun-kobun* relationships, see Ishino 1953; Bennett and Ishino 1963.) Even where other terms like *sensei* and *deshi* ("teacher" and "disciple") or *sempai* and *kohai* are preferred, the parent-child relationship tends to be the model. The same sort of symbolic filiation prevailed in the military life of prewar Japan. As pointed out by Hiroshi Minami, a social psychologist, military units formed pseudofamilies consisting of pseudoparents and pseudochildren. A former officer is quoted as saying, "The warrant-officer is like a housewife who takes good care of soldiers as a mother, while the company-commander may be likened to a father whose orders are strictly observed but who has the affection of kinship towards his soldiers" (1954:157).

The "child"-role player can expect to depend upon the "parent"-role player for security and protection by appealing to the latter's *oyagokoro* ("parental sentiment"), which is characterized as warm, benevolent, and nurturant. The *oyabun* may indeed display *oyagokoro* toward their *kobun*, the latter in turn responding with gratitude. However, as observed by Minami, *oyagokoro* can turn to cruelty, the *oya* demanding that the *ko* make unlimited sacrifices in return for the *oya's* given or expected benevolence.

> *Oya-gokoro*-ism among the Japanese leaders brings forth an eccentric tendency to seek for the sacrifice of their inferiors who are counted as their children. For instance, a commander of the Suicide Squad said: "With such a deep attachment towards my inferiors as any parents would have to their children, I wanted to

find a good chance for them at any risk to do some respectable service for the Emperor." (1954:158)

The point is that dependency on patronage cannot be obtained free of charge. Though the *oya's* benevolence may be unlimited, the dependency of the *ko* on that benevolence has to be coupled with his total dedication and sacrifice.

Dependency on patronage was naturally stronger and more common in prewar times, when the social structure was more authoritarian and when economic security for the average person was hard to come by. Postwar democratization, as well as the labor shortage and affluence, has weakened dependency of this type.

Dependency on Attendance: The Taboo of Status

A sort of inverse dependency relationship is that of a person of superior status being dependent upon an inferior who waits upon him and takes care of his personal needs. Such a caretaker is necessary to spare the high-status person daily chores that are beneath his dignity and to protect his status from exposure to the mundane. In Japan, where status tends to be tabooed, the higher up one goes on a status ladder, the more dependent one becomes on a caretaker in attendance.

Accommodative attendance may be provided not only by a hired servant but by one's occupational subordinate. The head of a department at a university would be waited upon by an assistant professor, who would, in turn, be attended by an instructor or a graduate student, whether in finding information at the library or in lighting a cigarette. All offices, academic, governmental, corporational, have *ochakumi* (literally, "tea servants"), who are most often recruited from the ranks of female office workers (much to the chagrin of Japanese champions of women's liberation), as if self-service were incongruous with certain statuses. Executives, university presidents and deans, and many others holding important positions depend upon the services of chauffeurs for transportation. Accustomed to seeing such dependency in persons of high status, I was shocked to come across an American university president in a grocery store, doing his shopping as I was mine.

At home, the husband depends upon the wife for domestic care. The husband is helpless in housekeeping tasks, such as doing the laundry, cooking, cleaning, and child rearing. He may be ignorant of what is where in the house; if his wife is away from home for some reason his colleagues will immediately sense it from his sloppy appearance. The widower becomes dependent upon a daughter, sister, or other available female. This shows that male status is tabooed and that men must be protected from mundane chores.

Although dependency on attendance correlates with status, most Japanese regardless of status seem eager to be waited upon. Men like to do their drinking at a bar instead of at home partly because they can better satisfy this dependency need through the immediately available, professional, feminine service of the hostesses. It is even more pleasurable to a bar patron to be surrounded by several hostesses, instead of one, competing with each other to serve him. Foreign visitors have reported finding themselves at a loss when a group of hostesses or waitresses swarms over them in a Japanese bar or restaurant. The hostesses' behavior undoubtedly has an economic motive, since the multiple service will be reflected in the customer's bill. But it is also a response to a common Japanese desire to be pampered. It might be added that women enjoy receiving this kind of service, too.

Like the other kinds of dependency, dependency on an attendant's service satisfies one's wishes but also binds one in obligation. A chief who expects to be waited upon must forgo his freedom. On the other hand, if, in order not to lose his freedom, he chooses to care for himself rather than be waited upon, he will not be popular. Dependency has a price. That even Japanese who ordinarily prefer dependency on attendance sometimes become aware of its constraints and wish to be independent is revealed when they travel abroad. While staying in America, where autonomy has been institutionalized in the many self-service operations, Japanese travelers miss the personal service so abundantly available back home. But they also clearly enjoy the discovered freedom. I have seen a number of Japanese professors and other academic figures, in temporary residence in the United States, do shopping and other domestic work without a blush; a dean looked frankly happy pushing a cart at a supermarket and confessed he liked it, although he added he would not do it in Japan.

Dependency on attendance is complementary to dependency upon patronage in that two individuals, hierarchically graded, can exchange the two types of dependency. This means that a superior and inferior can be perfectly interdependent without losing their status difference.

Dependency on Indulgence: *Amae*

Dependency is also an emotional state that appeals to and is fulfilled by another's indulgence. This type of dependency is epitomized by *amae*, a term made famous by Doi's work (1962, 1971). *Amae* is the noun form of the verb *amaeru*, in Doi's definition, "to depend and presume upon another's benevolence." "Because this term is associated with the pleasant gustatory sense of *amai* ("sweet"), *amaeru* has a distinct feeling of sweetness and is generally used to describe a child's attitude or behavior toward his parents, particularly his mother" (1962:132). An *amae* relationship can bind two mature adults, however. Through his psychiatric practice, Doi came to realize the importance of this dependency need from the way his Japanese patients showed their wish to *amaeru*.

Doi applies this concept broadly, so broadly that one might get the impression that almost all Japanese behavior including political behavior can be explained by the motivation of *amae*. For our purpose of typological clarification, it is necessary to restrict the meaning of this term to an indulgence relationship. Furthermore, if *amae* behavior is so common, its complementary role behavior should be equally common.

The role of expressing *amae*, called *amaeru*, must be complemented and supported by the role that accepts another's *amae*. The latter role is called *amayakasu*. Doi did not take into consideration the necessity of role complementarity between *amaeru* and *amayakasu*, perhaps because of the role asymmetry in the therapeutic relationship, where the therapist is inhibited from indulging the *amae* wish of the patient.

Once role complementarity is taken into account, it is apparent that both *amaeru* and *amayakasu* can take active or passive forms, although Doi looks at *amaeru* only in its passive form. The following fourfold definition emerges:

	Active (Initiating)	*Passive* (Accepting)
Amaeru	To solicit Alter's indulgence.	To accept Alter's indulgence.
Amayakasu	To solicit Alter to wish indulgence from Ego.	To accept Alter's wish for indulgence.

(Though they are verbs in Japanese, I will use *amaeru* and *amayakasu* here as adjectives and nouns, for convenience.)

There are no fewer candidates for an *amayakasu* role than for an *amaeru* role in Japan. When it goes too far, the *amaeru-amayakasu* relationship is criticized because it involves a lack of discipline on the part of the dependent person. Older siblings and even neighbors will tease, for remaining too long an *amaekko* ("*amae* child"), a young child who, for example, insists on accompanying his mother wherever she goes or demands her breast at bedtime every night. *Amae* sometimes refers to self-indulgence, as in the expressions *jibun ni amaeru* ("*amaeru* oneself") or *jibun o amayakasu* ("*amayakasu* oneself"), both of which usually imply disapproval for not taking responsibility seriously. To be an *amai* person is to be one who is uncritically indulgent or too naïve to be prepared for the hardships of life, and therefore one who cannot be relied upon.

Despite these negative implications of *amae*, the *amaeru-amayakasu* relationship is a desirable and often irresistible one. The person who knows how to *amaeru* has an easier time in Japan than one who does not, for the *amaeru* role player is readily responded to and accepted by the *amayakasu* role candidate. This calls attention to the strategic manipulability of *amae* in interpersonal relations. Ego can manipulate Alter's wish to be nurturant by exhibiting or withdrawing his willingness for *amae*. Ogino (1968) goes so far as to argue that *amae* is a solution to the conflict between a need for independence or aggression and a need for dependency. In this process of conflict resolution, social bargaining takes place between the *amaeru* role player and the *amayakasu* role player. Ogino's argument implies that *amae* is a result of judgment by an independent actor and that a totally dependent person is incapable of *amaeru*. Whether one takes this extreme position or identifies *amaeru* with dependency, it is clear that the *amaeru-amayakasu* interaction is immensely desirable or useful to most Japanese. This is further demonstrated by the popularity of lullabies among the Japanese, regardless of age. Incongruous though it might appear to foreigners, it would not be unusual to see a bunch of tough karate athletes singing a lullaby together at a social gathering. A familiar lullaby undoubtedly stimulates a longing for the days when *amaeru-amayakasu* interaction was uninhibited. Japanese adults in general feel a strong nostalgia for their happy childhood.

Dependency on Pity: Appeal for Empathy

Finally, we must consider the type of dependency that is based on Alter's pity aroused by Ego's plight. Here dependency and empathy are exactly complementary. Ego presents himself or appears in the eyes of Alter as helpless, miserable, defeated, and in desperate need of help. This does not fail to stimulate Alter's pity. It is not a coincidence that traditional love songs deploring hopelessness are sung in a despairing, tearful voice to appeal to the empathetic chord of the audience; one's tears mingle with another's in *morai-naki* ("sympathetic weeping").

The Japanese who is under a strain, physical or emotional, will not keep it to himself, as Americans might, but will feel compelled to reveal it to someone who will listen and "understand." Even if the listener does nothing more to help the sufferer, the latter will feel relieved. Conversely, if the sufferer does not find someone understanding to talk to, the situation will become unbearable for him. "Nobody understands me" is a commonly heard utterance of despair.

That empathetic pity is easily, and sometimes compulsively, aroused at the sight of helpless or suffering people can be illustrated by the following recollection of the behavior of Japanese soldiers in China during the Sino-Japanese War.

> There were many small children abandoned on the battlefield. These children, it turned out, were looked after and loved with remarkable tenderness by the Japanese soldiers who were called Oriental devils and were indeed destructive and cruel otherwise. As far as my company was concerned, the importance of following military rules came only after the need to protect the abandoned children of the enemy. Toward evening, after a day's march of fifty kilometers, we would enter a village and find children abandoned there. The soldiers would not begin their routine duties of the military life, such as taking care of horses and guns, until they had cooked the little food they carried and had fed the children. Even though I, as platoon leader, yelled at them, they paid no attention to me, saying, "The kids are crying, sir." . . . There was no one who committed atrocities on a child, and any soldier who was not kind enough to children was looked down upon as subhuman. (Furukawa 1972:18-19)

The point here is not to deny the cruelty of Japanese but to emphasize that, despite their cruelty, the apparent helplessness of even enemy children could stimulate their tender side.

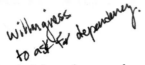
Willingness to ask for dependency.

The helpless do not always remain passive nor are they always looked upon as objects of pity. They may take the initiative in soliciting pity and asking for help from others. Compared with independence-oriented Americans, the Japanese have much less resistence to begging for help. The supplicant would say, "Please do this for me; look, I am begging you with my head as low as this." The person addressed would feel pity and would be likely to say, "When you ask me so earnestly, bowing so deep, I cannot say no." Appeal for empathy is articulated verbally by the supplicant when he says, "Please try to put yourself in my position."

Pity does not come exclusively from a person higher in status than its receiver, unlike patronage. A sick father may appeal to his daughter's pity by asking her to remain unmarried to look after him, to marry a rich man in order to support him, to work as a prostitute to earn the livelihood of the family, or, as in prewar Japan, to sell herself outright. The dependent person, thus conceived, is more or less parasitic, whereas the person depended upon is obliged to make a sacrifice. The prewar moral education curriculum called *shūshin* ("self-discipline") contained an abundance of stories, actual and fictional, about a child on whose sacrifice the whole family, parents and siblings, depended for survival. The object of such stories was to inculcate filial piety and willingness to sacrifice in schoolchildren, but one might wonder how such dependency by the family on a child could be tolerated. To be fair, it should be added that not only children but parents and adults were described as making sacrifices for children. Mothers were often depicted in moral lessons as the incarnation of sacrifice based on empathetic nurturance.

KEY DEPENDENCY RELATIONSHIPS

The foregoing ideal types of dependency do not exist discrete from one another in real life. An actual dependency relationship is a mixture of all four with varying degrees of emphasis. Let us examine the actual operation of dependency in three significant dependency relationships.

Mother and Child

The dependency relationship takes a typical and total form when expressed in mother-child interaction. It is here that all four types of dependency intertwine to form a culturally idealized relationship. First, the mother has power over the child, the latter being totally dependent on her for security, protection, and survival. Second, the mother is an overall caretaker for the child, responsible for his feeding, toilet control, clothing, and health. The child is dependent on the mother's attendance. Third, the wish for indulgence is fully gratified in the mother-child relationship. The mother can *amayakasu*, while the child can *amaeru*, in the most intimate manner, without much inhibition. Finally, her whole life being devoted to the welfare of the child, the mother symbolizes the ultimate in empathy and sacrifice, on which the helpless child depends.

There has been a postwar change in the image of the Japanese mother. While the prewar mother was quiet and submissive, the postwar mother is depicted in the mass media as aggressive and domineering. Nonetheless, the mother has been characterized consistently as dependable and helpful to her child. The child, for his part, does not renounce his deep attachment to his mother even after he matures, which offers another contrast to the American adolescent, who struggles to acquire independence from his mother and father. The mother's boy is not teased or made fun of as much as the henpecked husband is in Japan, whereas the reverse may be true in the United States. It should be added that the American child's compulsion for independence is a counteraction against the mother's compulsion for domination, which seems also strong in the United States. The dominance and possessiveness of the Japanese mother is either balanced by or hidden behind her sacrificial attitude or posture. Again we are reminded of the difference between individualistic, possessive inclinations in the one culture, and role adjustment and sensitivity in the other.

All this amounts to a reexamination of the Freudian hypothesis on psychosexual maturation. Freud's belief in the need for emancipation from parents, especially from the mother, for maturation or developing masculine identity, must be revised on the Japanese cultural scene where a sexual identity is established differently; it is a matter of occupying a proper place and acting out the role prescribed for that place, as a man, or as a woman. This does not necessarily require rejection of dependency on one's mother: in fact it is the mother who constantly indoctrinates the child to be a boyish boy or a girlish girl.

In Western culture, emancipation from maternal dominance is so compulsory for masculine identity that it becomes a traumatic pass-fail test. The Japanese do not regard passing such a test as necessary or desirable. Few, thus, are marked as failures. There may be many "mother's boys" in Japan, but they do not stand out as they do in a society where that test is imposed.

Japanese masculinity is threatened more by a lack of resoluteness or courage, indecisiveness and cowardice being regarded as feminine traits. Masculinity is asserted more against the opposite sex than against one's mother or other males.

The mother remains a lifelong object of attachment, not only because she is the source of all kinds of gratification, but also because she symbolizes the weakness and inferiority of the female sex in a male-dominant society. "The male world gives orders and expects obedience; the female world threatens and pleads, but can always be made to yield if the male is sufficiently strong and persistent in his aggression. The female world is loved, ill-treated, and despised" (Gorer 1962:320). This is another reason why the Japanese adolescent does not feel his male ego threatened by his attachment to his mother. This curious mixture of dependability and inferiority seems to make the mother the most idealized cultural heroine—one who is, simultaneously, the object of yearning, sympathy, and guilt. It is no accident that the mother's role has been a persistent theme in popular songs, stories, plays, and movies, and that incidents on that theme are filled with tearful scenes that never fail to move the audience to tears.

Mother as a feeder is symbolized by her breasts, which are frequently mentioned in conversation, plays, poems, and songs. I recall a nursery song that went something like this:

> Twos, twos, what comes in twos?
> Your eyes, one and two, they are two;
> Your ears, one and two, they are two.
>
> What else comes in twos?
> Your hands, see, aren't they two?
> Your feet, too, are two, aren't they?
>
> Aren't there better things in twos?
> Those round things, Mama's *oppai*,[1]
> Aren't they two?

In Japan, woman's breasts have been adored more as a symbol of maternal nurturance than of sex.

In attachment to one's mother, the Chinese seem even to

---

1. Meaning both the mother's breast (or nipple) and milk.

surpass the Japanese. Analyzing Chinese family relations as manifested in classic Chinese operas, Jing Hsu and Wen-Shing Tseng (n.d.) single out the intense emotions held by a grown-up son for his mother, which override those of all other relationships including the conjugal one. Devotion to mother takes priority even over loyalty to the country. The closeness between Chinese mother and child, as described by Hsu and Tseng, sounds like an absolute imperative for the child. The Japanese counterpart is more relativistic: which relation claims primacy depends upon circumstances and situations, although dedication to the nation tends to be primary.

Finally, it should be noted that mother-child dependency is not unilateral, but that the mother depends upon the child as much as the converse. In Japan, the mother, while sacrificing herself for the sake of her child, may remind him verbally or behaviorally of her heavy, sometimes exclusive, dependence upon him as the bolster for her life. She would say, "Remember, my child, you are the only one I have to depend upon; you are my life goal." Given such overwhelming dependency on the child, it is understandable why middle-class mothers in Japan today are prone to become *kyōiku-mama* (mothers obsessed with education who constantly press their children to study, especially in preparation for entrance examinations). This is another reminder that social behavior such as dependency is interactional: dependency leads to interdependency.

The mother-child relationship will be examined in more detail in chapter 8, on socialization.

Heterosexual Relationship

Dependency is extended to the heterosexual relationship such as in romance or marriage. The husband and wife alternate in playing a dependent role outside and within the house. Outside the house, it is the wife who is dependent, as if she were unable to make any judgment independent of the husband's opinion. The common pattern in public life still remains *fushō-fuzui* ("the husband initiates, the wife follows"), and a *tanomoshii* ("dependable") husband is regarded as ideal by many women. The Japanese, who are accustomed to women's dependency outside the domestic realm, are impressed with American wives who do not hesitate to express their own ideas and beliefs regarding politics, social problems, or religion. The same point was made by Nakane (1970:11) in mentioning that Indian women openly disagree with their husbands.

A step inside the house, the dependency role is reversed. The husband depends on the wife for housecleaning, cooking, and child rearing, of course, but also for taking care of his personal needs, such as helping him change his clothes after work. The husband usually gives his whole paycheck to his wife, who is responsible for budgeting, monthly payments, and savings. She may dole out an allowance to the head of the house as well as to the children. Having exclusive responsibility for financial management, she may also be able to accumulate a "secret savings" (*hesokuri*). In most cases the husband is ignorant of the regular living expenses of the household. Accumulation of *hesokuri* is so commonly practiced, however, that it ceases to be really secret; indeed, the husband comes to depend upon this "secret" savings for emergencies. Economists, both Japanese and foreign, have noted the strong Japanese inclination toward saving, which has contributed to Japan's economic development. Perhaps the penny-wise housewife deserves much of the credit.[2]

If dependency is not merely a matter of need but an expression of emotional attachment as well, dependency probably has a place in the romantic relationship. Indeed, the so-called pure-love stories (*jun'ai mono*) popular among high school girls, typically involve one partner's dependence upon the other. One partner, male or female, may be fatally ill, while the other partner, fully aware of the hopelessness of their love affair, looks after the sick one and dedicates himself or herself to keeping the other happy. The audience seems overwhelmed by the subtle communication between the dying and the selfless person with no expectation of future reward. The one partner is totally dependent upon the other's protection, attendance, indulgence, and empathy. Sickbed or deathbed scenes seem indispensable to the climax of love-story movies. It is no mystery that Segal's *Love Story* has been a bestseller in Japan ever since it was published.

Nor is it unreasonable to assume that, given the desirability of dependency coupled with the idealized mother-child relation-

---

2. When the husband has an irregular extra income, he might keep it secret from his wife and spend it as additional self-allowance. This countersecret savings is also called *hesokuri*.

ship, love or marriage involves maternal nurturance. Marital harmony is often achieved or restored by the wife's taking a maternal role in relation to the husband, tolerating, as a mother would with a son, the husband's neglect of his marital responsibility. When sexual passion is replaced by maternal indulgence, the husband acquires more freedom but at the same time becomes more dependent upon his wife. Maternal love can be shown even when marriage has broken down.

In the novel *Kanojo no Ottotachi* [Her husbands] by Harumi Setouchi, Kōta, the husband, confesses to his estranged wife: "Since I cannot live alone, I shall marry another woman after our divorce." The wife who knows whom he is going to marry, says promptly: "I agree. It is indeed inconvenient for a man to live alone. I did not worry [while I was away] because I knew Chie was living with you. Otherwise, I would not have left you all by yourself such a long time." (Setouchi 1968:Mar. 18). This is a passage from a fiction, yes. But it shows a culturally ideal way of life for women: women can attain spiritual serenity by taking a maternal role vis-à-vis their husbands and thus freeing themselves from sexual jealousy. The wife in the passage quoted above once was a little jealous of her future successor, Chie, but "now she felt she could trust Chie to take care of Kōta [in her place]." Kōta, the husband, appears as a helpless child who should be looked after by one of the two "mothers."

That this novel was written by a female writer may mean that this is a faithful projection of women's view of marital life. Regardless, such a view is not uncommon at all. A *sewa nyōbō* ("caretaker wife") is ideal in the final analysis. A television serial drama called *Magokoro* [The true heart] protrays Maresuke Nogi, the greatest army general of Meiji Japan, as quite helpless without his wife. His mother, on her deathbed, asks her daughter-in-law, Maresuke's wife, to become a mother to him after her death. In analyzing the culturally shared conceptions of mother, Yoshiaki Yamamura has drawn upon a series of popular television dramas with the collective title of *Okāsan* [Mother], which ran from 1959 to 1967. In one story the mother, kneeling on the floor, tells her son's new bride, "My son has shortcomings, but from now on please take my position [literally, "be my substitute"] in giving him support" (1971:81). Similarly, another story has a mother say to her son's fiancée, "Please listen, my dear. I beg you. Will you please look after my child forever. This one, this child of mine is mentally delicate, you see, and needs a lot of care" (p. 95). In such stories, the daughter-in-law, in turn, tries to be like the mother-in-law. Hence, the wife becomes a mother to her husband. The man also has that expectation. Yamamura quotes a man saying to his girlfriend, "I had a mother who took good care of me. Her hand reached wherever I felt itchy [a figurative expression for sensitive, considerate, helpful care]. This made me want to find a woman like my mother to be my wife—that is why I have remained unmarried until today" (pp. 95-96).

This dependency pattern is duplicated in an extramarital affair. The mistress is economically dependent upon the man who provides her a house and living expenses. On the other hand, she begins to play the same role as his wife in taking care of his routine needs, preparing supper, cleaning and ironing his clothing, and so on. On such service, this illegitimate husband becomes dependent.

Escape from such domesticity is sometimes sought in a Lolita syndrome, as when a fifty-year-old man falls in love with a seventeen-year-old bar girl who has no inclination toward the caretaker's role. Here the man plays a fatherly role (the girl is likely to call him "papa"), thus retaining a dependency relationship.

Physical Dependency: The Sick, Aged, and Dead

The emotional desirability of dependency leads to the likelihood that an emotionally satisfying relationship can exist when one party is wholly and justifiably dependent upon the other, as when one is ill and under the total care of another person. Caudill (1962) noted from the Japanese responses to the Thematic Apperception Test that sickness provides a social occasion for emotional communication, for offering and accepting sympathetic care. The Japanese thus like to go to bed with mild illnesses, Caudill observed.

The sick person, particularly if hospitalized, draws the attention of his friends and colleagues. The hospital room, with the patient surrounded by sympathetic visitors, becomes a place for confirming and restoring group solidarity. The desire for belongingness and togetherness is well gratified. The patient's dependency seems to strike a sympathetic chord in people who might be indifferent otherwise. From the point of view of *amae*, it appears that one person's obvious need to *amaeru* has aroused in another the wish to *amayakasu*. In Japan, sickness, enabling such free exchange of emotions, should be observed in light of its social significance, of the role the patient can play vis-à-vis his nurse or visitors.

In this connection, Caudill (1961) also took note of the role of the *tsukisoi* for Japanese psychiatric hospital patients. A *tsukisoi* (meaning "attached") is a caretaker, in a hospital context, assigned to a patient in a one-to-one pairing on a twenty-four-hour basis. The *tsukisoi* role is assumed by a hired subprofessional nurse if the patient can afford it (Caudill limited his study to such nurses), or by the patient's mother, wife, or other female relative if the hospital permits it. The *tsukisoi* nurse feeds the patient, sits and sleeps by the patient so as to be available any time the patient needs help, and serves tea to visitors. The existence of such a role indicates the deficiency of hospital facilities in meeting patients' nonmedical personal needs. It also suggests the Japanese patient's inclination toward total dependency, necessitating such an overall caretaker.[3]

That the sick role gratifies one's dependency wish and is thus regarded as desirable is demonstrated by a familiar Japanese greeting pattern: Ego says to Alter, "How are you? What's the matter—You look pale" or "You look tired." Alter appreciates such concern on the part of Ego. Conversely, when Alter asks how Ego is, Ego willingly and specifically tells what is wrong with him, whether it is a terrible hangover or diarrhea.

Just as the sick person is expected to be dependent, the aged person is expected to and does depend upon the younger. In the traditional social structure, dependency of the aged is tied to the institutional requirement to perpetuate the *ie*. The aged and retired parents depend upon their son and successor and his

---

3. Even in the rational setting of a modern bureaucracy, Japanese prefer an "overall caretaker" to a professional, businesslike person as a boss. Attitude surveys done in the 1960s bear this out (Tōkei Sūri Kenkyūjo 1961:236-238; Hayashi, Nishihira, and Suzuki 1965:69). The respondents were asked which of the following two types of men they preferred as a section head: (1) a businesslike manager who neither demands extra work nor looks after his men outside work, or (2) one who overloads his men with work but who also helps them in their personal lives "as if he were their parent." The overwhelming majority of respondents favored the latter type, which the authors label *ninjō kachō* ("section chief with human feeling").

family for security, comfort, and emotional support. They are also concerned over who will take care of the funeral, ashes, and tablets, the grave, and memorial services for them and their ancestors. Attainment of peace of mind in one's late years and salvation after death is thus closely connected with this sense of dependency upon the succeeding generation. The successor is expected to be dependable, willing to prove his filial piety by gratifying their dependency wish.

The dependency of one generation on another thus involves role reversal in conjunction with one's stage in life: a child is dependent on his parent, while the latter in his old age becomes dependent on his child and successor, who is now mature. Such lifelong interdependency will be dealt with in chapter 6, on reciprocity.

The dead person, when envisioned in a trance, also shows dependency by asking the bereaved to pay more attention to him or by complaining of their neglect. Informants in the Salvation Cult were found to have been possessed in an overwhelmingly high frequency by a dependent type of spirit asking its host to help it attain salvation (more on this topic in chapter 14).

The last point leads us to speculate on the possible relationship between a culture's image of the supernatural and its dependency orientation. In a culture where the supernatural appears not self-sufficient but dependent, people may feel less inhibited about expressing dependency wishes than those in a culture where the supernatural is almighty. There may be mutual role emulation between the supernatural and human in this sense.

"Parthenogenetic" Independence

For most Japanese, as we have said, a dependency relationship is a desirable one. However, their attitude toward dependency is. no freer from ambivalence than toward any other cultural values. As indicated in connection with the types of dependency, one must pay a price for satisfying one's dependency wishes. Nor is it always possible to maintain a harmonious relationship between the dependent and the depended-upon. An apprentice or *kobun* may suffer under a system of patronage and put up with all kinds of interpersonal conflict with his master or *oyabun* because he hopes to be able to stand on his own feet some day. Becoming *ippondachi*, "independent," is the ultimate reward for all the hardships. On another level, despite the overwhelming power and influence of gigantic corporations, Japan has sustained a large number of small, independent businesses. There seems to be as much compulsion to set up one's own shop as to be employed and looked after by a large company. This longing for independence has nothing to do with a postwar change in values. It may even be said that the more tightly dependency is institutionalized, the more zealously one may wish to extricate oneself from that institutional yoke.

It is interesting to glance at how independence was acquired in the traditional occupational structure and how it was interlinked with the system of dependence. Historically, becoming *ippondachi* meant, first of all, branching out from the parental stem, namely, setting up a branch house or its equivalent. This was true with commercial shopkeepers, craftsmen, artists, scholars, and other tradesmen. The employee-apprentice-"child" branched out from the employer-master-"parent," normally with the permission and support of the latter. Such independence was earned through long years of dependence. It was not true independence, however. As long as one assumed the status of a branch, one was subject to the control of the parental stem or at least obligated to give formal consideration to the latter's wish. In an interview, a retired *geta* (wooden footwear)-maker in his seventies revealed that he still never failed to pay respect to his former master by visiting his grave and by offering a gift to his descendants twice a year.

Secondly, becoming *ippondachi* represented the initial step toward assuming the status of employer-master-parent with one's own dependent employee-apprentice-children. The latter would eventually branch out and the whole cycle would thus be repeated.

Dore has described these processes of mobility and career production as "parthenogenesis" (1967:120). This term captures remarkably well the cultural interlinkage between two opposed values: dependence and independence.

CHAPTER 5

Occupying the Proper Place

In this chapter we shall look at Japanese behavior from the point of view of commitment to the social structure, particularly as it involves concern with occupying the proper place. By proper-place occupancy I mean one's awareness of the place assigned to one in a social group, institution, or society as a whole; one's capacity and willingness to fulfill all obligations attached to that place; and one's claim to recognition of that place by others.

THE CONCEPT OF *Bun*

Most illustrative of this orientation is the Japanese word *bun*, meaning "portion," "share," "part," or "fraction." The Japanese use this term very frequently in such idiomatic expressions as: *bun o wakimaeru* ("to know one's *bun*"), *bun o mamoru* ("to adhere to one's *bun*"), *bun ni hajinai* ("not to disgrace one's *bun*"), *bun o tsukusu* ("to fulfill one's *bun*"). Compound nouns with *bun* are as often used, including *honbun* ("true *bun*"), *mochibun* ("the *bun* that one holds"), *toribun* ("the *bun* that one takes"). A student may be told to fulfill his *honbun* as a student, that is, to study hard instead of getting involved in a student movement, which would be outside his *bun*. Interestingly, even the term for self is a *bun* compound noun, *jibun*.

The concept of *bun* has three implications, which all derive from the image of society as an organic whole, individuals being parts of that organism. First, the individual is conceived as a fraction. To the extent that he derives his self-identity from his *bun* he does not count as an integer but only as a part or fraction of the whole. The individual as such is a nobody but becomes a somebody through occupying a fractional place and contributing to the whole society or group.

Second, *bun*-holders are interdependent. The individual, as a *bun*-holder, cannot be self-reliant but must be dependent on other *bun*-holders. The awareness of one's self-insufficiency and interdependence with others is an essential concomitant of the *bun* concept.

Third, every member of society is supposed to be a *bun*-holder. While an individual counts only as a fraction and depends on other individuals, every individual is provided with such a fraction, which makes his life meaningful. Japanese feel that everybody ought to have a *bun* and that if anyone happens to be *bun*-less something must be wrong with society. One of the responsibilities of an administrator or leader is to see that every member of his group holds a proper place (*onoono sono tokoro o eseshimeru*). If everyone holds a *bun*, then it follows that, given the above-mentioned interdependence among *bun*-holders, no one is expendable; everyone can claim his social significance.

Having a *bun* or a place presupposes that one belongs to a social group. This is where the present subject intermeshes with the subject of chapter 2, belongingness.

Bun may be translated into the anthropological and sociological terms status and role. These two terms, often overlapping and used interchangeably, have been analyzed by many specialists, notably Linton (1936:113-115), Parsons (1954), Goodenough (1965), and Nadel (1957). Selectively drawing upon their works, I shall analytically distinguish status and role respectively, in terms of rights and prerogatives vs. obligations and responsibilities, passive vs. active, and quality vs. performance. Status is occupied, whereas role is carried out. Furthermore, status refers to a position in a hierarchical structure, whereas role does not necessarily imply a hierarchy.

Status and role, thus defined, can be viewed in two ways. First, they are relational concepts in that a status or a role exists only in relation to or contingent upon another status or role, as the status or role of teacher, leader, or employer can exist only in relation to that of pupil, follower, or employee. A status in a hierarchy holds a higher or lower position relative to another status in this sense. Second, status and role can be conceptualized independently, for example, status and role attached to sex (woman's status), age (adult status), physical attributes (the status of the handicapped), or occupation (carpenter). (For a more elaborate analysis, see Nadel 1957.) The latter may be labeled classificatory as distinct from relational status and role. The following discussion will include both, with varying degrees of emphasis.

STATUS ORIENTATION

The norm of *bun* occupancy is clearly reflected in status orientation. *Bun* is sometimes used as synonymous with status, as implied in such phrases as: "to be contented with one's *bun*"; "not to disgrace one's *bun*." Status here refers to a position in a hierarchical social system. When Benedict characterized Japanese behavior in terms of "taking one's proper station," she referred to a hierarchical structure and its associated behavior (1946:43-75). Similarly, Nakane (1967) identified Japan as a *tateshakai* ("vertical society"), bringing into focus the hierarchical orientation of the Japanese.

Sensitivity to Rank Order

Status orientation first involves sensitivity to the rank order according to which behavior must be differentiated. Ego is sensitized to the status he holds relative to Alter on a hierarchical scale, to whether he is higher or lower. The ethos of social relativism is fully mobilized for two reasons: one's status does not exist by itself but comes into being only in relation to other statuses; and Ego can enjoy his status only if Alter recognizes and respects it. Sensitivity to rank order, called *joretsu ishiki* in Japanese, is derided but characterizes the behavior of many Japanese nonetheless. Often when a list of names is printed as of the coauthors of a book or in an advertisement endorsing a certain product, a footnote is added saying, "the order of names is alphabetical, or "no order implied." Such a statement is made to avoid offending anyone on the list by the placement of his name and to ensure that no reader takes the list as a hierarchical order.

Respect for status is shown by the common affixing of titles of honor such as *sensei* ("teacher" or "master") to a person's name. When it is necessary to omit such titles to avoid cumbersomeness, as in a list of many names, a special footnote again is needed:

"Titles of honor are omitted." Japanese resist making untitled reference to someone who deserves a title. A social psychologist (Hamaguchi 1966:74) confessed that in writing a paper for a professional journal he had difficulty deciding whether he should omit titles like Dr. and Professor in the names of scholars whose work he cited, particularly those who were his own teachers or *sempai*. In the course of overcoming his initial resistance to calling them simply by their surnames, he realized that his reaction was quite Japanese.

Dichotomization of Behavior

Sensitivity to rank order entails a dichotomous differentiation of behavior—the up-faced orientation toward a superior, and the down-faced orientation toward an inferior. Such dichotomy is indicated in the Japanese language, especially in the variation of verbs. Verbs tend to be associated either with upward or downward action. Giving something upward to a higher-ranking person is distinguished from giving downward to a lower-ranking person. Receiving is also distinguished between that coming from a higher-ranking person and from a lower-ranking person. The point is not that the Japanese language lacks in verbs that indicate horizontal motion, but that it is rather poor in status-neutral vocabulary, whereas status-indicative expressions are rich and elaborate. This is particularly true of spoken Japanese.

Upward speech vis-à-vis a superior has two aspects: exaltation with reference to Alter's behavior or state and humility with reference to that of Ego. It is because of this differentiation that Japanese can tell whom the conversation is referring to without indicating "I," or "you," or "he." The verb "go," for example, is *irasshaimasu* or *oide ni narimasu* in exalted form, and *mairimasu* in humble form. Ego uses the former expression to refer to the action of someone else to whom or about whom Ego is speaking, whereas he uses the latter expression to refer to his own action. There are situations, however, where an action involves both Ego and Alter, or where conversation refers to a third person who holds a status higher or lower than either Ego or Alter. Consequently, the style of speech can become fantastically cumbersome and error-ridden (for common errors in respect speech, see Sugano 1972).

The upward-downward dichotomization is expressed in interaction behavior other than speech. Ego's actions tend to move along a scale of respectfulness or rudeness according to the status he holds relative to Alter. Such behavioral dichotomization would not present a problem in the interaction of two persons of different ranks: one person would be polite and respectful, while the other would be condescending, relaxed, or even rude. A problem of behavioral adjustment would arise where three rank-ordered persons interact with one another. Both the highest and the lowest can maintain a status-fitted attitude consistently, but the person in the middle must dichotomize his behavior between upward and downward depending upon whom he is speaking to at the moment. This problem is usually solved by the middle person addressing only the higher person in disregard of the lower person.

The cultural dearth of ways to express horizontal or status-neutral relationships forces the actor to make a binary choice between respectful, formal behavior and disrespectful, informal behavior. This dilemma has been felt in postwar education, where equality is emphasized as a basic value. One of the main objectives in the moral education of prewar Japan was to inculcate the awareness of rank distinction, respect for superiors and elders, and familiarity with the proper usage of polite, respectful forms of speech and manners. Mastering the elaborate vocabulary of *keigo* ("respect words") was a difficult but necessary part of training for schoolchildren. There was, for instance, an Imperial vocabulary reserved exclusively for use in speaking of the emperor and his family, and to make an error in its usage was considered most serious.

Postwar schoolchildren are spared the learning of elaborate *keigo*, and as a result old-timers complain that young people today do not know how to speak. To be fair to the prewar generation, the gap caused by the loss of respectful speech indeed tends to be filled by disrespectful speech under the above-mentioned condition of binary choice. In extreme cases, status reversal takes place, as when militant students yell at professors "downward" in the rudest possible language while the professors answer "upward" with respect words. A psycholinguist observed this situation and noted the dilemma between the linguistic and the psychosocial pressures therein:

It is linguistically interesting to watch a meeting between so-called radical students, on the one hand, and administrators and professors, on the other. Radical students make it a rule to attack the traditional usage of the Japanese language as part of the Establishment, and in addressing administrators and professors, they deliberately use the lowest form of pronoun (*omae*) and the straight imperative form, e.g., *damare* (shut up). To them, the use of honorific language signifies a linguistically imposed submission to the existing Establishment and thus they avoid using it. In contrast to these students, administrators and professors typically keep using honorifics and the indicative or subjunctive mood to express their requests. In such a linguistic situation, a sensible dialogue is difficult, and a meeting often becomes unproductive. A Japanese-speaking person is well aware that when a subordinate or inferior person stops using honorific language and starts using the imperative form and the familiar style of address in talking with a superior person, he is declaring hostilities; and this act often creates an irreversible hostile relation between the two. (Higa 1972:54)

Avoidance of the command form of speech in postwar Japan, according to Higa, stands out also in Japanese commercial advertisements, compared with their American counterparts. When use of the imperative mood is unavoidable for effective appeal, it is made to be uttered by comedians, coquettish women, and children so that its offensiveness is reduced. "This phenomenon indicates that as long as the speaker somehow clearly manifests his inferiority to the listener, even in an artificial way, he can use the imperative mood" (pp. 55-56).

This remark confirms that the Japanese are still basically bound by a hierarchical frame of reference, lacking in alternatives, even when they compulsively try to be equalitarian. This status orientation is further supported by the cultural bias for empathy and dependency, inasmuch as baby talk is effective in commercials in appealing to the audience's nurturant empathy for the helpless, as well as in gratifying their sense of superiority.

Behavioral dichotomization along a vertical scale also underlies the Japanese tendency to differentiate ranks infinitesimally, instead of lumping together nearly equal ranks into one. The slightest difference in age, graduation time, the time of entry into a company, and so on, makes one person higher than another. Although there is a term to indicate a person of equal status, such as *dōhai*, Japanese tend to differentiate one another as *sempai* and *kōhai* on the basis of a negligible rank difference.

All this motivates and reinforces the Japanese tendency always to be sensitive to rank order.

Status Display

Status orientation includes a motivation for status display involving competition and one-upmanship. The *meishi* used for self-introduction invariably indicates one's status. More tangibly, one may exhibit the possession of the latest-model commodity, of the newest words and knowledge. Faddism, which we discussed in the context of conformism, gains momentum under the pressure of this one-upmanship. One must possess, display, or consume what is most modern or most famous of its type. Decades ago a typical item was the world's best Swiss watch, a Dunhill lighter, a Parker pen, a German camera, Johnny Walker Black Label, Chanel perfume; by the time the energy crisis hit the country, "mai kā" (my car) had become a widespread possession. And now the Japanese compete for world-famous works of art and antiques.

As these examples indicate, status symbols are found among Western products. When it comes to one-upmanship, Japanese seem to forget their national pride supported by the strong sense of belongingness. The same is true in language or knowledge. The Japanese are notorious for their uninhibited usage of English or other European words in such forms and pronunciations as sound hilariously amusing or atrociously offensive to the native speaker. Since these are used intermixed with Japanese words within a Japanese sentence, not just the borrowed foreign words but the Japanese language itself is spoiled from the point of view of linguistic purity. A British scholar, well versed in Japanese, was appalled by the "linguistic pollution" of Japanese with borrowed English that was demonstrated at an international symposium on Japanese literature. He made a list of Japanized English words used by Japanese participants in Japanese presentations. Examples are: *tēma* ("theme"), *wansaideddo* ("one-sided"), *kaba* ("cover"), *puran* ("plan"), *tekisuto* ("text"), *ekizochikku* ("exotic") (Morris 1970). More typical "Japlish" is found in the abbreviations, initials, or Japanese-English combinations that no one but the Japanese can understand: *rimokon* for "remote control," *nonpori* for "nonpolitical," CM for "commercials," SF for "science fiction," *angura* for "underground bar," *mai hōmu shugi* ("my-home-ism") for family-centeredness. Many Japanese themselves deplore this sort of Western cult or xenophilia, but Japanese journalism keeps feeding its audience such "polluted" language, and the latter absorbs it with undiminished appetite.

Intellectuals enjoy playing the game of one-upmanship through the display of their repertoire of Western knowledge. This is what David Riesman calls the "cultural humility" of the Japanese, which goes curiously side by side with their "clannishness." He mentions the tradition of a Japanese intellectual finding a Western mentor, be it Talcott Parsons, Harold Lasswell, C. Wright Mills, or Riesman himself, and becoming "a kind of vicarious *deshi*" ("disciple") (Riesman 1964). It looks as if status-focused identity for a Japanese can be found only in association with Western culture. In fact, the Japanese are enormously curious about what is going on in the West and are such avid readers of translated literature that their culture could be labeled a "translation-culture" (H. Kato 1972:38). Here is a wide market for cultural brokerage, and a bicultural or bilingual person can easily make a career out of it.

The snobbish appeal of a foreign institution was well demonstrated when a Japanese opened a foreign language school in Tokyo that he named Harvard Foreign Language Center. President Nathan Pusey of Harvard University protested, complaining that Harvard University had nothing to do with the center. It was reported that that name was given just because "it sounded good" (*Honolulu Star Bulletin* 2/6/70). All this reflects a Japanese ambivalence toward their national identity that is suggestive of an inferiority complex. We should hasten to add that this does not hold true for foreigners other than Westerners. Disdain toward "backward" peoples, including Asian neighbors, has been revealed through the rude behavior of Japanese tourists in Southeast Asia.

Within the domestic market, too, Japanese take pride in shopping at the "best" stores in the whole country; nationally famous candies or pickles are used as gifts, wrapped in the particular store's wrapping paper that can be identified immediately. Best often means oldest, which shows a persistent traditionalism side by side with faddism. To give examples of recent fads, the shibboleths denoting desirable possessions during the fierce commercialism and general prosperity of the 1960s were the "three C's," car, cooler (air conditioner), and color television, and the "three P's," plane, place (land), and pool.

Status Elevation

The Japanese also subject themselves to a long-range effort to elevate their status through education and occupation. Coupled with an optimistic belief in the efficacy of strenuous personal effort in attaining a goal, the Japanese individual expects to work hard in his teens and twenties as a necessary investment in eventual status elevation. Not only *doryoku* ("strenuous effort") but *kurō* ("suffering") is expected of a young person who has ambition. Under the current system of formal education, both *doryoku* and *kurō* are invested in the "infernal" examination that every person has to go through.

The final effort for status achievement is made in preparing for a university entrance examination if the university is the highest in reputation, or for an employment examination after graduation if one's alma mater was second-rate. Once this stage is passed successfully, the person can relax as if he were on an escalator that would take him upward without much effort on his part. Given such a reward structure, it is understandable that a youngster who has failed the examination for a first-rate school would rather try for the same school the following year, assuming *rōnin* (derived from the word for a masterless, floating samurai) status for a year, than accept admission into a second-rate school. There are so many *rōnin* students at any one time that "*rōnin*" is recognized as a social status, as demonstrated in letters to the editor signed "*Rōnin* student."

Competition is such that regular classwork does not provide adequate preparation for entrance examinations. Candidates usually go, every day after regular school, to "cram schools" that are exclusively devoted to preparing students for entrance examinations. There are an amazing number of such preparatory schools; they are distinguished from each other by how many successful candidates they have produced. Competition, then, includes the system of preparatory schools, so much so that the candidate must first pass an examination to enter the best preparatory schools! The result of all this is an oversupply of "examination-smart" kids who are quick in responding to questions but lack self-motivated interest in a particular subject aside from the desire to get a good grade (Tashiro 1970).

In their orientation toward status elevation and strenuous competitiveness, Japanese resemble Americans. Some differences can be noted, however. Status orientation for Americans is kept from going too far by their compulsive equalitarianism, while the control mechanism for Japanese is their cult of belongingness, with its stress on solidarity and cooperation. Second, status achievement for Americans involves an effort spread over a lifetime, whereas Japanese maximize that effort during youth to the point of exhaustion and begin to enjoy relaxation thereafter. In the sentence-completion test, the responses to "If you persevere through all the hardships that you encounter" revealed this expectation: 24 percent of adults and 18 percent of youths specifically referred to relaxation outcomes, for example, "You will have an easy life" (see the Appendix, Table 1).

To sustain the orientation toward status achievement, Japanese social structure allows for status mobility, although many statuses are ascribed ones, such as those from sex, age, birth order, lineality, and ancestry. There was mobility even under Tokugawa feudalism, and modern Japan has openly fostered ambition for *risshin shusse* ("rising in the world") in schoolboys—boys only. Mobility means vertical mobility within one organization since one's choice of occupation involves total commitment to a single organization. In prewar Japan, careers in government or the military offered the greatest status mobility within an organization. One could rise as high as cabinet minister or general, commanding the whole nation. In postwar Japan, where ministers are no longer imperial appointees and the militaristic value is in disrepute, the pursuit of status has shifted, it seems, to the business and professional worlds. University professorship ranked highest as a desirable status, at least before students started to harass professors through what is called *taishūdankō* (literally "mass negotiation," but actually the imposition of students' collective pressure to induce "confession" and repentance in an abducted professor), which was rampant in the latter half of the 1960s.

Alienation from the traditional aspiration for *risshin shusse* has been observed among the younger generation today, which appears more interested in the gratification of present needs. Nonetheless, the same youth continue to attend cram schools.

Vertical Alliance

The strong motivation for status elevation throws peers into fierce competition, since one's success precludes another's in the same market. In contrast, the same motivation induces a superior and inferior to play complementary roles, the former pulling the latter up, and the latter pushing the former up. Solidarity is thus easier to create among unequals on a hierarchical basis than among equals. Japanese Ego is more at ease with a superior or an inferior Alter than with an equal Alter, unless the latter is in an intimate relationship with Ego. *Oyabun-kobun, sensei-deshi, sempai-kōhai* are among the institutionalized names for role pairs in vertical alliance, interlocked in dependency orientation as well as in parthenogenetic mobility. More important than parthenogenesis for status promotion is "succession" to the parental status, which requires an even tighter alliance between a superior as the status-incumbent and an inferior as the would-be successor. To be nominated as the successor to the retiring head of a department in a university or of a shop is more honorable than to assume a similar position in another university or to be allowed to branch out and open a new shop. In expectation of this ultimate reward, the inferior will be totally devoted to the superior.

The ethos of social relativism may also underlie the inclination toward vertical rather than horizontal alliance. In this ethos, Ego's action is contingent upon Alter's action and vice versa. In an exactly equal symmetrical relationship, Ego may have too much uncertainty about what Alter is going to do, and Ego may thus be unable to take action: Ego's humility might be taken advantage of and reacted to in arrogance, whereas Ego's status display might arouse enmity. A vertical relationship does away with this uncertainty and riskiness since the actions of a superior or inferior Alter are more predictable.

This last point accounts for the greater Japanese propensity toward "complementarity" rather than toward "symmetry" in social interaction (Bateson 1971). Status complementarity is expressed and stabilized through what might be called linguistic dimorphism, where one party "talks down" and the other complementarily "talks up." This sort of dimorphism appears most clearly in heterosexual interaction where the Japanese male speaks a dominant, masculine language that the female complements by a language of feminine inferiority. If a man wants to avoid the dominant, masculine style of speech to show his sexual equalitarianism, he must choose either a formal, nonintimate style or a feminine style. It is not surprising, therefore, that the informal speech of young men today has been feminized. Along with speech, the whole mode of physical appearance seems to be moving toward femininity, including the use of cosmetics.

Vertical alliance at the expense of horizontal alliance is often responsible for group fractionation, as manifested by the formation of *batsu* (cliques) within a group. Such fractionation is controlled, again, by the sense of belongingness counteracting the pull of status.

Status Propriety

Status orientation, primarily with regard to classificatory status, involves an endorsement of status-proper behavior: one is encouraged to behave "like" the holder of one's status, "like" being expressed as *rashii* or *rashiku*. A child should behave *kodomo rashiku* ("like a child"), a woman should be *onna rashii* ("like a woman"), a man *otoko rashii* ("like a man"), and so forth. Among manlike behaviors are suppression of the emotions and not "talking too much." One of the best-known commercial catchphrases in recent years is: "*Otoko wa damatte Sapporo bīru*" ("Men silently drink Sapporo beer"), which is uttered by Toshiro Mifune, the John Wayne of Japan. A man of high status or wealth is also supposed to be generous and indifferent to pecuniary matters.

Status inhibition refers not only to behavior but to one's external appearance, including attire and material possessions. The color, material, and style of one's clothing, for example, should match one's status, which is defined by age, sex, occupation, and so forth. A male university professor would be expected to wear a dark suit, white shirt and subdued tie, and well-polished leather shoes. Visiting Japanese scholars in Hawaii often express shock at the casual dress of American scholars and professors who wear aloha shirts and *zori* sandals. In Japan, red, pink, and other bright colors have traditionally been considered feminine, so a man would refuse to carry a red umbrella in the rain even when there is no other alternative. But neither can all women enjoy bright colors; the status of age enters in. Fabrics for kimono are age-graded in color and pattern from the bright to the subdued: the salesclerk at the kimono counter will tell you to what age group a certain fabric belongs, the thirties, the sixties, and the like. The use of cosmetics is also considered status-proper for women. Externally visible possessions, such as a briefcase, watch, or fountain pen, should also match one's status; an executive, or even a section chief, should not carry around shabby things.

Since most Japanese conform to the status-corresponding codes of behavior and appearance, it is easy to guess the status of a stranger from a glance at him. Japanese sensitivity to rank order, as discussed above, is thus aided and reinforced by this orientation. Additionally, Ego is constantly reminded of his status identity by address terms, such as *sensei*, applied to him by Alter. Age status is called to attention by Alter's addressing Ego by quasi-kin terms like "Elder sister," "Auntie," "Grandma." These terms are an important mechanism for resocializing an individual through different life stages. The same logic applies to the prevalence of "baby talk" with babies.

The dependence of a superior upon an inferior for caretaking service, as discussed in the previous chapter, is an indication that a mundane task is considered incongruous with high status. Such status inhibitions end up confining a high status holder to nothing more than a ritual, figurehead role, and, historically, the ultimate in role ritualization was embodied in the emperor.

Shame

An appearance, behavior, or performance that is incongruous with a given status generates shame. If so, it may be said that the more status-conscious one is, the more vulnerable he is to shame. This is not to endorse Benedict's view of Japan as a "shame culture," for there is much guilt as well. However, I do agree with Benedict that the Japanese are sensitive to shame, primarily, I believe, because of their status orientation. In a previous paper (Lebra 1971a), I went so far as to argue that shame is generated or triggered in conjunction with status occupancy, and that one is vulnerable to shame when one poses as a status occupant. "Shame results," I wrote, "from whatever happens to undermine or denigrate the claimed status by revealing something . . . of the claimer which is inconsistent with the status" (p. 246). Status inhibition, then, is a necessary strategy for avoiding shame.

Status is linked to shame when two conditions are satisfied. First, status-incongruous behavior will not generate shame unless the status in question is recognized and identified by an audience. The Japanese are sensitive and vulnerable to shame not only because they are status-oriented but more specifically because they tend to display their status, which makes status easy for others to identify. True, there are occasions when status remains anonymous, as when one is traveling abroad as a private citizen. On such occasions, the ordinarily status-inhibited Japanese can afford to be "shameless". As a proverb says, "A traveler can do anything without shame."

The second condition is that status-incongruous behavior must be subject to exposure. As long as there is no danger of such exposure, one can be free from shame, if not from guilt. The high status holder is more protected from such exposure than a low status holder, protection being provided by a caretaker. Furthermore, this implies that Ego is sensitive to shame only in relation to an Alter who maintains some ritual distance from Ego; without distance there is no privacy and thus nothing to be exposed. Intimate kinship or friendship thus does away with shame. The Japanese may be said, then, to be shame-sensitive because they pay special attention to those people with whom they interact at a ritual distance. This aspect of shame will be analyzed in more detail in chapter 7.

Status orientation with a deep sense of pride and shame is among the factors embedded in Japanese culture that keep dependency from going too far. A proud person will not automatically ask or accept help from others; he will first weigh the risk of shaming himself by having to be helped against the risk of going without needed help to keep his status intact.

Use of Status as a Strategy

Finally, let us discuss the manipulability of status orientation, or what might be called the "status game," as we did with other behavior patterns in previous chapters. Status manipulation by a superior to persuade an inferior is perhaps to be expected, but the reverse can also happen. Let us assume that most people are preoccupied with status, concerned with maintaining dignity, vulnerable to shame, and susceptible to self-inflating flattery. Ego can manipulate these weak spots in Alter if he is willing to play the deviant. In negotiation with Alter, Ego may put himself in a humiliating, despicable position as a flatterer or a supplicant or both. It is not uncommon that a Japanese negotiator, apparently without bargaining power, succeeds in negotiation entirely by humbling himself, by bowing low and begging persistently. The persuasive appeal of the humble posture combines with Japanese empathy aroused at the sight of a helpless person. The negotiator succeeds, it seems, by causing the other party pleasure and at the same time guilt for keeping him in such a shameful posture. Refusal of a request made at such a cost of face would call for retaliation.

What is implied here is that insofar as status is a value it can be exchanged as a commodity for something else: one can gain something in exchange for one's status by humbling oneself. It follows that the higher the status, the more bargaining power one has in negotiation. When a superior person assumes a humble posture in asking the help of an inferior, his persuasive appeal is overwhelming. In *Shiroi Kyotō* [The gigantic white tower], a novel by Toyoko Yamazaki portraying the fierce power politics in a medical school, a high official of the Education Ministry is thanked by the head of the medical school for expediting the financial appropriation for construction of a new building for the school. In reply the official says, "I did so because I was asked by Azuma-san [professor and head of the Surgery Department, who was present]. Azuma-san is a *sempai* from my hometown and a great *sempai* from the university I graduated from. When he asks me with bowed head, I cannot say no" (1965:111). Here, not only the status difference between *sempai* and *kōhai*, but also shared belongingness to a hometown and a university, made the official vulnerable to persuasion.

In a vertical alliance, the inferior must be careful to support and protect the superior's status even at the cost of his own status. Goro Zaizen, the hero of *Shiroi Kyotō*, who is an assistant professor of Surgery and expected to succeed to the departmental headship, errs in this respect because he allows his own professional reputation to rise beyond that of Azuma, the head. Azuma, no longer able to stand this humiliation, begins to retaliate by plotting to bar Zaizen as his successor. A total breakdown of vertical alliance thus ensues.

Status can be manipulated by the holder of an attendant status. He can take advantage of the status inhibition of his master and make the latter totally reliant upon himself. The servant's eventual takeover of the master's power may well follow.

The ritualization of status, in turn, necessitates status borrowing to justify a cause, movement, or coup d'etat. Historically, a political movement to overthrow the existing power was often justified by inviting a man of high status to be the movement's figurehead, whether he be a powerful noble, a collateral descendant of an emperor, a royal prince, or an emperor himself.

In the publication industry, it is not uncommon, in order to promote sales, to publish a book under the nominal authorship of a well-known, prestigious person, with mere acknowledgment of "assistance" from its real writer. Compromise may be made by juxtaposing the names of the two authors, nominal and actual, the former presented as "supervisory editor." Nominal authorship is usually bestowed upon the real author's superior or assumed by the latter as his just due, as when the head of a department claims "supervisory" or even exclusive authorship for the book written by his subordinate. Most readers know who did the work. Despite this, the practice is continued by publishers. As a result, the higher one ascends a hierarchy of prestige, academic or otherwise, and the more administrative responsibility one assumes, the more publications one can claim.

ROLE PERFORMANCE

Let us turn to the role aspect of *bun*. This aspect is implied in phrases like: "to carry out one's *bun*," "to fulfill one's *bun*."

Role Commitment

Japanese show a strong commitment to a given role. In the first place, role commitment is a mirror image of status orientation. It is assumed that for one to maintain or elevate his status he must satisfactorily perform the role corresponding to that status. Failure in role performance will impair his status, which he will experience as shame. Hence, the more the individual identifies himself with his status, the more committed he should be to his role. When DeVos (n.d.) identified the single-minded cathexis of one's social role as an explanation for suicide in Japan, he meant role commitment in that sense. He called this attitude "role narcissism," particularly in association with a professional or occupational role. Role narcissism among the Japanese, argued DeVos, tends to be acute and can drive one to commit suicide when one's role responsibility has not been met as expected (more on this in chapter 11).

Another source of role commitment is the sense of belongingness, including strong identification with a collective goal. To the extent that they identify with the group goal, its attainment gives gratification to the individual members. Role commitment to a group goal is particularly manifest when achievement of the goal promotes the status of the group in relation to other groups. Recall how eagerly the Japanese contributed to nation-wide preparations for the Tokyo Olympics in 1964. The sense of belongingness, then, motivates the individual to carry out whatever role he is assigned, since an error in his performance may lead to a breakdown of the whole project. The internalized negative sanction for such an error would be guilt rather than shame since he would feel he has harmed other members of his group.

Thirdly, role commitment, associated with either status or belongingness, receives cultural support from the internalized moral value of work. This work ethic, which is regarded as an equivalent to the Protestant work ethic, may relate to the historical fact that the aristocracy in Japan, compared with its European, Chinese, and Indian counterparts, has formed a less distinct cultural elite, less separate from the working mass (Hasegawa 1966). The working man covered with sweat and dirt was a morally idealized figure that, of course, was fully utilized by the samurai elite of feudal Japan, who were parasitically dependent upon diligent peasants. In addition to such a social-structural explanation, some offer an ecological explanation for Japanese diligence: the dependence of wet-rice agriculture on intensive labor, leading to the equation of the more labor, the more yield (Koike et al. 1969).

Belief in the work ethic seems to have survived the postwar value change. The responses to my sentence-completion test included a great number of references to "hard work," "diligence," and "making an effort" as a necessary condition or means for attaining a goal. For instance, in completing the sentence fragment "In order to build an ideal home life," 19 percent of adults and 33 percent of youths referred to energy expenditure, such as "I will work hard," or "making an effort is necessary" (see the Appendix, Table 7: category 1). A more conspicuous result can be seen in responses to "That he has achieved success," where more than 70 percent of both groups attributed the success to energy expenditure (see the Appendix, Table 8: category 1).

There may be many other conceivable explanations, and no single explanation would be adequate. The point is that the Japanese do not share a contempt for labor with, say, the Indians, but rather tend to glorify it as a virtue of endurance and perseverance, and this certainly contributes to role commitment.

Related to this is a fourth source of role commitment, the belief in social utility as a basis for self-identity. Japanese derive self-worth from the confidence that they are socially useful. To be good-for-nothing is as bad as being lazy—another indication of social relativism.

Finally, role commitment is facilitated by the Japanese taste for regimentation. Collective action in an orderly manner has been a major part of school training and was reinforced through military regimentation. By prewar education at least, the Japanese as a whole were disciplined to play a role allocated within a regimentalized system, whether educational, military, or industrial.

That personal identity is established on the basis of the primary role one holds is demonstrated by the practice of referring to or addressing people by their role names, especially occupational role. In a neighborhood community where the residents know one another on a face-to-face basis, people are often identified by their occupations, shops, or trade names, for example, *sakaya-san* (Mr. or Mrs. wine shop), *haisha-san* (Mr. dentist), *tabakoya-san* (Mr. cigarette store), or *Mishimaya-san* (Mishimaya being a shop name). Even a stranger, if identifiable by an external insignia such as a uniform, may be addressed as "*gakusei-san*" (Mr. student), "*omawari-san*" (Mr. policeman), and the like. Sociocentric role names may override egocentric kinship terms. The head of a house is often called "father" by all members of the house regardless of particular kin relationships between the caller and the head; hence a mother may call her son "father" if he is head of the house in which she lives. This differs from teknonymic practice, as observed in Korean kinship terminology (Lee and Harvey 1973), which is more strictly kinship-oriented. The kinship identity is often replaced by an occupational role identity in Japan even when one is referring to one's kin. One informant during my fieldwork in Eastern City referred to her daughter, who, not having a brother, succeeded to the family business, as *mise no okāsan* ("mother of the shop"). A more intriguing example was provided by another informant telling about her mother-in-law. The mother-in-law evidently called the informant *nēsan* ("elder sister"). Asked why, the informant said that she ran a cabaret-type entertainment business and that her clients called her by this term.

Similarly, holders of high rank are not only referred to but addressed by their role names, such as *shachō* ("company president"), *kachō* ("section head"), *jichō* ("deputy head"). This, of course, elucidates status orientation as well as role identification. The role-status identity may be more specifically shown by such terms of address as *kōchō sensei* ("school principal"), *eigyō-buchō* ("head of the business affairs division").

Role Versatility

Role commitment among the Japanese can be so strong that, as the term "role narcissism" implies, the role becomes the core of the individual's self-identity. The incidence of suicide due to an error in role performance demonstrates that role can become identical with self or can come to represent all meaning in life. One's existence becomes affixed to and trapped by one's role.

Such role entrapment is only one side of the picture, however. Since roles are played in a social setting, one can perform a role perfectly without internal commitment. Role orientation involves versatile adjustment to whatever role one is expected to play. Excessive identification with a single role will be detrimental to one's skill in playing the variety of roles he is assigned. Japanese culture does not neglect to emphasize the need for one to fit his role and to change behavior as his role shifts. Carrying over one's previous role behavior into a new role is met with negative sanction. A young man is expected to play a young man's role, to be like a young man, but on reaching adulthood he should behave like a mature adult: he had better abandon his dream or ideal cherished in adolescence. It is common knowledge that most of the former Zengakuren leaders, who once fought for "filiarchy" (Feuer 1969:214) against gerontocracy, have converted and become members of the Establishment since graduation. An imperial combat soldier was supposed to kill himself before he could be captured, but, once captured, history shows that he played the role of "good" prisoner in spite of himself. Not that he was conflict-free, but precisely because of his role commitment as a Japanese soldier and the acute conflict resulting from his role-failure, he had to resort to another alternative available in Japanese culture, namely role versatility, which offset his previous role identity.

In sum, role orientation for the Japanese takes two forms: extreme role commitment and versatile adjustment. Role is internalized in one, while it remains external in the other. In the former, the self is absorbed in the role, whereas in the latter, the self is not affected by the role. These two forms are different manifestations of the ethos of social relativism; which form predominates depends on the social situation and on mutual expectations between Ego and Alter. Let us contrast this with an individualistic culture.

In an ethos characterized by the individualistic principle, one's role, especially the occupational role, may be taken as the realization of oneself on the one hand, and, on the other, as a calling from a transcendental being, as in the Puritanism characterized by Weber (1958). In both cases social relativism has little to do with one's occupational identity. It is as if role commitment were a result of independence from social ties. The individualistic culture is dramatically expressed, at one end, in the Dionysian frenzy and aggression glorified by Nietzsche, and, at the other end, in the low emotional temperature of a Puritan detached from human sentiment and excitement. The latter relates to a Western invention, the concept of a rational bureaucracy, where rules speak for themselves without interference from human emotions. Both forms of individualism reflect the asocial emphasis of Western culture. The social role is inundated by the Nietzschean personality on the one hand, and is identified, on the other hand, either as a divine mission or an impersonal cluster of rules. In Japanese culture, in contrast, the personality is enveloped by the social role and yet is not as impersonalized as in the Western bureaucratic model since role involves social interaction demanding an exchange of emotions. Love and hate among the Japanese are not as strong and compulsive as among Westerners (E. Ishida 1961); but neither is the total suppression of emotions characteristic of the Japanese.

Related to this cultural difference is the concept of sexuality. Sexuality for Japanese seems foremost a role concept. To be a woman means to play a woman's role in relation to others. Femininity thus may be consciously or deliberately displayed in external adornment as well as behavior and speech. It may be speculated that the Japanese individual's sexual identity, so caught up with role playing (and status maintenance), does not become as internalized at the unconscious level of the personality as happens in a culture that identifies sex with intrapsychic passion. Male actors playing female roles in kabuki plays can thus be accepted more readily by Japanese.

Role Vicariism

Both commitment and versatility in role assumption prepare one for taking a substitutive role for someone else. For Japanese there is nothing unusual in playing the role of a parent for a child, in becoming a substitute parent, or in entering into other substitutive relationships. Thus, an employer plays the role of parent toward an employee, a *sempai* employee plays the role of an elder brother toward a *kōhai* employee, and so forth. The common phenomenon of symbolic filiation, as referred to in relation to dependency, or of symbolic fraternity, may be partly understood in light of the ease with which role vicariism takes place among the Japanese.

Related to this is the common practice of *muko yōshi*, adopting a daughter's husband as a son and successor to the headship of the house. This combination of actual matriliny and symbolic patriliny is inconceivable unless the adoptor is willing to play the role of a substitute parent, and the adoptee has a corresponding attitude. In this form of role substitution, the daughter's husband can act as if he were the son and successor of the house, whereas the daughter can act as if she were a daughter-in-law. Role vicariism is based on the capacity and willingness to take such "as if" roles.

The same is true with the traditional institution of *ie*, which historically would incorporate a servant, tenant worker, or other nonkin into its membership as if they were adopted sons. The *dōzoku*, a Japanese version of lineage consisting of a main house and branch houses hierarchically organized, was merely an extension of the same principle in which some of the branch houses might have no "real" kinship relationship with the main house. F. L. K. Hsu's study of the institution of *iemoto* gives further insight into role vicariism interwoven with social structure (1971). *Iemoto* is associated with schools of the traditional arts, for example, tea cult, flower arrangement, drama, dance, music, archery, and so on. It refers to the main house, which supposedly has descended from the school's original founder and thus has inherited the secret principle and techniques unique to the school; it also refers to the headmaster of that house. The apprentice-student, after receiving training and a license at the *iemoto*, is permitted to open his own school as a branch house of the *iemoto*. Hsu sees the *iemoto* as a general type of social organization that permeates Japanese society. To him the *iemoto* is thus a basic pattern unique to Japan that corresponds with the clan for China, the caste for India, and the club for America. The fundamental principle governing *iemoto* is what he calls "kin-tract," combining a kinship model with a contract model (1971:302-333). As applied in our present context, it would be impossible for two strangers to come to contractual terms as student and teacher and at the same time to be tied in a kinship bond, without the cultural background of role vicariism.

The vicarious kinship goes farther than fictive kinship. Ego may address the family of his friend in the same terms that the friend would use: he may call the mother of his friend "mother" by vicariously taking the role of his friend, not necessarily because a fictive mother-child relationship has been formed. I am tempted to label this "vicarious kin terms." This practice may flow from the Japanese inclination for empathy, which urges one to imagine oneself in another's place. Vicarious kin terms are an expression of such empathy.

Empathetic role vicariism may go as far as *migawari* ("body exchange"), or self-sacrificial action in behalf of another person. One might hear a Japanese say, of someone very close to him who is ill or dying, "Oh, I wish I could do *migawari* for him!" Herein lies a complete union of role orientation and emotions whereby Ego identifies himself with Alter in *ittaikan*.

Role substitution can provide compensation for failure in status elevation. An ambitious man who has not achieved his desired status is likely to expect his son or somebody else to attain it in his place. In *Shiroi Kyotō*, Mataichi Zaizen tells his *muko yōshi* (his daughter's husband and his adopted son), Goro Zaizen:

> You are the one I spotted as promising. I want you to become professor of a national university—the position I could not get—by all means. Practitioners feel lonely no matter how many patients they attract and how much money they earn. Even someone like me who is resigned to be a common doctor in the commercial city of Osaka feels discontented, you know. After making money, men want to have fame, and I believe fame is the ultimate object of human desire. Money and people follow you if you are famous, but money alone remains nothing more than money. I want you, my daughter's husband, to satisfy that desire for fame which I could not. I am making money, you should know, only to that purpose. (Yamazaki 1965:38)

Even more common is a mother's vicarious satisfaction from her son's success in his career.

Reciprocity

The foregoing chapters have stressed that the Japanese patterns of social interaction reflect an ethos of social relativism as distinct from an ethos dominated by the pursuit of individual autonomy and self-interest or of transcendental absolutism. This chapter deals with reciprocity as another manifestation of social relativism. Although inseparably interwoven and interlocked with dependency and proper-place occupancy, reciprocity can be viewed as an analytically distinct concept.

RECIPROCITY AND *On*

Before examining a culture-specific aspect of reciprocity, it is necessary to define the concept of reciprocity in general terms. As I advanced in an earlier paper (1969), reciprocity can be summarized by the following interrelated aspects of social action between two individuals (or groups), A and B:

1. *Bilateral contingency*
   A acts in a certain way expecting B to respond in a certain way.
   A's favor to B obliges B to repay.
2. *Interdependence for mutual benefit*
   A gives something to B because B has something else that A needs.
3. *Equality of exchanged values*
   What A gives to B is equivalent to what he receives from B.

These symmetric aspects of reciprocity were emphasized by Malinowski (1959), for instance, when he characterized reciprocity as "sociological dualism," economic give-and-take, and mutual legal obligations of repayment. Gouldner (1960) insisted on point 3, particularly with reference to the fair (nonexploitative) distribution of rights and duties, in his distinction of reciprocity from the Parsonian notion of complementarity.

Reciprocity thus characterized excludes wholly unilateral types of action, whether they are sacrifice and devotion, generosity and benevolence, dominance and exploitation, or compliance and submission.

When applied in the Japanese cultural setting, reciprocity immediately suggests the concept of *on*. It might even be argued that *on* is a culture-bound notion of reciprocity for the Japanese. Under the initial stimulus of Benedict's work (1946), several Japanese specialists have undertaken self-examinations of this concept (Sakurai 1961; M. Yoshida, Fujii, and Awata 1966; Lebra 1969).

On is a relational concept combining a benefit or benevolence given with a debt or obligation thus incurred. What makes this word difficult for foreigners to comprehend is that it is not a discrete object but is imbedded in the social relationship between the donor and receiver of a benefit. From the donor's point of view, *on* refers to a social credit, while from the receiver's point of view, it means a social debt. An *on* relationship, once generated by giving and receiving a benefit, compels the receiver-debtor to repay *on* in order to restore balance. *Ongaeshi* means repayment of *on*, and *onjin* means *on* benefactor, both of which are among the most commonly used Japanese vocabulary.

If Japanese society is bound by social relativism, it is safe to say that the society's reward structure derives from this "socially contingent" reciprocal exchange that is morally sustained by the norm of *on*.

THE *On* TRANSACTION

First, let us look at *on* reciprocity from the point of view of the social exchange, trade, or "transaction" that creates, sustains, or cancels social debt and credit.

The Debtor's Response: Gratitude and the *Giri* Constraint

An *on* receiver is a debtor who is compelled to repay the debt.

This compulsion is derived from two mutually opposed sources within the debtor's attitude, which implies bipolarity in the debtor's response.

First of all, the *on* receiver is expected to feel, and does feel, grateful to the *on* giver. A strong sense of gratitude, interlocked with *on*, has been inculcated as a foundation of the Japanese moral character. Gratitude may be expressed verbally and demonstrated eventually by the action of repayment. The moral significance of gratitude, however, lies not so much in an external demonstration as in Ego's awareness of being in debt, Ego's internalization of Alter as a benefactor, and Ego's retention of the memory of having received the *on*. Not to forget a received *on* is as important, if not more so, as to repay it; to be forgetful of a received *on* or to refuse to repay it would equally incur the accusation of being *on-shirazu* ("unaware of *on*," implying "ungrateful").

Gratitude is usually expressed as *arigatai* ("grateful") and, in conversation, as *arigato* ("thank you"). Often, however, "grateful" is expressed by *sumanai*, which can also mean "sorry" or "unpardonable." Doi has noted that *sumanai* is used for expressing both gratitude and apology (1971:26). Perhaps the *on* debtor feels at the same time grateful to and sorry for the *on* creditor, either because he is aware of the creditor's sacrifice in his behalf or because he feels incapable of repaying the debt fully. When a Japanese wants to express sincere gratitude, he feels urged to say, "I am sorry," since "thank you" does not sound sincere enough. This is one of the typical mistakes Japanese make in their interactions with English-speakers, the latter being likely to say, "Why sorry?"

Gratitude to the *on* donor thus involves guilt feelings toward him—a point that I have elaborated upon before (1971*a*, 1972*b*). The linkage between gratitude and guilt in the Japanese mind is further reflected in the religious teachings of many sects, old and new, stressing the importance of *kansha* ("gratitude") and *zange* ("apology" or "repentance").

The concept of *on* constitutes a basis for Japanese morality to the extent that it involves deep gratitude and guilt. *On*, however, does not always elicit such a morally positive response. It is often identified as a heavy burden that one would like to unload as soon as possible. Receiving *on* can mean losing freedom. This burdensome aspect of *on* is expressed as *giri*, although *giri* has other meanings as well.[1] As it relates to *on*, *giri* implies a sense of constraint under which the debtor feels bound in his actions toward the creditor. The *giri*-bound debtor then makes efforts to repay, not so much out of a spontaneous willingness to express his gratitude as out of a strong compulsion to get rid of the debt and thus restore his autonomy. The overwhelming feeling of *giri* is the undesirability of being an *on* debtor.

Receiving *on*, therefore, is not always appreciated. Strong disapproval is directed against those who "sell" an unsolicited *on*, who impose *on* without consideration of the receiver's feelings. Discretion is required not to impose *on* even unwittingly, and the *on* giver may stress that he has no intention of imposing *on* upon the receiver. This sort of consideration underlies the Japanese giver's habit of belittling his gift, to the effect: "This is of such poor quality that I feel embarrassed to offer it. I beg you to be kind enough to accept it although it is beneath a person of your status." Most illuminating of the ambivalence felt by the favor receiver is the term *arigata-meiwaku*, which might be translated "gratitude-imposing nuisance." The *on* creditor, then, does not always arouse gratitude and guilt in the debtor; his action may at times foster hostility.

---

1. For other meanings, see Kawashima (1951*b*) and Benedict (1946). Kawashima, in his attempt to integrate the meanings of *giri*, discovered how variably the term is used: *giri* is identified as *iji* (which implies the will to maintain honor) by one scholar; as "honor" by another, as *gimu* between equals, and also as *tsukiai* ("social intercourse"). The villagers whom Kawashima studied defined *giri* as *okaeshi* ("return," that is, repayment for *on*), while among the definitions given by geisha was found "vanity" (p. 761). Dictionaries, too, give different definitions. Kawashima feels that none of these definitions is wrong, and none is exclusively right. He goes on to offer his own definition, which is meant to be an integration of past studies. Since I find it the most plausible of all the definitions made so far, it may be worthwhile to summarize it here. *Giri* refers to a social order consisting of a set of social norms that assign every status holder a certain role to be carried out. More specifically, *giri* is generated by and in turn maintains gemeinschaft relationships between particular individuals. The gemeinschaft relationship involving *giri* can be characterized by: (1) duration (not a temporary relationship but a permanent one, for example the *giri* of regular gift-giving), (2) total involvement, the relationship occupying not just a small part of life, such as a pupil learning a skill from a teacher, but the whole sphere of life, including the pupil's marriage and family, (3) an imposition on the individual by virtue of his status, as when *giri* is contrasted with *ninjō* ("human feelings"), (4) a personal, particularistic relationship involving face-to-face interaction in a physical sense, (5) emotional ties (instead of a contractual relationship maintained from calculations of self-interest—this is where *giri* becomes identical with *ninjo*; even when self-interest is indeed calculated, the relationship must preserve the facade of emotional solidarity), and (6) a hierarchical relationship involving an unequal distribution of obligations.

Ego, on his part, is warned against the ready acceptance of an offered favor: "Don't accept a free drink." This warning operates against the otherwise pervasive readiness for dependency. Polite refusal of an offered favor is justified under the guise of *enryo*, the virtue of reserve and modesty. Excessive dependency on someone's help, whether patronage, attendance, indulgence, or pity, may eventually place Ego in the undesirable status of a debtor, *giri*-bound hand and foot. Avoidance of *giri* may be sought in a free-floating, isolated, independent life.

Data from my sentence-completion test indicate an intergenerational difference in the relative emphasis upon spontaneous gratitude or the obligatory sense of *giri*. In response to "Because I once received *on* from that person" (Appendix, Table 6), more youths than adults expressed the obligation of repayment (category 1), for example, "I must repay some day"; where as more adults showed a willingness to repay (category 2), for example, "I would like to help him," "I want to make every effort to repay," and the like. A wider discrepancy was observed in the general attitude, than in specific action of repayment, of the debtor toward the benefactor. Twenty-three percent of the youths, in contrast to only 4 percent of the adults, expressed the sense of inhibition or constraint felt by the debtor (category 3), such as "I cannot talk back to him," "I cannot raise my head," "I must make concessions in everything," "I don't want to face him." Conversely, about 20 percent of the adults, but only 4 percent of the youths, responded with an acknowledgment of gratitude or unforgetfulness (category 4), such as "I am grateful," "I must not forget that under any circumstance." Whether this difference is due to the postwar change in values or merely reflects two different stages of life remains to be determined. The findings at least show the range of variation in a debtor's response.

In summary, we can say that *ongaeshi* ("*on* repayment") is motivated by a bipolar orientation—gratitude and guilt or *giri* constraint or a mixture of both. Figure 1 depicts this bipolarity:

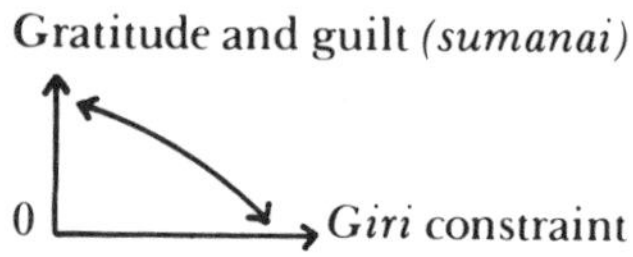

Gratitude and guilt *(sumanai)*

0   *Giri* constraint

Figure 1. Debtor's Response

The two-pointed arrow shows the range of variation or fluctuation between the two responses on the part of the *on*-receiver.

The Creditor's Expectation and Strategy

Given the compulsion for repayment on the part of the debtor, whether motivated by gratitude or *giri* constraint, the *on* donor is likely to consider himself a creditor and expect to be repaid in one form or another. Indeed, he can take advantage of his creditor status to manipulate the debtor. Likewise, when Ego contemplates helping Alter, he considers his action a social investment that will pay off some day.

At the same time, the creditor must be cautious, because of the ambivalence felt by the debtor, not to offend the debtor by crudely demanding repayment. The blunt expectation of a payoff is in fact so offensive that one avoids appearing anything but altruistic. It is interesting to see that the sentence-completion-test responses to kindness (Appendix, Table 3) are divided into two large groups, one pointing to reciprocity and the other alienated from it. In response to "If you are kind to others," a large number of both adults and youths referred to the expected repayment, either in the form of kindness or something else (categories 1 and 2). But, as many respondents emphasized either the autistic satisfaction of the kind actor, regardless of payoff, or the benefit to society (categories 4 and 5). Autistic satisfaction was demonstrated in such sentences as, "You will feel better," or "Your heart will be brightened," and the benefit to society in, "The world will be at peace," or "Society will become easier to live in."

Expectation of payoff, constrained by the need for apparent altruism, must be communicated with extreme subtlety to avoid offending the debtor and being charged with bribery or blackmail. The power politics surrounding the appointment of a new department head in a medical school, as described in *Shiroi Kyotō*, consists primarily of ruthless, yet subtle, psychological bribery. Both Zaizen, who aspires to the position, and Azuma the incumbent, who wants to block Zaizen's promotion, try to collect supporters through the game of reciprocity. In both cases, Ego tries to establish his creditor status, either by subtly reminding Alter of the past debt he, Alter, has not yet paid, or by offering a benefit; Ego also covertly promises to do something for Alter provided the latter supports Ego.

Accumulation of *on* credit can be regarded as social insurance to be cashed in in a crisis. The *onjin* does not have to ask for help, since the debtor will rush to his aid as soon as he is informed of the predicament of his *onjin*. Giving of *on* serves as an "insurance policy" only when the debtor does not repay the debt immediately but waits for an opportunity, the best opportunity being an emergency the creditor cannot meet without others' help. Japanese culture, like other cultures, endorses opportune repayment and disapproves immediate return, unless the transaction is a purely economic contract or conventional gift-giving.

Success stories used in prewar moral education alluded to the reliability of such social insurance. A talented, diligent boy from a poverty-stricken family finds a benefactor who, recognizing the boy's potential, gives generous support for his education. After he has completed his education and has successfully "risen in the world," the *on* debtor happens to learn that *onjin*, now old and sick, is also penniless. The former protégé finds himself in a position to repay his debt with an enormous interest. Status reversal thus goes beautifully with the norm of reciprocity.

The strategy of reciprocity may involve a triad rather than a dyad when A chooses to influence C through B. If A is an *onjin* to B, and B is an *onjin* to C, the two kinds of credit can be interlinked through B so that A can influence C. This relationship may be termed "transitive reciprocity." To the extent that it involves the substitution of one creditor-debtor relationship for another, transitive reciprocity may be utilized only where role vicariism is not resisted. In the above example, C would comply with A, either by vicariously taking the role of B or by regarding A as a vicarious player of B's role.

SPECIFIC RECIPROCITY: GIFT-EXCHANGE

Although we started from a general definition of reciprocity, it should be realized that there is wide variety in actual reciprocal relationships. One way of bringing order to the variety is to dichotomize reciprocity into general and specific types. Some reciprocal exchanges are more specific than others, although the term *on* applies to both types of reciprocity.

Let us first look at specific reciprocity, which is best exemplified by conventional gift-giving.

Prescribed Occasions for Giving

Conventional gift-giving is associated with specific, well-defined occasions that call for celebration, condolence, or the ritual expression of gratitude or good will. Such occasions pertain to the life cycle, calendrical cycle, emergencies, special events, and visiting. Though the occasions are thus diverse and the gift-givers may vary from case to case, the occasions are consistently well defined and associated with particular ceremonies.

Beginning with the life-cycle ceremonies, or "rites of passage," the most important occasions of life that call for gift-giving are birth, marriage, and death. For these events the gift is addressed to and received by the family as a unit (or by the head of the house as the family representative) rather than the particular individual involved. The reason is obvious in the case of birth or death: neither the newborn baby nor the dead can acknowledge a gift. But in marriage also, it is not so much the new couple as the two families that acknowledge gifts, even though the couple probably in turn receives them from their families. (For more on this, see Befu 1966-1967.)

The intervals between birth, marriage, and death are also punctuated by ritually defined growth phases of childhood, including *miyamairi* when the infant is taken to a local Shinto shrine to be introduced to the deity, and the rituals for three, five, and seven year olds (under the traditional age-counting system); by an initiation ceremony (for adulthood; or in old Japan, for joining a youth group); by phases of aging (marked at the sixty-first year of life, followed by the seventieth, seventy-seventh, eighty-eighth, and so on). Nowadays it is fashionable to hold wedding anniversary celebrations. Not only the "life" cycle but the postmortem cycle also occasions gift-giving, as for example, on death anniversaries.

The life-cycle-anchored celebration also includes one's educational and occupational advancement or success. Passing an examination to enter school is an occasion for gift-giving, along with *gōkaku-iwai* ("celebration of success in examinations"). This is followed by *sotsugyō-iwai* ("graduation celebration"), which usually shortly precedes *shūshoku-iwai* ("celebration of being employed"). Unusual promotion in occupational status may be another occasion for celebration.

Gift-giving occasions are also regulated by the calendar. Twice a year, at midsummer and the end of the year, everyone in the nation becomes engrossed in buying, giving, and receiving gifts. The midsummer gift is called *chūgen* (which originally referred to July 15, when the dead were supposed to receive special care and sacrifice), the year-end gift is called *seibo*. *Chūgen* and *seibo* calendrically tie in with the time workers receive a special semiannual bonus, which often amounts to two or more months' salary. The so-called *bōnasu-būmu* ("bonus boom") can be observed in the crowds filling department stores to buy *chūgen* or *seibo* gifts. While these are gifts for adults, children receive New Year's gifts from adults as a token of a year gained.

Third, an emergency that causes a sudden unexpected deprivation provides another kind of occasion for gift-giving. Among common emergency occasions are serious illness, fire, and major robbery. Giving gifts to the victims is intended to help them economically as well as to express sympathy. Such gifts are called *mimai*.

Fourth, some special events, falling in none of the preceding categories, also prompt gift-giving. Examples are construction of a house, opening a store or new business, or the taking of a trip. The gift for the person who is going away from home either temporarily or permanently is called a separation gift. It may represent concern about the dangers involved in traveling, a wish to contribute to travel expenses, or a regret over temporary separation.

Fifth, visiting someone at home, whether on business, to establish friendship, or to renew an old acquaintance, is accompanied by gift-giving. An "empty-handed" (*tebura*) visitor may be criticized for his ignorance of etiquette and therefore is likely to apologize for coming *tebura*. This may explain in part why visiting in Japan is voluntary and often unexpected rather than at the request of the host.

Calculability of the Gift's Value

Reciprocity in gift-giving is specific not only in terms of the occasion but in the calculability of the value of the gift. The price of most gifts purchased at a store can be roughly estimated. And many gifts are in the form of cash, which is not presented boldly but is wrapped in a special envelope with a symbolic decoration suited for the particular occasion. The envelope is inscribed with the giver's wish (such as "to celebrate," or "tiny intent," belittling its content) and his brush-written name, and sometimes the amount of money is marked on the reverse side.

Cash is given almost always for important life-cycle events such as birth, marriage, and death, for emergencies and for traveling—occasions on which cash is needed above everything else. Particularly the funeral gift, called *kōden*, is paid in a generous amount of cash, though some may give both cash and food or flowers to be offered at the altar. The semiannual gifts, *chūgen* and *seibo*, tend to be of commodities, such as clothing, accessories, electrical appliances, sundries, food, or sake. However, gift certificates, a disguised cash gift, are now in popular usage for *chūgen* and *seibo*.

Associated with the calculability of gifts is the idea that when it comes time to give someone a gift in return, its value should equal the value of a gift received from that person. On an occasion like a funeral, when many people visit and present gifts, the receiver's memory is inadequate to record his obligations; instead, a written record is made of who gave how much to facilitate proper reciprocation later. The Japanese are aware of the cynicism involved in calculating funerary gifts while crying over the death of a kinsman. Embarrassment is avoided by the mutual-aid system in which neighbors or colleagues take the roles of receptionist and recorder of *kōden*-gifts in behalf of the bereaved.

Repayability

Finally, some reciprocal relationships are considered specific because the gift can be repaid by a counter-gift; repayability is a measure of specificity. Repayability takes two forms: immediate repayment and symmetric repayment.

First, many of the gifts mentioned above are answered by an immediate return gift so that the initial receiver will not remain a debtor too long and thus incur interest upon his debt. A separation gift is repaid by the traveler in souvenirs of his journey; Japanese tourists often end up being too busy buying souvenirs to enjoy their travel partly because of this pressure to repay separation gifts. A *mimai* gift in an emergency like a fire may be matched by a token return, while a *mimai* gift for sickness may be repaid by inviting the givers to a celebration of recovery.

Feasting is the most common form of immediate return for a gift associated with a ceremony. Ceremonies for birth, marriage, and other celebrations include feasts given for invited guests. Here the immediacy of repayment is complete, since the host is simultaneously giving the feast and receiving gifts from his guests—it is by no means clear which side is the giver and which is the repayer in this case. If the feasting alone is not considered an adequate return, the host will deliver an *orei* ("appreciation") gift after the ceremony that may range from a symbolic token to a more substantial gift.

The gift from a visitor is reciprocated immediately by tea and food served by the host, unless the gift happens to be more than a little *temiyage* (modest "hand-carried gift"), which would require a better-matched return gift.

Second, repayability is assured by the possibility of a symmetric repayment duplicating the initial giving through counter-giving on a similar occasion and with a similar gift. A gift for the matriculation of Ego's son will be reciprocated by a counter-gift for the matriculation of Alter's son. A cash gift may be repaid by a cash gift, and so on.

At this juncture it should be realized that symmetry in repayment, although ideal in terms of balancing the exchange, is difficult to maintain. Except in the case of cash gifts, it would be senseless to exchange the same thing. In many cases it is difficult or even impossible for the recipient to wait for the same life-cycle event or emergency to be experienced by the initial giver. First of all, symmetric repayment defies the requirement of immediate repayment since the initial receiver may have to wait for a long time before a similar gift-deserving occasion is experienced by the giver. Nor is immediate repayment always endorsed.

Exact repayability is thus far from being a fact. There always remains some uncertainty as to how much one owes whom, even in an extremely specific gift-exchange. Nor is it necessarily culturally desirable to be either debtless or creditless: keeping the reciprocal book in perfect balance means cancellation of social ties. There ought to be uncertainty, overpayment, or underpayment. Furthermore, if the reciprocal partners are in touch with each other on a more or less continuous basis, there is no pure "giving"; as Befu observed, "most gift-giving in Japan is actually gift-returning." All gifts seem to refer to the past relationship between the giver and receiver (Befu 1966-1967:166). And once the relationship is taken into consideration, it is no longer the value of the gift alone that affects the balance. As Befu continues:

> What constitutes equivalence and cancellation of debt is not easy to state. It in part depends on the economic value of the gift, of course. But that is not the only variable. Relative status difference, degree of intimacy, economic disparity between the two, among others, are also part of the equation. (p. 167)

This brings us to the other type of reciprocity—generalized reciprocity.

GENERALIZED RECIPROCITY: THE MORALITY OF *On*

Reciprocity must be distinguished from pure economic exchange in that its significance lies in the creation or maintenance of a social relationship rather than in the transfer of goods from hand to hand. What is exchanged may well be of economic value, as in the exchange of gifts discussed above. However, if part of reciprocity, such an exchange is coupled with an exchange of noneconomic values such as love, respect, pride—the values that are the ingredients of a social relationship. The vocabulary of reciprocity is "giving," "accepting," and "returning," rather than selling, buying, and paying or borrowing and lending.

Reciprocity is further to be distinguished from a contractual relationship, in which the mutual rights and duties of two parties are specified through legal documentation, in which default incurs legal penalties, and in which dates of beginning and end are delimited. Reciprocity is more diffuse, informal, and personal, and its effectiveness is derived from the partners' memories.

These considerations lead us to realize that reciprocity tends to deviate from its ideal type, characterized at the beginning of this chapter as (1) bilateral contingency, (2) interdependence for benefit, and (3) equality of exchanged values. It is likely that reciprocity also involves some degree of unilaterality or asymmetry (Blau 1964). This is another way of saying that reciprocity tends to become generalized.

The Japanese concept of *on* derives its moral strength precisely from a cultural generalization of reciprocity. Although *on* can refer to a specific gift-exchange as well, its moral implications lie in the relationship between generalized benevolence and generalized obligation.

Generalized Benevolence

Generalized benevolence is a moral virtue stressed in Japanese culture under such names as *shinsetsu* ("kindness"), *nasake* or *jihi* ("compassion"), *awaremi* ("pity"), and *omoiyari* ("empathy"). The Buddha is the ultimate embodiment of unlimited benevolence. One should keep one's heart warm, the Japanese have been taught, with benevolent sentiments not only toward fellow humans but toward animals, including insects. Prewar *shūshin* lessons, as well as Buddhist sermons, contributed to the inculcation of the imperative of benevolence.

Of greater moral importance than the need for benevolent action is Ego's awareness of Alter's generalized benevolence, which again reflects the essence of social relativism. Unlike conventional gift-giving, generalized benevolence is not limited to a specific occasion, nor is it economically calculable or repayable. Generalized benevolence refers to the benefactor's overall attitude and pattern of action rather than to the value of the object given or to a certain act. All this means that Ego as a receiver of generalized *on* must be aware and unforgetful of the whole attitude and good will of the *onjin*.

Thus, generalized *on* is associated with diffuse, ill-defined terms like *sewa* ("taking care" or "looking after"). Ego feels deeply grateful and obligated to a generalized *onjin* because he has received so much *sewa* from him. If asked what kind of *sewa,* he may find it difficult to answer because any attempt to define the content of *on* in this case would be felt inadequate in conveying the unlimitedness of the *on*.

The most generalized *on*, which is impossible to pinpoint, is felt toward one's parents, particularly one's mother. Her *sewa* for children is spread in time throughout the day, all year, and over a lifetime—far from being limited to specific occasions. Maternal care cannot be estimated in its amount and intensity and is therefore unrepayable. The parental *on* is identified not only as *sewa* but as *shimpai* ("worry") and *kurō* ("suffering"). A man may feel grateful and guilty toward his aged (or deceased) mother because she worried so much for him. He is guilty because it was he who caused her *shimpai* and *kurō*. Thus, generalized benevolence typically involves sacrifice by the benefactor. It is no coincidence that the main source of guilt for Japanese is in the unrepayable *on* owed to one's mother (DeVos 1960).

Generalized Obligation

Generalized benevolence produces generalized obligation in its receiver. First, the receiver of generalized *on* remains indebted always, sometimes all his life. A permanent debtor, he is supposed not to forget the *on* even for a moment, and he should make every effort to repay even though his repayment would amount only to "one ten-thousandth" of what was received.

Second, the unpayability of generalized *on* rules out the possibility of symmetric repayment and necessitates, instead, complementary repayment. A common form of complementary repayment is overall compliance, submission, or loyalty to the benefactor, thus forming an interdependent tie between the generous *on* creditor and the compliant *on* debtor. This is why the morality of *on* is often attached to a hierarchical relationship, with emphasis upon the virtue of obedience.

Third, since generalized *on* involves one's total life, a chance for repayment may come at a point in one's career when status reversal has taken place between the benefactor and debtor. The mother, now aged and helpless, may come under the total care (*sewa*) of her son or daughter, the generalized debtor, who is now at the prime of his or her life. The generalized *on* may thus be repaid not only through economic support for the benefactor, but also through *sewa*, *shimpai*, and *kurō*. A similar status reversal may occur between a nonparental benefactor and his protégé, as is often referred to in success stories containing the moral lesson of *ongaeshi*. The *onjin*, formerly wealthy and powerful, may now find himself saved from poverty, sickness, or even death by the *on* receiver, who has risen from extreme deprivation in his childhood to nationwide fame, thanks to the *on*.

The orientation toward status elevation, which was examined in the preceding chapter, is interlocked with the morality of *on* to compel the *on* debtor to fulfill his obligation through status achievement. *On* repayment does not necessitate status reversal, though, and may take the form of vicarious enjoyment of the debtor's success by the benefactor since he contributed to the success. The mother would feel her sacrifice repaid not merely because she now can rely upon her·son for her security but because she shares and enjoys his success.

Structural Support

Generalized reciprocity may arise from an accidental, unintended experience or action. Being rescued from drowning, for example, is accidental and yet the rescuer will be thanked as a lifesaver and will become a permanent *onjin*. However, the generalization of *on* is not always of such a precarious nature but is systematically supported by the following structural factors.

Ascribed on. An *on* relationship cannot be created or terminated merely by the mutual consent of the partners involved. Morally significant *on* is especially deeply imbedded in the traditional social structure based on the premise of lineal succession of ancestral legacy. One does not simply engage in an *on*-relationship but is born into debtor status vis-à-vis one's parental and ancestral benefactors, who have all contributed to bringing one into this worldly existence. One is born, in other words, with a birth-debt (far from birthright). Both *on* credit and *on* debt are thus ascribed, so equality in bargaining power between *on* partners is ruled out at the very beginning of one's life. The benevolence of the ascending generations should be regarded as pure and unlimited, and it should be matched only in total devotion by the descending generation. *Ongaeshi* for ancestors and parents is thus demonstrated through *kō* ("filial piety").

Ascribed *on* is also owed to the place or group into which one is born. *On* to one's society and country should be remembered and repaid, since individuals would enjoy no security or happiness outside it.

In the sentence-completion test I tried to find out whether the respondents would show a sense of generalized indebtedness and, if so, to whom. The sentence fragment "That we can live as happily as we do now" evoked expressions of indebtedness primarily to two objects: the country or nation and ascending generations (Appendix, Table 5: categories 1, 2, and 3). It is interesting to note that adults were oriented toward ancestors and other deceased generations as *on* donors, whereas youths attributed happiness to the parental generation only. Indebtedness to the country cut across the samples. Intergenerational differences fully taken into consideration, it can be still argued that both groups revealed a sensitivity to ascribed *on*.

Hierarchically based on. Such asymmetry in the distribution of *on* is more clearly revealed in the relationship between *on* and the hierarchical order of society. The general impression is that *on* flows downward so that the superior in the hierarchy assumes the status of *on* creditor, the inferior that of *on* debtor. This impression may be historically traced to pre-Tokugawa feudal times, when a warlord rewarded loyal vassals with land and other assets confiscated from his enemy—such a reward was called *on*. The practice of *on*-granting is historically so imbedded in a hierarchical order that some observers, Sakurai (1961) among them, consider an *on* relationship to exist only between unequals. I do not agree with this view since there are other kinds of *on* relationships, but I do agree that a very significant part of *on* morality is linked to the hierarchical social structure.

What is essential here is not so much the benevolence of a superior as the indebtedness of an inferior by virtue of his inferior status. An *on* debt is thus owed by the young to their elders, by a pupil to his teacher, by a *kōhai* to his *sempai*, by a henchman to his boss, by a section member to his section chief, by an employee to his employer, and so on. The traditional form of *ongaeshi* by an inferior-subordinate to a superior-master is called *chū* ("loyalty, devotion"), which was considered one of the two main pillars of Japanese morality, the other being *kō*. The ultimate benefactor to whom the maximal *chū* should be devoted was, of course, the emperor.

Chū and *kō* may come into conflict, as when Ego's parent and master are hostile toward each other and each demands compliance from Ego. In Japan the general solution to this conflict has been to give priority to *chū* at the expense of *kō*, unlike in China, where *kō* has been absolute. However, these two principles are not usually contradictory in the Japanese mind, for *chū* ultimately merges into *kō* by the master's taking a vicarious parental role.

Collectively shared on. As I have suggested, the individual Japanese is not a self-sufficient, autonomous whole but a fraction constituting a part of the whole. Belongingness is a necessary basis for establishing identity. The unit of action, then, is the group rather than the individual. We saw that gifts are given and received by the group rather than the individual. The *on* relationship, too, is extended over and beyond the initial partners to the two groups of which they are members. Such group sharing of an *on* relationship is another structural support for the generalization and stabilization of *on* reciprocity.

The most elementary unit for sharing *on* is the household. Sharing of a member's *on* by other members of the household involves intergenerational inheritance of *on* from parent to child. The father's *on* debt to his boss will be inherited by the son, who will try to repay it if his father dies leaving the debt unpaid. Likewise, if the boss dies before his *on* credit is paid off, his child will succeed to the creditor's status and benefit from it. Here again role vicariism is activated.

The Pervasiveness of Indebtedness

Given these structural factors in favor of generalized reciprocity, the moral principle underlying the concept of *on* is uniquely assymetric, with the emphasis upon one's awareness of being obligated to everyone and at all times. Bellah has viewed the idea of the unpayability of *on* as an equivalent to the Western concept of original sin, assuming "a fundamental 'flaw' in human nature which cannot be overcome by man alone but only by some intervention from above" (1957:73). The similarity between *on* and original sin is not complete, however, and Bellah hastened to note that "the theory of *on* holds for superordinates within the social system, such as parents or political superiors, in exactly the same terms as it holds for entities above the social system, gods or Buddhas, etc."

Japanese morality, in short, is characterized by an overwhelming sense of unpayable debt to countless benefactors, which makes one at once humble and obligation-bound. From the standpoint of the sociology of law, Kawashima characterized the Japanese as *gimu chūshin* ("obligation-preoccupied"), in contrast to the Western *kenri chūshin* ("right-preoccupied") orientation (1967).

Even politicians, whose prime motivation might be thought to be a desire for power, credit their sense of obligation as motive for seeking office. The defeated Socialist candidate for governor of Tokyo in 1963, Masaru Sakamoto, wrote an essay after the election that gives a clue to the Japanese *gimu-chūshin* orientation (1963). In it is a detailed account about how he was compelled to accept the Socialist Party's nomination. He had planned, he wrote, to terminate his thirty-five-year political career and to devote the rest of his life to writing, even though he was being urged to run for a third term as the governor of Hyōgo Prefecture. When many people visited him and tried to persuade him to run for governor of Tokyo, he firmly refused, sometimes angrily:

> For the past thirty-five years, I have been elected a member of the House of Representatives, Mayor of Amagasaki City, and Governor of Hyōgo Prefecture. Yet, have I once said I wanted to run for any of these? Is it not true that I have always yielded to your persuasion and forced myself to run, and won? It may sound

immodest, but I feel I have carried out my task as a pioneer. And finally, did I not win the election for governor as a radical party candidate, which was considered difficult, and work for two gubernatorial terms? Does not your *ninjō* allow me to retire to my study—the thing which I have long been looking forward to?

But, instead, "reality" forced itself "like a gigantic ship" against his will. The night before Tokyo representatives of the Socialist party visited his home, he discussed the matter with his family. He tried to persuade his wife and son to approve of his candidacy. He was born, he said, under the star of dedication to the party. How could he refuse to run when the party could not find any other candidate. Winning or losing was not his concern. "My wife cried, my son cried. Bathed in tears, I made up my mind." At the formal meeting with the party representatives, he said, "Please use me if you consider me useful. I shall leave everything to your decision."

The candidate then moved to Tokyo for the election campaign, with some hesitation because he had the obligation, as the first son of his family, of looking after the ancestral graveyard in his hometown. He justified the move on the basis of sacrificing a smaller obligation to a greater obligation. He was not successful in the election. In deep repentance at having run for the office and in anger at the corruption of the conservative party, he wrote this essay. It concluded with his resolution to stay in Tokyo instead of returning to Hyōgo Prefecture because he felt indebted to the 1,630,000 voters who had supported him, total stranger though he was. He felt it his fate to live permanently in Tokyo to repay their kindness. How could he carry out his *giri* if he went back to his hometown? At the same time, this decision meant that he owed an apology to the residents of Hyōgo Prefecture: "For these reasons I have decided to be a Tokyo resident. I have no adequate words to apologize to you. All I can say is that you have long been kind to me, worthless as I am. My feeling is much more than gratitude. I am only bowing to the fate that has befallen me."

While this is an exaggeration of the norm of obligation, reflecting as it does the irrational state of an unsuccessful political candidate, it does elucidate Japanese thinking with regard to generalized obligation.

NONRECIPROCAL COMPENSATION

The asymmetry of the *on* relationship discussed above imposes an unfair burden upon the structural debtor. Both *kō* and *chū*, if taken seriously, will lead the debtor to feel that he has overpaid and that he deserves compensation. Given the social structure in favor of the asymmetric *on* relationship, the over-payer must look for nonreciprocal compensation. By this I mean the compensation Ego obtains not from Alter, with whom he is reciprocally related, but from a third person. Perhaps we can call this triadic compensation.

Three-Generational Compensation

One of the major compensatory mechanisms involves three generations interlinked by the chain of debt and credit. A's over-payment to a member of the ascending generation, B, is paid off by C, a member of the descending generation. Ego's *kō* to his parent is expected to be returned in the form of *kō* from his own child to himself. There is a cultural conviction of a smooth and equitable transference of debt and credit in this manner involving a lineal triad: "If you are devoted to your parents, your children will be devoted to you." This conviction may have an empirical basis in that the child, watching the parent's devotion to the grandparents, is likely to learn and emulate the behavior of *kō*. It is also linked with a transcendental belief in the karmic chain of restitution from generation to generation. In my sentence-completion test, trust in the lineal triad as a compensatory mechanism was revealed in adult responses, but not in youth responses (see the Appendix, Table 4). Responding to "If you carry out obligations of filial piety," 40 percent of the adults and only 1 percent of the youths wrote "You, too, will be the receiver of filial piety," "Your child will emulate you," and the like (category 2). Interestingly, the youths seem less concerned with com-pensation than with empathetic optimization of parent's pleasure or comfort (category 3): "Your parents will be pleased."

In the case of a woman, usually patrilocally married, this type of compensation involves three generations of in-laws: Ego's de-votion to her mother-in-law is compensated for by Ego's daughter-in-law's devotion to her.

Rank-Ordered Compensation

The same logic applies to the hierarchical order, where a lower-ranking person, culturally commanded to be unilaterally obligated, tends to overpay to the higher person. A's overpayment to his superior B is paid off by his inferior C. Here is another moral lesson: "If you are loyal to your superior, your subordinate will be loyal to you."

These triadic systems of compensation may offer an outlet for retaliation as well, however, if the compensation is not voluntarily offered by the third person but must be forcefully demanded by the frustrated overpayer. In the three-generational system, the mother-in-law syndrome is a case in point. The hierarchical system generates what Masao Maruyama calls "transference of repression" in his characterization of Japanese political behavior (1956:21). In the hierarchical system, A's overpayment to his superior B is demanded back from his inferior C, involving A's overbearing attitude toward and exploitation of C.

Distinct from this but still as a means of compensating for hierarchical exploitation is the emergence of an informal hierarchy within a formal one. While the formal hierarchy is based upon a formal system of rank order and promotion, the informal hierarchy may find its basis in sheer longevity. Historically, these two coexisted in a distinct form, paradoxically, in the Japanese military, where the most rigid form of hierarchy was supposed to exist. The formal hierarchy was staffed, from the bottom up, by private second-class, private first-class, superior private, sergeant, corporal, and so on. The informal one consisted of first-year servicemen, second-year, third-year, old timers, and so on. It has been said that the power of this informal hierarchy based on longevity was often superior to the power of the formal hierarchy, so that a university-educated first-year officer could not command a third-year private. According to Yamamoto (1972), it was lynching by the informal power manipulator, not formal sanctions, that was most dreaded and detested about military life. When the informal hierarchy overshadows the formal hierarchy, the compensatory chain takes the form of *gekokujō* ("control of superiors by inferiors") or "topsy-turvy democracy" as referred to in chapter 1.

CHAPTER 7

The Three Domains of Situational Interaction

PATTERN PERSISTENCE VERSUS SITUATIONAL FLUCTUATION

Belongingness, empathy, dependency, proper-place occupancy, and reciprocity have been delineated and analyzed as normative components of social relativism. As "normative," each represents an internalized pattern of behavior that most Japanese follow and reveal fairly consistently. In other words, what has been described so far characterizes Japanese behavior as it has persisted over time and across situations. An individual may deliberately repress one or another of these culturally patterned values, say, a dependency wish, in a certain relationship. But this repression is not likely to last long; instead, the dependency wish will pop out perhaps in another relationship. This is what I mean by the persistence or consistency of a behavioral pattern. One might call this cultural entrapment.

This argument is based not so much upon the psychoanalytical belief in the recalcitrance of the unconscious or upon the widely held view that a value, once internalized into a personality, is difficult to get rid of. It is based essentially on the fact that one value is so interlocked with another that one cannot be dispensed with without affecting another. This applies particularly to a culture in which social relativism predominates. I remember a Japanese visitor praising American academic institutions for the freedom they allow all staff members regardless of rank, which is unheard of in Japan. He complained about Japanese universities, where lower-ranking faculty are totally caught in *oyabun-kobun* bondage. As that complaint is often heard from visiting Japanese academics, one wonders why no change has taken place in the Japanese academic establishment—and evidently there has been little change despite the campus unrest of the late 1960s. The answer was given unwittingly by the visitor: "In America, when an assistant professor gets in trouble, like being arrested for drunken driving, I was told his department head will not come to bail him out. Is that true? I am afraid I could not live under such an insecure system." Implied herein is the lesson that one cannot demand freedom and equality unless one is willing to forgo the security derived from all the values that we have discussed so far—belongingness, empathy, dependency, proper-place occupancy, and reciprocity. As long as socially anchored security holds primacy over other values, the Japanese cultural pattern is unlikely to lose its force.

This chapter departs from the general patterns elucidated in the preceding chapters to take a more microscopic, short-range view of Japanese behavior. Here we are concerned with "situational" interactions, those triggered and guided by a given situation. While evincing a trans-situational persistence in behavior patterns, the Japanese also show sensitivity to situational change and readiness for situational adjustment. This is consistent with the ethos of social relativism, which fosters sensitivity to social situations. The Japanese often single out and dramatize a special situation that requires corresponding behavior by the participants in that situation. This aspect of Japanese behavior was noted and referred to as "a sense of occasion" by a Western observer (Kirkup 1970). With "a sharp awareness and appreciation" of an occasion, the Japanese "instinctively adopt the behavior suited to the time and the place" (p. 273). From the point of view of commitment to an ethical standard, such situational fluctuation of behavior has been identified as "situation ethic" or "situationalism" by Japanese as well as Western observers. It would be dangerous, however, to infer a lack of moral integrity in this situational adaptability. Situational fluctuation constitutes only a part of Japanese behavior, and fluctuation often takes place at a surface level or for a reason that does not bear on ethics.

THE THREE SITUATIONAL DOMAINS

Situations vary in time and in place. Since we cannot possibly exhaust all situational variations, the following scheme is proposed for identifying situational domains in which behavior is likely to change.

First, the Japanese distinguish one situation from another according to the dichotomy of *uchi* and *soto*. *Uchi* means "in, inside, internal, private," whereas *soto* means its opposite, "out, outside, external, public." The Japanese are known to differentiate their behavior by whether the situation is defined as *uchi* or *soto*. That distinction perhaps characterizes human culture in general, but it is essential in determining the way Japanese interact. Where the demarcation line is drawn varies widely: it may be inside vs. outside an individual person, a family, a group of playmates, a school, a company, a village, or a nation. It is suggestive that the term *uchi* is used colloquially to refer to one's house, family or family member, and the shop or company where one works. The essential point, however, is that the *uchi-soto* distinction is drawn not by social structure but by constantly varying situations.

The *uchi-soto* dichotomy is a necessary criterion for defining a situation, but not a totally sufficient one. A situation has to be characterized by a second dichotomy, *omote* and *ura*. *Omote* refers to "front," or what is exposed to public attention, whereas *ura* means "back" or what is hidden from the public eye. One may note an overlap between *uchi* and *ura* and between *soto* and *omote*. Nevertheless, they are mutually independent dichotomies. Four combinations of these dichotomous variables are logically possible:

uchi-omote	*uchi-ura*
soto-omote	*soto-ura*

The *uchi-omote* combination, namely, a situation both "inside" and yet "front," is unlikely to occur. However, the other three combinations are perfectly valid. Let us depict these combinations as a scheme of situational domains.

	Omote ("Front")	*Ura* ("Back")
Uchi ("In")	—	Intimate
Soto ("Out")	Ritual	Anomic

Uchi and *ura* combine into an intimate situation, *soto* and *omote* into a ritual situation, and *soto* and *ura* into an anomic situation. The dashes refer to an empty set that does not exist in reality.

In the intimate situation, Ego both perceives Alter as an insider and feels sure that his behavior toward Alter is protected from public exposure. Opposed to the intimate situation is the ritual situation, where Ego perceives Alter as an outsider and is aware that he is performing his role on a stage with Alter or a third person as audience. Confidentiality, which characterizes the intimate situation, is lacking in the ritual situation. Finally, the anomic situation contrasts with the intimate situation in that Ego defines Alter as an outsider, which rules out intimacy between Ego and Alter; it contrasts with the ritual situation in that Ego is freed from the concern that an audience is watching his behavior. The anomic situation is likely to occur when Ego finds Alter or a third person to be a stranger or enemy who does not share Ego's norms and whose approval is irrelevant to Ego. It is in this sense that the anomic situation combines *soto* and *ura*.

Ego finds himself in an intimate situation at one moment, in a ritual situation the next moment, and so forth. Even when Alter remains the same, the situation may change from intimate to anomic, for instance, when intimate friends become estranged. An intimate situation may be suddenly replaced by a ritual situation when an intimate dyad happens to be exposed to a third person who does not share the intimacy. The situational fluctuation to which Ego is constantly subject is represented in Figure 2.

Under the effect of social relativism, the Japanese tend to be sensitive to these three situational domains and to vary their behavior in accordance with them.

The outline above of the three domains is far from satisfactory, but to make it more satisfactory we cannot dwell on situations as such but must proceed to interaction behavior. It is easy to see that the three situations are respectively matched by three interaction patterns—intimate, ritual, and anomic. There is a dynamic interchange between a situation and interaction behavior. If both parties wish it, for example, a ritual situation can be changed into an intimate one by behavioral manipulation, as when one party breaks the ice at an encounter by a show of intimacy. However, let us first characterize each of the three behavior patterns as if they rigidly corresponded with the three situational domains.

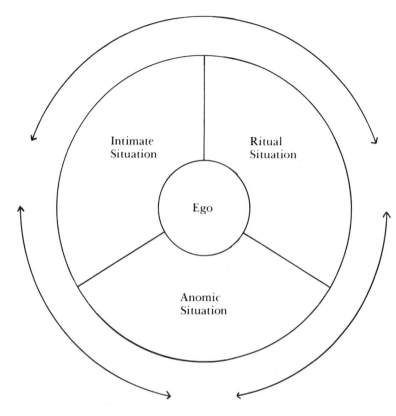

Figure 2. Situational Fluctuation

Alters for intimate interaction are naturally recruited from those with whom Ego has interacted (or wants to interact) most, through co-residence, co-working, co-playing, and so on. Such social backgrounds correspond to what Nakane calls a frame. However, any given situation can bring two strangers into intimate interaction temporarily, as will be discussed below. For instance, Ego will display intimate behavior toward a stranger provided the situation is defined as intimate. Intimate behavior is manifested in two ways: communication of unity between Ego and Alter, and display of spontaneity.

Communication of Unity

Intimate behavior is first characterized by expression and confirmation of unity, oneness, or solidarity, based on mutual liking and emotional attachment. The opposite of intimate behavior, then, is an expression of distance or alienation. Unity is communicated outwardly and inwardly. The outward communication of unity typically takes the form of play and enjoyment—doing pleasurable things together. Small wonder that Japanese go in for group participation in eating, drinking, singing, and dancing. Even sleeping and bathing together with one's peers is a culturally endorsed expression of intimacy. "Doing things together" necessitates "being together," occupying the same space. Among the Japanese, the physical proximity in intimate interaction is further reinforced by tactile communication: touching, pushing, slapping, and shoulder-to-shoulder togetherness are common expressions of intimate interaction.

Inward communication of unity and solidarity stems from the notion that in perfect intimacy, Ego does not have to express himself verbally or in conspicuous action because what is going on inside him should be immediately detected by Alter. The Japanese glorify silent communication, *ishin denshin* ("heart-to-heart communication"), and mutual "vibrations," implying the possibility of semitelepathic communication. Words are paltry against the significance of reading subtle signs and signals and the intuitive grasp of each other's feelings. The ultimate form of such communication is *ittaikan* ("feeling of oneness"), a sense of fusion between Ego and Alter. Ego then feels Alter's pleasure and pain as though they were his own. All this sounds like a reiteration of what has been said with reference to belongingness and empathy. The difference is that here a situational boundary, not a relationship, permits such intimate behavior. Ego may interact intimately not only with close kin or a friend but also a stranger, such as a customer at a shop, if the situation is so defined. Social unity is activated here by situations rather than by established social relationships. Even an intimate relationship like that of mother and child is not always acted out in intimate behavior.

Spontaneity

Intimate behavior, secondly, is characterized by the actor's spontaneity, freedom from inhibition. Ego's natural inclinations and wishes are expected to be expressed freely and without penalty from Alter. To show inhibition and reserve in an intimate situation may even be disapproved as *mizukusai* ("strangerlike").[1] Relaxation is the norm of intimate interaction.

When spontaneity is carried to extremes, intimate behavior takes the form of what might be called social nudity. Here Ego reveals his natural self, stripped of all face or social mask. A heart-to-heart talk is expressed in Japanese as a talk "with the body exposed." Such nudity is often intensified by the deliberate violation of conventional manners and etiquette (*hame o hazusu*). For instance, Japanese, even intellectuals, tend to behave with childish excitement in childish games and play in situations permitting intimate behavior and social nudity, as if their usual sophistication had suddenly evaporated. This contrasts with the likely behavior of foreign intellectuals in a similar situation. Nakane has remarked:

> Dr. Tomonaga, a recent Nobel prize winner, once wrote to the effect that foreign physicists do not hesitate to discuss physics while eating and drinking, to have pencil and paper ready, to draw formulas as if they were under the spell of something—so much so that he could hardly keep up. (Nakane 1967:182)

Nakane herself had similar experiences and admitted that she used to be annoyed by foreigners' enjoyment of cerebral talk even during a meal or in a relaxed gathering. On the other hand, she continues, foreign visitors to Japan find themselves completely left out of communication as soon as their Japanese friends start drinking (Nakane 1967:182).

Infantility, stupidity, rudeness, vulgarity are thus released or deliberately acted out in an intimate situation. Boisterousness, crying, postural indulgence such as lying on the floor (which would be a grave *faux pas* in other situations), falling asleep in front of others while the party is still going on—such violations of conventional norms are permitted or even endorsed in intimate interaction. Even transvestism is encouraged, especially in stunt performances; and in games played in intimate situations each

---

1. *Mizukusai* literally means "smelling of water" or "watery." Here, *mizu*, "water," idiomatically means something that prevents or interferes with intimacy. Hence, *mizuirazu*, "with no water coming in," describes a situation in which intimacy may be fully enjoyed.

player may have to take off his clothes piece by piece every time he loses a score.

Social nudity is also manifested in the content of humor, which abandons human dignity and conventional taste. Intimate conversation typically involves humor relating to human bodily functions, such as sexual potency and intercourse, defecation, urination, flatulence, and so on. Incidentally, this behavior is culturally sanctioned by the principle of *yokubō-shizenshugi*, "desire-naturalism," mentioned in chapter 1.

The frankness expected in intimate interaction often leads to aggression, including impoliteness toward one's superior. Heated arguments, quarrelling, and even violence may ensue, which end up negating the very unity that is supposed to be reinforced in intimate interactions.

This last point makes it clear that the two characteristics of intimate behavior, communication of unity and spontaneity, are mutually distinct variables. At an extreme, one begins to correlate inversely with the other: the more spontaneity allowed, the less unity attained; or the more unity to be attained, the less spontaneity allowed. Intimate interaction in its ideal form must be based on a proper balance between the two. Figure 3 depicts these ideas.

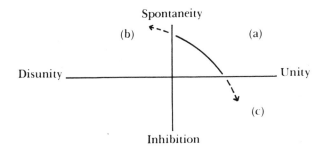

Figure 3. Balance in Intimate Behavior

Area (a) shows an optimal orientation, combining spontaneity and unity, for intimate interaction. Arrow (b) indicates an unbalanced orientation with excessive spontaneity at the expense of maintaining unity, and arrow (c) shows the reverse of (b), where the need for keeping unity results in suppression of feelings.

The Setting

Intimate interaction is facilitated by activities, resources, and settings that are tension-reducing. The ideal setting in that respect might be one's home. However, the home is not always ideal for communication of unity or spontaneous expression, for two reasons. First, home is where domestic chores must be done, and the family members are more or less task-oriented, not always ready for emotional communication of unity. Second, and more important culturally, the Japanese home, especially the middle-class home, is involved in the maintenance of status distance between its members on the basis of generation, birth order, and sex. Such distance is thought necessary for disciplining children. Thus, even husband and wife must maintain some ritual distance, at least in front of their children or parents—a case where a possibly intimate dyad must suppress intimacy in the presence of a third party. One cannot be totally spontaneous or relaxed under such conditions.

This suggests that the ideal setting for intimate interaction requires, first, separation from the setting of daily work. Intimacy seems maximized when actors engage in pure play or pleasurable activities away from work. Second, intimacy requires apparent equality among the participants in these activities.

Segregation of play from work for Japanese occurs in time and place. On a daily basis, workers spend their evening hours after work at bars enjoying intimate interaction with co-workers while drinking. The bars are likely to be situated somewhere between the working place and home. Intimate interaction away from work is reinforced by institutionalized recreation, on a seasonal or annual basis, for individual offices, departments, or a whole company. Seasonal group trips to hot springs, for instance, are eagerly looked forward to as occasions for intimate, relaxed interaction. Trips are ideal occasions, enabling complete segregation of the play scene (a hotel or inn) from the work scene (office or home). At the end of every year, various work units in companies hold *bōnenkai* ("the party to forget all the hardships of the year"). They take place in a private room in a hotel, restaurant, or teahouse, in whose homelike atmosphere one can relax, stretch out, and even sleep. With the tension-reducing power of sake, *bōnenkai* usually end up in boisterous merrymaking (*donchan sawagi*), without which the party would not be considered success-ful (Matsumoto 1970:27). What we have described as social nud-ity is most likely to result. Stupidity acted out on such occasions is actually considered a sign of manliness. *Santō Jūyaku* [The third-rate executive], a famous business-world novel written by Keita Genji, describes a *bōnenkai* attended by all the staff of a company, including the president. A young man performs a stunt called "catching fleas," involving scratching his body, feeling about for a flea, taking off his coat, tie, shirt, and so on, in search of a flea. This performance provokes uproarious laughter adding much to the levity of the occasion, and the same man dances with the president until, their wobbly legs entangled, they tumble to the floor and fall asleep (Genji 1961:347-350).

Such periodic gatherings, meant to reinforce intimacy, are enjoyed not only by groups of workers but by students or former classmates. The essential requirement is the segregation of the situation for intimate interaction from the workaday situation; social nudity freely expressed within that segregated situation is not supposed to be carried over into ordinary life the next morn-ing.

The second requirement for intimate interaction is equality of the participants. This may be achieved by limiting the Alters to Ego's peers, such as classmates or co-workers of the same rank. However, group activities often necessarily include people of different ranks, particularly when a party or a trip is sponsored by the company. There are cultural means of offsetting the rank distinctions of ordinary life and of creating the temporary ap-pearance of equality. Visible similarity is achieved by wearing uniforms; on an overnight group tour, all participants, superior and inferior alike, wear the uniform kimono provided by the hotel with its name on it. If it is a hot spring, they all bathe together in the same tub, where rank distinctions are easier to ignore. Here nudity is not just social or metaphorical but physical and literal. After drinking, eating, and merrymaking, they all go to sleep, lying side by side, in the same room.

The only problem would be that of sex. On the one hand there is the culturally imposed status distance between sexes. On the other, the above-described intimacy, including co-sleeping, might be thought to involve sexuality if the group happens to be heterosexual. Such complications did not emerge in the past, since intimate interaction in a group was sexually segregated. Even today, Japanese tend to believe that a truly satisfactory gathering must exclude the opposite sex. This is shown by the fact that parties are often held by men and men alone. Women, too, hold parties of their own at which they feel completely relaxed. Many middle-aged women belong to a local women's club that organizes annual trips.

On occasions when men and women are mixed in play, gatherings, or trips, an effort seems to be made to ignore sexual differences, not to let sex interfere with group unity. After a party held at a teahouse or a member's home, it is not unusual for participants to spend the night, sleeping in the same room without concern about sexual matters. Dore notes:

> It is common after late-night parties, either family parties or *geisha* parties, for all the assembled company, men and women, to sleep in the same room. The valued feature of this "mixed sleeping" (*zakone*) is the sociability it affords; the opportunity for conversation in fuddled comfort for as long as one feels like staying awake. There is no assumption that anything improper will take place. . . . (1958:48-49)

The temporarily assumed equality in rank and even in sex thus involves group regimentation, the extreme of which is again opposed to one of the two characteristics of intimate behavior, namely, spontaneity. Even such regimentation, however, may not be as uncomfortable as it seems, given the culturally tamed emotions, especially sexual emotions, described in chapter 1.

RITUAL BEHAVIOR

The ritual situation that elicits ritual behavior ranges widely, from the extremely structured situation, such as a ceremony, to the undefined, accidental situation, such as an unexpected encounter with an acquaintance on the street, from play scenes to work scenes. What links them all is that Ego defines Alter or a third person (or both) as an outsider whose opinion he cares for. The reasons may also vary widely, but, most generally, Ego cares because Alter has some influence over him and Ego thinks Alter would exercise his influence variably depending on Ego's performance. It should be stressed again that ritual behavior corresponds with a ritual situation, not necessarily a ritual relationship. An intimate relationship within a family may call for ritual interaction if the situation is so defined. The boundary between inside and outside moves according to the situation. Among the indicators of ritual behavior are posture (tense, unrelaxed way of sitting or standing), gestures and countenance (deep bowing, somber facial expression), style of speech (formal, polite style with honorifics, or ceremonial speech), and physical distance between Ego and Alter.

Ritual behavior closely relates to status orientation; the only difference is that ritual behavior is situationally defined and does not govern interaction between a superior and an inferior if the situation is defined as intimate. The ritual actor concerns himself with conforming to conventional rules, manners, and etiquette, presents himself with his social mask on, and manages his impression on Alter or a third-person witness in a manner well depicted by Goffman (1959). He tries to maintain face. There are two ways of maintain face, defensive and aggressive.

Defending Face

Face-defensive behavior is characterized by an effort by shame-sensitive Ego not to "lose face." The best way of doing that is to avoid behavior that risks causing him shame. Direct self-exposure is most risky. Hence, Ego must control his expression, suppress his natural feeling or spontaneity. In this way ritual behavior clearly contrasts with intimate behavior. Instead of acting out his feelings, Ego must first heed the ritual code of behavior and defend himself with ritual circumspection. This is the opposite of social nudity.

The required behavioral inhibition keeps Ego at a distance, not only physically but emotionally, from Alter, which is also in contrast to the social unity communicated in intimate behavior. The distance is behaviorally expressed by such gestures as bowing.

Suppression of spontaneity may extend to total inaction when Ego faces a new situation the ritual code for which is not immediately available. This may be observed when Japanese meet strangers, such as foreigners, whose approval they seek and yet whose expectations they are ignorant of. Rather than take a risk by exposing themselves, they simply freeze. Foreign observers tend to exaggerate the extent of this aspect of Japanese behavior—rigid, inhibited, unemotional—because it is what they see most often.

So far we have been discussing Ego's defense of his own face.

Ritual behavior involves the defense (or protection) of Alter's face as well (see Goffman's distinction, 1967:14). In fact, the Japanese, bound by the norm of empathy, have internalized the value of not embarrassing others as well as of watching out for their own face. Ritual interaction is thus characterized by mutual discretion as well as self-defense.

The following is a list of concrete mechanisms for defending face, both Ego's and Alter's, to which Japanese often resort in ritual interaction.

Mediated communication. Ego wants to negotiate with Alter on some delicate issue. Instead of exposing himself to Alter by direct negotiation, he asks someone else to transmit his message to Alter. If the mediator is skillful in manipulating the exchange of messages, neither Ego nor Alter loses face if a request is turned down. This is one of the merits of the system of arranged marriages. Mediated communication involves making dyadic communication triadic. In this triad, the mediator must appear to be the originator of negotiations, motivated altruistically to do good for both parties.

Refracted communication. A slightly different version of triadization is one in which Ego communicates with Alter by talking to a third person in Alter's presence. What Ego cannot directly express to Alter is expressed to the third person with the expectation that Alter will understand Ego's real intention. This happens within a family, when a married couple try to communicate affection or hostility to each other by talking to their child. Likewise, a daughter-in-law may scold her child with inordinately harsh words in front of the mother-in-law to express her exasperation with the latter. In short, an intimate dyad such as the mother-child pair is used to facilitate communication of a more ritual dyad, such as the husband-wife pair. If Ego feels intimacy toward a deceased kin, say, his mother, Ego may talk aloud to her in front of the household shrine or gravestone, so that Alter, with whom Ego really wants to communicate, will hear.[2]

---

2. I must hasten to add that triadic communication—both mediated and refracted—can be manipulated in a reverse direction. Parties to an intimate dyad may have lost the habit of articulately communicating with each other to the extent that such communication would be felt too formal and embarrassing to them. When they find themselves in need to verbally articulate their thoughts to each other, they may seek out a third person to whom they relate more ritually. The third person may take the role of a messenger as in mediated communication, or may be directly addressed in conversation as in refracted communication.

Acting as delegate. Ego meets Alter face-to-face but conveys his message as being that of someone else. Ego thus pretends to be a delegate or messenger for a third person. Instead of saying, "I want this," he says, "He wants this," or "I personally don't care but I am being pressed by these people to do this." The person on whose behalf the negotiation supposedly proceeds is usually chosen from acquaintances of higher status. In this connection one may recall the authority structure of Imperial Japan, which permitted many self-appointed delegates to carry out their own wishes by representing them as those of the emperor. The emperor himself was said to be fulfilling his obligation to imperial ancestors. This behavior ties in with the obligation-preoccupied orientation of the Japanese that was pointed out earlier.

Anticipatory communication. Ego does not express his wish but expects Alter or a third person to anticipate his wish. The burden of communication falls not on the message sender but on the message receiver. Instead of Ego's having to tell or ask for what he wants, others around him guess and accommodate his needs, sparing him embarrassment. This sort of anticipatory communication was referred to in the context of empathy.

The higher one's status, the more others strive to anticipate his wants. Males receive more such service from females than the other way around. Bachelors elicit anticipatory accommodation most since they are believed to be most helpless.

For anticipatory communication to be possible, Ego must be trained to be both receptive to the offer of such service by Alter and sensitive to Alter's unexpressed needs. The extreme of such sensitivity merges with silent communication in intimate behavior. *Omoiyari* ("empathy") cuts across the two situations, ritual and intimate, obviating verbal communication in both.

Self-communication. Avoiding the risk of face-to-face exposure, Ego may write down his thoughts and wishes as if he were doing so to his own satisfaction. This may take the form of a diary—a possible explanation for the Japanese habit of keeping a diary. The writer feels free to express his sentiments, for he is communicating with himself alone. The style of writing will be that of the monologue, status-free, distinct from the socially addressed spoken style. A poetic form of expression may be preferred because it dramatizes the private nature of the monologue.

Such self-communication can become socially significant if it is ever disclosed. In some instances, disclosure is expected by the writer. In *The Key*, a novel by Junichiro Tanizaki, the husband and wife write about their sex lives, including the wife's adultery, in their separate diaries. Each pretends to keep his diary secret but each fully expects the other to read it. This is fiction and rather grotesque at that, as are many novels by Tanizaki. What is more likely to happen in reality is that one would send part of one's diary to someone as a message. Diary exchange is not an unusual form of courtship. Self-communication by keeping a diary is used, incidentally, in one method of psychotherapy in Japan, and this will be discussed in detail in chapter 13.

Correspondence. Communication through the exchange of letters is a combination of self-communication and interpersonal communication—self-communication because the message is expressed while its sender is alone. Even when Alter is easily accessible in person, Ego may prefer sending written messages to talking. A letter, even though clearly addressed to Alter, makes the communication indirect enough that Ego is spared any possible embarrassment. Curiously enough, such written communication takes place often between intimate persons, such as lovers or a mother and her child. *Shōnenki* [Boyhood], a longtime bestseller by a psychologist (Hatano 1954), is primarily a true record of letters exchanged between mother (the author) and son, using the same notebook. A middle-school student, bright and sensitive, the son writes to his mother about his experiences with friends and teachers at school, with his father and brothers, about neighbors and relatives, about the ongoing war, and even about his mother, the very addressee of the letters. The mother responds to each of her son's letters, encouraging, explaining, sometimes scolding him. Mutual affection between mother and son seemed to be fully expressed only through their letters.

Understatement. The Japanese language, especially in its spoken form, allows subtle, implicit, open-ended, obscure understatement. This may be partly because syntactically it is not necessary to state the subject, and verbs and negatives come at the end of a sentence. By omitting subjects, verbs, and negatives, the speaker can avoid making a verbal commitment and thus risking the loss of face. Since a sentence can be left open-ended, the Japanese speaker is freer to retract what he has said, should his listener disagree. A Japanese often feels ill at ease speaking in English because he loses this sense of freedom and is compelled to make an assertive, committing, irreversible statement. Avoidance of premature self-assertion was also discussed, the reader may recall, in the light of empathetic concern for maintaining consensus.

As examples of understatement, let us look at some Japanese idioms for refusing an offer that are so subtle that no foreigner, unless familiar with them, will be able to tell whether the offer has been refused or eagerly accepted. The expression *Kekkō desu*, means both "I appreciate it," and "No, thank you." *Sekkaku desu ga* ("It's very kind of you, but") also expresses polite refusal and may be completed by *Goenryo sasete itadakimasu* ("Would you please let me constrain myself").

Unobtrusive behavior. Implicit in understatement is the avoidance of obtrusive behavior. The more obtrusive Ego's behavior is, the more liable Ego is to lose face or to injure Alter's face. Cultural wisdom encourages Ego to be unobtrusive. Modesty and subtle refinement can thus be considered necessary qualities to display to defend face. Even shyness, bashfulness, or anticipatory embarrassment may be viewed as defensive in this light. Humility, besides being a virtue, is a social weapon to defend one's own and another's face. *Enryo* refers to the restraint Ego imposes upon himself in interaction with Alter when he is offered help, a treat, a gift, and the like. The same term describes both polite hesitation to accept a desired offer and polite refusal of an undesired offer. Thus, Alter does not always know how to take Ego's expression of *enryo*. Since *enryo* refers to polite hesitation in most instances, Alter is generally supposed to keep insisting that his offer be accepted.

A contrasting situation is encountered in the United States. Doi's discomfort with his American host (mentioned in chapter 3) owed not only to the fact that Japanese are not used to choosing what they are offered, but also, in my view, to the culturally imbedded norm of *enryo* constraining the guest's behavior.

Ritualism. Face is most vulnerable in unpredictable situations. The most common means of keeping it safe, then, is to minimize the options and uncertainties that might arise in a situation. Ritualism is an answer. Ritualism refers to rigid, meticulous control of interaction behavior in a predetermined way so as to prevent embarrassing surprises. As manifested in formal social gatherings in Japan, ritualism requires elaborate preparation so that everything will proceed smoothly and exactly as expected. Extemporaneous conversation involving competitive one-upmanship in storytelling, which seems to characterize American cocktail parties, is to be avoided at ritual Japanese gatherings. (This does not mean that the game of witty remarks is not enjoyed at all by Japanese, but only within an intimate situation where one feels free to embarrass another by outdoing him in an exchange. The kind of joke expressed there is most likely to be an in-group joke that makes no sense to outsiders.) For one thing, the Japanese would find it rude to interrupt someone still talking, as it is customary to do at American-style cocktail parties. At a typical Japanese formal gathering called *enkai*, people are seated around a table, a number of preselected speakers give prepared flowery speeches in a predetermined order, and glasses of beer are emptied by all present on the voiced signal, "Kampai!" ("Empty the glass!"). Only then can the dinner, by now cooled, be eaten. One thing must be done at a time, participated in by everybody in unison.

Displaying Face

The same cultural matrix behind Ego's defense of face seems to tempt him to promote his face through social aggression. While defensive face demands inhibition and minimization of self-exposure, aggressive face necessitates self-exhibition and ostentation. One's dignity must be proven by exhibiting one's capacity or attribute that matches the claimed dignity. "Impression management" thus includes not only concealing what should not be revealed but also revealing what should be revealed in an ostentatious, dramatic manner. Such showing off is opposite to the norm of unobtrusiveness that is activated in defending face.

Moreover, Ego's aggressive face is maintained, promoted, or demoted in competition with Alter's face. The extreme of such competition is a sort of zero-sum game, in which Ego can enhance his face only by demoting Alter's. What we said about Ego's empathetic consideration for Alter's face—*omoiyari*—evidently does not apply here. Below some behavioral manifestations of self-exhibition are considered; they are listed from the more sociable to the less sociable.

Conspicuous generosity. Generosity is one means of establishing one's dignity. Generosity in rendering help, gift-giving, or entertaining guests is considered by most Japanese a necessary measure to maintain or upgrade one's face. This is why refusal of an entreaty redounds to the discredit of the refuser as well as the one refused. To be thought stingy is one of the worst stigmas for a person who wants to dignify himself.

In situational interaction, generosity is displayed, for instance, at a bar or restaurant when two or more people, after enjoying food and drinks, fight one another for the check. Such competition in showing generosity is precluded only if there is a clear-cut rank order in the group so that the highest-ranking person is expected to pay for all. (If it were intimate interaction, the wish for Dutch treat would be frankly expressed.) Japanese visitors to the United States are often shocked when the higher-ranking persons in a group do not appear ashamed to ask for separate checks.

Concern for generosity is coupled with the desirability of appearing indifferent to pecuniary calculation in daily life. It is well known that Japanese, especially male Japanese customers, do not count their change at stores, as if counting were indicative of stinginess. Nor are bills at restaurants examined. Even when the customer is aware of a miscalculation by the cashier, he prefers to keep quiet if not too much money is involved.

Indifference to pecuniary matters further relates to the tendency to join others in contributing money to a group project, such as buying a birthday gift for a member or giving a funerary gift to a member's relative. Refusal to contribute invites contempt from fellow members. Some members may try to outdo others in the amount contributed, in which case the action can be properly described as "aggressive." Other members may only try to "keep up with the Joneses," in which case the action is more defensive.

I hasten to add that generosity is not motivated solely by one's concern for face. Obviously, other factors are involved, ranging from genuine kindness to Alter to the wish to bind Alter by reciprocal obligations in future transactions. At present, we are looking at generosity only in terms of the ritual code in face-to-face interaction.

Self-praise. While generosity is a sociable form of aggressive face, self-praise is a more self-centered, asociable one. Ego's telling Alter how great Ego is runs solidly counter to modesty and humility. *Jiman* ("boasting") is strongly disapproved of by most

Japanese, and yet enough Japanese indulge in it to make it a cultural trait. This is only natural since Japanese are socially sensitive and concerned with social reputation. The desire to let Alter know Ego's distinction can be satisfied quickly by means of self-praise, though at the cost of modesty. A *jiman* talk is usually begun with the remark, "This may sound like *jiman*, but. . . ." The listener may tolerate the boast that follows out of politeness but be secretly disgusted. Or, the listener may respond with awe and admiration, either because he takes the speaker seriously or because he wants to please him. Role vicariism is also activated in *jiman* behavior, as when a man brags about his son's school performance—very common behavior indeed.

Arrogance. The least sociable form of self-display is arrogance, an attempt by Ego to promote his dignity by demoting Alter's dignity. The arrogant person is described in such terms as *otakai* ("high-browed"), *ibaru* ("overbearing"), "looking down on others," "making fun of others," "playing a big shot." Self-praise does not necessarily hurt Alter's pride, but arrogant behavior does. For this reason it is most detested by Japanese and sometimes elicits retaliation by the person who suffers a loss of face. There is thus relatively heavy cultural sanction against indulgence in arrogance; Japanese in general are careful not to look arrogant, to the degree that they appear overly humble. Nonetheless, arrogance seems to be an inseparable part of the complex of ritual interaction; it is usually latent but gets activated when the chips are down. I even contend that internalization of the value of humility is interlocked with internalization of its opposite, arrogance, and that the latter is simply recessive while the former is dominant. Humility, then, far from being exclusive of arrogance, is complementary to it.

There is more cultural elaboration for defensive face than for aggressive face, for the obvious reason that aggressive face, especially self-praise and arrogance, is not culturally approved. Exhibitionism may satisfy Ego's needs and thus be tempting to Ego, but will be detested by Alter, its victim. Some Alters, however, may try to win a favor from Ego by ingratiating themselves. Such Alters are as much disdained by other people for their lack of dignity as the arrogant Ego is disapproved.

These considerations lead us to conclude that ritual behavior, too, is based upon a proper balance of different values. Figure 4 depicts the balance.

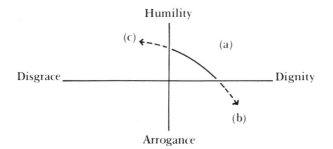

Figure 4. Balance in Ritual Behavior

The cultural ideal in ritual behavior lies in the range of (a), namely, in the balance between humility and dignity. One should be humble, modest, and polite but at the same time maintain one's dignity. When the pull of dignity is too strong, ritual behavior becomes arrogant, as is shown by arrow (b); when humility goes too far, ritual behavior reflects lack of dignity, as is indicated by arrow (c). Both (b) and (c) deviate from the norm of ritual behavior, although they exist side by side with (a) in actual behavior within the Japanese cultural complex.

Some Implications of Ritual Behavior

Violation of the cultural value of ritual behavior entails the serious consequences of being humiliated and of humiliating others through a breach of etiquette. Historically, the norm of ritual conformity was stressed most under the Tokugawa regime in an effort to suppress the belligerence of samurai warriors. The famous, dramatically embellished story of the Forty-Seven Samurai, associated with the golden period of the Tokugawa, reveals the seriousness of humiliation. The whole tragedy of that story—involving the forced *harakiri* ("disembowelment") of the feudal lord, Asano, and the subsequent confiscation of his estate, leaving his family, vassals, and retainers homeless and penniless—was triggered by Asano's humiliation at the shogun's court. Through the trickery of a corrupt court official (whose attempts at extortion Asano had once rebuffed), Asano was led to reveal ignorance, to err in seating himself, or some such minor error (the accounts vary), on a grand ceremonial occasion at court. Though aware of the possible consequences, Asano drew his sword to strike the official, wounding him. For this violation of the law, Asano was ordered to commit suicide. The point is that Asano was willing to sacrifice his life and property to redeem lost face. The story is still very popular among the Japanese and is played on the stage and in the movies year after year. True, the popularity may be based primarily on the loyalty of the forty-seven masterless samurai who finally avenged their lord Asano by killing the venal official. It also appears, however, that the Japanese audience shares Asano's humiliation and sympathizes with his reckless action. How would a Chinese audience react to this; would it not think Asano a fool? Would it not think it much more sensible to have bribed the official and thus been spared the humiliation at court in the first place?

If making ritual errors is so serious a matter, and everyone tries to avoid doing so, deliberate self-humiliation is of value for its scarcity. On the entertainment market one can sell self-humiliation as the player of a fool's role. The most common type of comedian in Japan, called *manzai*, specializes in undignified display, self-mockery, in breaching the ritual code, showing vulgarity, and making physical assaults upon the partner-comedian, such as hitting, kicking, and throwing. The Japanese audience finds the comedian's total "deritualization" hilarious. Deritualization would have little market value unless the audience were so used to ritual interaction.

There is another type of comedian, the *rakugo* comedian, whose role has a different bearing on ritual behavior. The *rakugo* comedian tells stories, in the fashion of American comedians; but while the American comedians are often appreciated for their ability at extemporaneous performance, *rakugo* comedians tell only the stories they have memorized in their apprenticeship with a master. Since the same stories are told and retold, the audience is often well versed in them. Yet *rakugo* lovers enjoy listening to the same stories and get a kick out of the same jokes. *Rakugo* performances are even advertised by the titles of stories, as well as by the names of the comedians. The comedian's creativity does not lie in making up a story but in his unique way of uttering words or in his way of setting up the audience for the punch line. It is not so much the content of the story that is appreciated as it is the subtlety and refinement expressed in the telling of it. Thus, where the *manzai* comedian entertains by total violation of the ritual code, the *rakugo* comedian entertains by a ritualistic display minimizing extemporaneity.

What we have said about ritual behavior also suggests the significance of intimate behavior. The ritually bound Japanese need culturally sanctioned occasions for indulging in social nudity. Thus tension is released periodically through these occasions, and people have an opportunity to "really" get to know one another.

ANOMIC BEHAVIOR

Anomic behavior is characterized as action toward an Alter who is defined as an outsider and yet with whom Ego feels no need to maintain a "front." It is different from intimate behavior in that Alter belongs to the outside world, but it is also different from ritual behavior in that there is no consideration of ritual code. Anomic refers to normless, the state where there are no definite norms to control behavior. On the one hand, Ego is not bound by face and thus can afford to be "shameless" or "thick-skinned." On the other, Ego does not have to consider Alter's face and is allowed to be "heartless" (Goffman 1967:11) and offensive. *Omoiyari* ("empathy") is irrelevant. The following situations are likely to give rise to anomic behavior.

Situational Novelty and Anonymity

If the situation happens to be totally new to Ego, anomic behavior is likely to emerge. Such a novel situation may be encountered by the person who has lived in a small, isolated village all his life and suddenly goes to a city; who has come into contact with a foreigner for the first time; who is traveling abroad for the first time, and so forth. In these situations his interaction cannot be guided and controlled by a set of norms. The likely outcome would range from total inaction—a refusal to interact—to uninhibited action in a "shameless" and "heartless" manner. Japanese visiting abroad tend to suffer from the uncertainty of this anomic state but also enjoy the sense of freedom it allows, at least until they develop a new set of social relationships abroad.

Both suffering and enjoyment derive from Ego's status of being anonymous or a "nobody" in the eyes of Alter and audience. Anomic behavior, then, may be said to arise in situations that make Ego anonymous. Anonymity can be created not only by novel situations but in crowds. It is often said that Japanese, who are extremely polite and even timid as individuals, do not hesitate to show rudeness and boldness in a group. This is not only because of their group orientation but because an actor in a group is more anonymous than an individual actor.

Struggle for Survival and Power Contest

Anomic behavior is occasioned when the actor's survival is at stake. The survival struggle makes Ego forget good manners toward Alter. A familiar example is found in Japanese behavior at train stations during rush hour. Hurrying to get to work on time and confronted with inadequate transportation service, people push one another and even knock each other down to get into the train. They seem oblivious to politeness or their own dignity. The usually well-mannered Japanese thus shock foreign observers by this total lack of etiquette at train stations. Other, rarer conditions bring out anomic behavior. The threat of starvation would drive Japanese, as much as other peoples, to search for food in disregard of their face and dignity. And in combat, both hostility toward the enemy and one's destructive power must be fully unleashed, polite gestures being not merely irrelevant but fatal.

Related to the struggle for survival is a situation in which two persons confront each other in a contest of sheer power. Here it is power or the difference in power, not a norm, that determines behavior. If the parties are about equal in power, their behavior is likely to exhibit mutual hostility, suspicion, and competitiveness. If there is a clear-cut difference, so that one party can dominate the other at the point of a gun, so to speak, the dominated party will have no choice but to cower in submission while the dominant party acts with arrogance and contempt, neither side exhibiting concern about face. Power is expressed in bodily strength, weaponry, wealth, but it is also expressed in the number of actors involved. Actors in a group may behave arrogantly toward individual actors outside the group not only because they are anonymous but also because they appear more powerful. The weaker party may submit not so much from respect as from fear. Under such circumstances both behaviors, arrogance and docility, are anomic.

This discussion of anomic behavior has alluded to basic conditions of human existence shared in all cultures. Cross-cultural differences seem to lie in the degree to which actors differentiate anomic behavior from other behaviors. I believe that more differentiation is observed among Japanese than, say, among Americans. The reason is obvious: Japanese have clear-cut definitions of intimate and ritual situations, together with cultural prescriptions of how to behave in either situation. For them the anomic situation is a residual category that is not covered and thus one that calls for a pattern of behavior all its own.

Let us recall Benedict's description of Japanese war prisoners. For a Japanese, capture by a foreign enemy would present all of the aforementioned circumstances calling for anomic behavior—a totally novel, anonymous situation, threatened survival, and compliance forced at the point of a gun. In my opinion, the captured Japanese soldier became a model prisoner not so much because he switched his loyalty as because he saw the situation as hopelessly anomic. On being captured, the Japanese soldier is said invariably to have demanded that the enemy kill him (Yamamoto 1972). His later compliance with the enemy seems to indicate anomic behavior more than anything else.

CROSS-SITUATIONAL BEHAVIOR

Japanese behavioral differentiation according to the situation takes striking form in cross-situational interaction. Some adjustment must be made when one situation, an intimate situation for example, coexists with another situation, such as a ritual situation, or when one situation is suddenly intruded upon by another situation. The following are some patterns of behavioral adjustment to such situational hybrids.

Ritualization

Suppose Ego is interacting with Alter intimately when a third person suddenly shows up. If Ego feels that he cannot share the intimacy with the third person but must maintain some ritual distance toward him, the initial dyadic intimacy is suddenly terminated and replaced by ritual behavior not only toward the sudden intruder, but also between Ego and Alter.

The situation need not involve a triad. Two strangers happen to meet and Ego behaves in a rude, arrogant, or hostile manner toward Alter because the latter does not appear to be very high in status and Ego does not care about Alter's opinion. This is a typically anomic situation. All of a sudden Ego discovers that Alter is a relative of his employer. Ego's behavior is most likely to shift into a ritual pattern involving extreme embarrassment, sincere apology, correction of posture from a relaxed into a formal, rigid style, respectful speech, and so forth.

These examples show that when an intimate situation or anomic situation is mixed with or intruded upon by a ritual situation, priority goes to the ritual situation, and intimate or anomic behavior is replaced by ritual behavior. I call this cross-situational behavior "ritualization."

Ritualization may take place in an extreme situation like a rush-hour train boarding, a situation typically anomic. After knocking down everyone else to get in the train and secure a seat, Ego no sooner sits down than he finds an acquaintance standing in front of him. He will suddenly change his behavior and make a formal greeting, attempting to bow low in a sardine-packed train, where there is absolutely no room for body movement. He will even get up to give the acquaintance his seat, over the latter's protests. It certainly strikes one as strange to see such a pair competing with each other in showing polite gestures while the rest of the crowd, totally exhausted, looks covetously at the empty seat.

Collusive Disperception

Some situations call for two behavior patterns at once. Suppose a person meets an unexpected visitor approaching his house. As soon as he sees the visitor, he would naturally be inclined to express surprise and joy at meeting him again—in short, to engage in intimate interaction. However, he is at the same time bound by the ritual code governing the receiving of a guest. The guest, too, feels he must follow the etiquette for a guest. Thus, host and guest do not start to talk immediately on seeing each other, but wait until both get ready to bow in formal style and to greet each other in the conventional manner. Sometimes they cannot get ready until they have reached the drawing room and are sitting face to face. It would appear to a stranger that the parties had not recognized each other until then. This kind of collusive disperception in host-guest interactions has been well observed by Hulse (1962:305).

Analogous to this situation is the relationship between traditional stage actors or dancers and their audience. On the Japanese theatrical stage not only actors, but also auxiliary staff, are present to help actors make costume changes on stage and to see that the actors' attire hang properly. Other helpers bring in and remove props. Unless the audience were capable of disperceiving the informal part and concentrating on the formal part of the action, it would be intolerably distracting to see the auxiliary personnel on stage. Japanese theater-goers claim that once they get involved in a play they cease to see the assistants and that to be disturbed by them indicates a lack of artistic sophistication. Even Japanese puppet shows, in which puppet operators are fully visible to the audience, are said, if successful, to make the audience oblivious to the presence of the operators.

Sequentialization

To prevent a collision of two situations, one situation may be made to follow another so that two different behaviors can be exhibited sequentially. The formal social gathering called *enkai*, for example, is so bound by ritual requirements that many of its participants satisfy their desire for relaxation and spontaneous interaction after the formal part of the gathering. It is common to hold an informal party called *nijikai* ("second party"), in another place, immediately after the formal one. The *nijikai* is composed of intimate friends from among those attending the first party. It is at the *nijikai* that *enkai* participants have real fun, with unrestrained conversation and even arguments and quarrels. The ritualism of a formal party is tolerated, it seems, because of the anticipation of what is to come afterward.

Such a sequential shift may take place in host-guest encounters. As soon as the host recognizes his guest coming toward him, he may express his surprise or pleasure spontaneously or the two may engage in a moment of friendly conversation. The guest is then invited to the drawing room, and when he and the host are seated face to face they will exchange formal greetings, bowing low, apologizing for not having seen each other for a long time. This formal gesture is then followed by relaxed, intimate conversation.

A researcher from Japan came to an American research institute for a ten-month stay. A month before he was to leave he came to say good-bye to the staff. The staff wondered why he did so then instead of a month later. It turned out that his formal appointment had ended, and he thought it required a formal farewell. He stayed on for another month as a "private" researcher and reappeared to make a final but informal leave-taking.

A similar pattern is followed in the conventional form of letter writing. Ordinarily, a letter is begun with a conventional description of the season and weather, followed by inquiry into the addressee's health and a report on the writer's own. Only after a rather long, ritualized greeting of this sort is the real intent of the letter disclosed in a less formal tone in a new paragraph, which begins with an expression like *sate* or *tokoro de*. These expressions, meaning "by the way," warn the reader that now that formalities are completed he should be ready for the real message. If the letter writer wants to get into the issue right away, he may prepare the reader by beginning, "formalities omitted."

Actual situations vary from case to case, but the cultural principle governing cross-situational interaction is simple and clear: one situation should not be mixed with another. Situational mixture is avoided by giving priority to one situation over another, by ignoring one and dealing with another, or by sequentially arranging one situation after another. To make *kejime* ("discrimination") from situation to situation is a part of moral discipline, as well as a sign of maturity for Japanese: the person without *kejime* cannot be depended upon. The sense of *kejime* is reinforced by the common practice of having a certain ceremony at the beginning and end of a meeting: in prewar classrooms, for example, and to a certain extent in postwar ones too, students stood up to greet the teacher at the beginning of class and again to thank him at the end.[3] This concern for maintaining *kejime* may contribute to the Japanese person's keen awareness of the discrepancy between *honne* and *tatemae*. *Honne* means one's natural, real, or inner wishes and proclivities, whereas *tatemae* refers to the standard, principle, or rule by which one is bound at least outwardly. This cultural pressure for situational discrimination may also underlie the Japanese recognition of what BenDasan (1970) calls "law behind law," "reason behind reason," and "word behind word."

---

3. The recent fad is to use English initials when describing the criteria of *kejime*—T.P.O., which stands for time, place, and occasion.

CHAPTER 8

Early Socialization

This chapter considers the socialization of the Japanese child, which consists of the learning (by the child) and teaching (by the parent or a parental figure) of the beliefs, values, and norms of the culture. From the standpoint of culture, socialization means the transmission of a cultural system from individual to individual and from generation to generation, thus insuring its persistence. From the standpoint of society, socialization serves to keep the society supplied with qualified members.

In anthropology, socialization has been a key concern of the subfield called culture and personality, which has long been under the influence of Freudian psychoanalytic theory. This is no coincidence because it was Freud who stressed the importance of the experiences of early childhood in the formation of the adult personality. The psychoanalytic bias has resulted in an emphasis and often exaggeration of cultural differences in the psychosexual training of children, such as weaning and toilet training, to the neglect of other more important aspects of socialization. Many anthropologists have pointed out this oversight. (Among them, see Hammond 1971:408, with regard to studies on Japanese child-rearing.) I shall not be bound by this traditional approach.

As clear from the definition of socialization above, two parties participate in socialization, the one being socialized and the other doing the socializing. The one being socialized, the trainee, is the child, and the socializer is the parent, grandparent, or older sibling within the family, and a playmate, schoolteacher, neighbor, or similar significant figure outside the family. It is true that socialization seldom operates in a unilateral way; a teacher learns, through teaching, as much as the learner and thus is resocialized. In this sense socialization is a lifelong process. However, in this chapter we shall ignore the mutuality of socialization and focus primarily on preschool socialization in the family. Most crucial in family socialization is the mother-child relationship.

Interdependence between Trainer and Trainee

First, let us consider how the child interacts with his trainer. A glance at interaction patterns in a Japanese family leads us to believe that socialization in Japan builds up and reinforces interdependence and solidarity between the trainer and trainee. This takes the forms of physical contact, appeasement, and sensitization to loneliness and dependency.

Physical Contact

Foreign observers often remark on the physical closeness of the Japanese mother and her child, not only physical proximity but actual body contact, or what the Japanese call "skinship." This is found particularly in infant care.

A common practice that regularizes body contact between mother and infant is breast-feeding. The mother holds the baby in her arms or lies down by the baby in such a way that it can secure her nipple in its mouth. Breast-feeding has been believed to be nutritionally necessary and psychologically natural and was practiced without inhibition even in public until foreigners expressed "cultural shock" at it. Under the influence of governmental recommendations and women's magazines, "modern" mothers have switched to bottle-feeding. But there still is overwhelming resistance to exclusive bottle-feeding, and Japan's Doctor Spock, Dr. Michio Matsuda, has been influential in pushing Japanese mothers back to the old custom. He has been especially critical of those "cultural mamas" who simply imitate the Western way in total disregard of the experience and wisdom of "thousands of years" (Matsuda 1964).

Breast-feeding persists not only for nutritional reasons but for emotional reasons. Japanese mothers generally enjoy nursing; weaning is difficult for them as well as for the baby, as observed by Benedict (1946:261). The breast is often given not so much for feeding as for playing with. Matsuda stresses this emotional gratification as a merit of breast-feeding:

> Nursing a baby is not just a matter of nutrition. It seems enjoyable to a woman to show love for her baby this way—the way only women can. . . . Think how the baby feels. I see babies nursing almost every day and find that the breast-fed baby looks happier than the bottle-fed one. . . . I think the child, when brought up feeling his mother's love all around his body, will develop something unique at the depth of his psyche. (p. 82)

The time chosen for weaning depends upon a number of variables, including the mother's health, education, and need for nondomestic work, the arrival of a new baby, and regional custom. Generally it is not completed until one year after birth, sometimes two or three years. Breast-play lasts longer, facilitated by the custom of the child's sharing the same bed with his mother. It may last until he is forced out of his mother's bed when a new baby is expected.

Another daily practice that necessitates body contact is bathing. The Japanese caretaker bathes with her baby. First of all, Japanese as a people enjoy bathing, soaking in the deep Japanese bathtub (*furo*). This pleasure is doubled by co-bathing. The baby is held tight to the mother's body and together they sit and soak in the tub. This is done in a public bathhouse as well as in private baths; the women's section of a public bathhouse is usually furnished with a row of baby beds. During bathing, as well as nursing, the mother and infant share physical pleasure and communicate to each other through body contact.

An emphasis upon body contact and body communication has been noted in general patterns of interaction between mother and infant, in addition to nursing and bathing. Caudill and Weinstein (1969) conducted a systematic study of maternal care and infant behavior comparing Japanese and American urban middle-class families. With a carefully controlled sample and methodological rigor, they observed the behavior of three- to four-month-old infants and their mothers. They came to the conclusion that there are cultural differences, not so much in care relating to biological needs as in "the styles in which infants and mothers behave in the two cultures" (p. 29). One of these differences is that the Japanese mother seems to communicate with her baby more in a physical than a verbal way, whereas the American mother more often chats with her baby. The Japanese mother picks up her baby, carries and rocks him to soothe and quiet him; in contrast, the American mother talks to her baby, looks at him, and stimulates him to be active. These differences are reflected in the babies' behavior: the American baby is active, vocal, and explores his environment, whereas the Japanese baby is quieter, more passive, and less restless.

Along with infant care, the sleeping arrangement is another indication of the cultural bias for physical contact and togetherness between the trainer and trainee. The Japanese family tends to congregate for sleeping in fewer rooms than are available, suggesting that the members choose to sleep together rather than being forced to by population density and space limitation. Dore has noted that the Japanese prefer the intimacy of crowded sleeping to being isolated in separate rooms (1958:49).

Caudill and Plath studied parent-child co-sleeping patterns among urban Japanese (1966). They found that parent-child co-sleeping occurs so often that it interferes with or overrides marital co-sleeping. The father and mother may even sleep in separate rooms, each co-sleeping with one or more children. Extended kin, especially the grandmother, also play a significant role in co-sleeping arrangements. When a baby is born, he inevitably co-sleeps with his mother; an older child who has been sleeping with the mother may then go to sleep with his father, or more likely his grandmother. Siblings also co-sleep. This sort of sleeping arrangement would not work well if any member of the family had an incestual awareness or inclination. Sexuality does not seem to enter into the awareness of Japanese co-sleepers. Thus, a father may share a room with his daughter, a mother with her son, and a brother with a sister.

Sharing the same bedroom involves body proximity and exposure but not necessarily skin contact. Sharing the same bed would be more relevant to our present context of body contact in socialization. The following is my impressionistic generalization about co-sleeping in the same bed. A newborn infant sleeps in his own small bed, nowadays often in a crib. At several months of age, he may be placed in his mother's bed so that she can nurse him easily. He loses this privilege as soon as another pregnancy takes place, when he is placed into his own bed or moved to someone else's bed, such as his grandmother's. It may be generally said that a preschool child has chances to share a bed with an adult. The Japanese bed mats (*futon*) facilitate co-sleeping: they can be spread close to each other so that a child can roll around from one bed to another; he may go to sleep in his mother's bed and wake up in his father's bed. Even when every member of the family has his own bed, children can roll around, consciously or unconsciously, sharing beds in the same room. Thus, inevitably children have body contact with siblings or with adults, intentionally or unintentionally, during the night.

The body warmth experienced in co-sleeping is likely to be retained in the child's memory and recalled with pleasure after he attains maturity. An example cited in Caudill and Plath is illustrative of the impact of co-sleeping upon one's adult life:

> The twentieth-century social reformer, Toyohiko Kagawa, as a child prized—and later vividly remembered—opportunities to sleep by his elder brother. As a seminarian he was deeply impressed when a missionary offered to share his bed even though Kagawa was tubercular. When he recovered, Kagawa in turn shared his bed in the Kobe slums with criminals, alcoholics, the ill, and the destitute. (p. 364)

Skin contact is further observed in the way a mother may transport her child. As Japanese do not hire babysitters, the mother usually takes her child with her wherever she goes, unless someone in the family stays home to watch the baby. A buggy may be used to transport a child who cannot yet walk. The more traditional common form of transport is papoose-style (*onbu*), on the back. The child is secured to the mother's back by means of a long sash, with his legs spread, one toward each side of her torso, and his hands on her shoulders, in such a fashion that his whole body rests on her back. When carried this way, the child either sleeps or looks over his mother's neck or shoulders. Mother and child feel each other's body warmth. In winter, the exchange of body warmth was facilitated by a kimono-styled, quilted coat that covered both mother and child. *Onbu* is so enjoyed that some children are able to fall asleep only on the mother's back.

Onbu is used not only to transport a child, but also to insure his safety while his mother is busy working. If she has no time to watch over a crawling child, the mother might prefer to carry him around on her back, leaving her hands free. If not the mother, the grandmother or older sister may carry him on her back at home. *Onbu* is associated more with a female caretaker; the father carries the child in his arms, or, when the child is old enough, on his shoulders, for fun. It should be noted that this kind of transport is enjoyed by both parties, even when the child can walk (Befu 1971:156). Parental affection, it seems, is expressed most easily through the body contact provided by such means of carrying a child.

Thus, the Japanese child quickly learns to find pleasure and security with and near his mother. Vogel and Vogel (1961) noted a grade-school child sitting on his mother's lap when guests were present. Infant-care practices—including breast-feeding and bathing, co-sleeping, transport on the back or in the arms, and, I might add, the practice of helping the child eliminate by holding him above the toilet—all sensitize the child to the *ittaikan*, the feeling of oneness, that adult Japanese seek in intimate interaction.

Body contact is observed not only between the baby and his mother or other family members, but also between the baby and adult neighbors or houseguests. It is very common to see a baby surrounded by many adults who hold and play with him in turn.

Appeasement

There is a general belief among Japanese that the child, particularly the preschool child, should be free from frustrations and tensions. Child care is thus largely oriented toward appeasement of the child's emotions. This is what strikes foreign observers as a total lack of discipline among Japanese children, which stands out in marked contrast to the rigid inhibition required of adults. Impressed by this, Benedict characterized the life cycle typical of a Japanese individual as "a great shallow U-curve with maximum freedom and indulgence allowed to babies and to the old." Maturity and adulthood represent the peak of obligation and responsibility, leaving little freedom to the individual. This U-curve is exactly reversed in the case of the American, who enjoys utmost freedom in the prime of his life (Benedict 1946:254). It is questionable whether old age in Japan is as enjoyable as childhood, as suggested by the U-curve. The high rate of suicide among the aged seems to refute Benedict's proposition, and the U-curve should probably be replaced by an L-curve. In any event, the preschool child is most indulged.

The most common infantile expression of frustration is

crying—or, rather, the Japanese mother interprets her baby's cry as a sign of frustration and pain. Crying, therefore, is to be prevented or stopped as soon as possible. Appeasement takes the form of nursing or providing comforting body contact such as was described above. The baby soon learns to expect that as soon as he utters a cry he will be picked up, offered the breast, carried around, rocked, and thus completely soothed in his mother's arms.

In this connection, the study by Caudill and Weinstein (1969) mentioned earlier found a cultural difference in infants' vocal expressions: the American infant makes "happy" utterances, whereas the Japanese infant's vocalization is "unhappy," and both are correlated with the mother's "chats." The authors conclude that "the American mother would appear to be using chatting as a means of stimulating, and responding to, her infant's happy vocals. The Japanese mother, however, would appear to be using chatting to soothe and quiet her infant, and to decrease his unhappy vocals" (p. 35).

The need to appease a crying baby is so taken for granted that if the mother is busy and unable to attend to her screaming baby immediately, she may even apologize to him saying, "Forgive your mama for neglecting you."

Dr. Matsuda encourages mothers to appease their babies, rather than to ignore their crying, with the warning that if one leaves a crying child unattended to teach him that crying will get him nowhere the child might develop a protruded navel or hernia from the overexertion (1964:60).

This cultural attention to the minimization of crying leads to two types of child behavior. On one hand, the child, "even at a very early age, learns that crying is not permitted under any circumstances, and that whatever tensions he has will be satisfied by the nearby mother" (Vogel and Vogel 1961:163). The child then tends to be quiet and contented (Caudill and Weinstein 1969), and trustful. On the other hand, the appeasement policy in socialization may produce an undisciplined, spoiled child who knows that the most effective way of getting whatever he wants is to throw a temper tantrum. This was noted and interpreted as aggression toward the mother by Benedict (1946:263-264) and by Norbeck and Norbeck (1956:660). According to Benedict, "Not all little boys, of course, have these tantrums, but in both villages and upper-class homes they are looked upon as an ordinary part of child life between three and six. The baby pommels his mother, screams, and, as his final violence, tears down her precious hair-do" (p. 264). I am tempted to suggest that an analogy may be drawn between a child in a tantrum and a god in the Japanese pantheon who vents his anger by causing trouble for humans. Both the child and the god are expected to be placated and quieted down by some sort of pacifier. Indeed, the folk belief has it that a child is a god's gift or a god himself to be looked after.

Sensitization to Loneliness and Dependency

The child learns that his needs will be taken care of immediately by his mother or surrogate mother, who is always around him, and that his security is dependent upon his caretaker's presence. This sense of security, tied up so closely with the immediate presence of his mother, is lost when he finds his mother absent. "Thus there is a great anxiety about the mother's being absent and a real fear that he will be unable to solve his problems and tensions if she is absent" (Vogel and Vogel 1961:163).

This tendency seems reflected in and reinforced by the mother's caretaking behavior. Caudill and Weinstein discovered that the Japanese mother stays with her baby while he is asleep, whereas the American mother leaves her sleeping baby alone. Further, "caretaking for the American mother is largely an 'in' and 'out' affair. When she is in the room with the infant she is usually doing active caretaking, and upon finishing this she goes out of the room. The Japanese mother, although not engaged in active caretaking any greater amount of the time, is passively present in the room with the infant to a greater extent" (1969:32). Infant care for the American appears largely to be a matter of work and tasks, whereas the Japanese regard it as an opportunity for the caretaker and infant to enjoy each other's presence. Many an infant gets used to going to sleep only while being held by the mother or while the mother, lying next to him, nurses him or sings a lullaby. When the baby falls asleep, the mother gently places him on the bed or slips out of the bed so that he will not wake up. He often does wake up the moment he is left alone and cries for his mother to come back.

The child shares much time and space with adults, even when adult guests are present. There is no clear demarcation line between the adult's and the child's worlds, not so much because children are believed able to participate in adult conversation as because they cannot be physically isolated.

Incidentally, the baby version of the popular game hide-and-seek may reflect the fear of being alone and the joy of togetherness. An adult hides his face with his hands, saying, "I am not here, I am not here"; then he bends close and reveals his face to the baby, saying, "Bah!" The baby, tense at first, responds to the revealed face with a great squeal of joy. This game appears a little different from the American game of peek-a-boo in that the Japanese player emphasizes his "absence" rather than his "peeking."

The child is thus sensitized to the fear of being left alone and to the feeling of loneliness, as well as to dependency on his mother for gratification of his wishes. This means a problem of adjustment for the child when he enters school. Japanese kindergarten children tend to show more fear, bashfulness, and mutism than American children (Vogel and Vogel 1961). We can see that socialization has contributed to the sensitivity to loneliness and the urge for togetherness exhibited by Japanese adults.

DISCIPLINE

Though the family socialization of a preschool child is generally oriented toward indulgence and appeasement, training and discipline are subtly under way. Certain behaviors are encouraged and rewarded and others are discouraged and punished. Some aspects of this training are not peculiar to Japanese culture but are shared by other cultures, such as the American, whereas others are more distinctively cultural, as documented by Lanham (1956; 1966).

Content of Discipline

What kinds of behavior are encouraged and what are discouraged? Lanham (1956:574) enumerates the do's and don'ts most frequently mentioned by a sample of mothers in a small city in central Japan (in order of frequency):

To Do:	Toilet habits, polite sitting position, eat properly, manners, washing hands before meals, use chopsticks, say arigato ("thank you"), words to say preceding and following a meal, return things to their places.
Not To Do:	Play outside without footgear, soil clothes with urine, quarrel, let food fall from the table, envy (want things others have), throw stones.

This information, findings in other research, for example, the study of child training in a fishing community by Norbeck and Norbeck (1956), and personal observation have led me to the following analysis.

Basic Abilities. Even though socialization in Japan sensitizes the child to interdependence between himself and his socializer, he is nonetheless trained and encouraged to develop basic abilities of his own. In this respect Japanese socialization may differ least from that in other cultures.

First, the child is encouraged to learn to control himself physically. Toilet training begins by encouraging the child to signal his urge to the family, to show no resistance when the caretaker holds him over a toilet to help him eliminate, and ends with the child's being able to go to the toilet by himself. Japanese mothers are not severe in toilet training, however; they tend to wait until the child becomes old enough to "understand," although they will praise the child's occasional earlier success in toilet performance (Norbeck and Norbeck 1956; Lanham 1956).

Oral training involves weaning, the child's acceptance of food from a spoon, marked by a ceremony for *kuizome* ("beginning to eat"), which is held when the child is about a hundred days old, and finally his ability to handle his own spoon or chopsticks. Mothers often resort to severer discipline in weaning, such as covering the nipple with hot pepper.

The child is also given training in posture and locomotion. The family encourages the baby to turn over in a lying position, to crawl around, to sit up, to stand up, and to walk. Though the mother is aware of the undesirability of overtraining the child in this way, she also wants her child to grow normally, and she constantly anticipates the next stage of growth. As the proverb says, "The crawling baby is told to stand up, the standing baby is told to walk—such is the parental wish."

Along with physical training, the child is exposed to intellectual training, involving vocalization. He learns the names—often baby words—of things in his immediate environment or belonging to his body: names for the mother's breast (identical to the name for mother's milk), urine, and feces, the mother and other family members, and so forth. Although verbal skill is generally not stressed in this culture, the child is trained in speaking, and precocity in learning adult vocabulary is often cherished. The importance of being smart or having a good mind is constantly stamped on the child's mind: the mother praises her child for being *rikō* ("smart") and scolds him for being *baka* ("stupid"). The smart child draws attention not only from the family but from neighbors and others outside, is asked what kind of great person he wants to become, and hears people praise him to his mother.

Learning the *kana* syllabary, reading and writing, and simple arithmetic starts before the child enters school. Recently there has been an increasing tendency to overtrain preschool children in this respect, partly in anticipation of the entrance examination required for some exclusive kindergartens.

Preschool children, especially in middle-class families, also learn to draw pictures, to sing and dance, or to play a musical instrument; some are sent to a special art school. Lanham reported that Japanese nursery-school children are maturer than their American counterparts in such activities (1966:331):

> An uninterrupted attention span of long duration was characteristic of the Japanese but not of the American children. Activities when painting are illustrative. In Japan, four-year-olds scurried back and forth with jars of paint as needed. Concentrated attention was devoted to the project and soon it was finished. The American children used paints affixed to an easel so their untidy habits would be under control. The hand moved slowly, sometimes two or three times over the same line and occasionally the procedure was accompanied by daydreaming.

Orderliness. Generally speaking, however, there seems to be no outstanding difference between Japanese and American children in basic training in the sense inferable above. More distinctive is the Japanese stress on orderliness or tidiness in daily life. The child is taught to be neat, not to drop food from the table, not to soil clothing, not to drop things on the floor, not to poke the paper shoji, to place shoes on the shoe shelf, to return things to their original places, to close opened doors, and so on. The child comes to learn that tidiness in such external forms manifests an alert and moral mind and indicates one's trustworthiness. Sloppiness is taught as a sign of moral degeneration.

Manners. Cultural distinction in child-rearing is even more noticeable in the stress the Japanese family places on conventional manners and etiquette in disciplining its youngest members. The child learns how to sit properly and how to bow. When called, or when asked to do something, he is taught to answer, "Hai!" ("Yes, I am here," or "Yes, I will do it"). Conventional greetings are learned, such as "Good morning," "Good night," "Good-bye," and so on. Even the child on his mother's back is told to bow and say hello to acquaintances she meets on the street. Emphasis is consistently placed on expressing thanks for favors and apology for wrongdoing. The stylized expressions of appreciation for food, to be said before and after every meal, must also be learned in early childhood. As he grows older, the child also learns to say, "I'm leaving" when going out and "I'm back" when he gets home.

Behavioral modesty is stressed in training girls particularly. The practices of co-sleeping and co-bathing are coupled with training in controlling body exposure. A little girl learns how to be modest while nude in the bath, and how to place her legs while sleeping. If her sleeping posture is too unrestrained, with legs wide apart, she will be teased by the family, saying, "You slept like the character of *dai* [with both arms and legs spread apart]." The importance of the ritual control of behavior is thus instilled in a preschool child.

Interpersonal Harmony. Despite the overall indulgence and gratification characteristic of a Japanese childhood, the child is taught to prize interpersonal harmony and to restrain himself to avoid conflict. This is emphasized for older children who have begun to interact with playmates and others outside the family. "The most serious misbehavior of older children is quarrelling with persons outside the family" (Norbeck and Norbeck 1956:661).

Not only outright quarrelling but envy toward peers is prohibited (Lanham 1956:581), and not causing trouble for others is prescribed. "A mother praises her little boy for informing her about breaking a window because otherwise 'No one would have gone to apologize or pay the damage and you would have caused the people much trouble' " (Lanham 1966:329). The morality of honesty and good conscience is involved here, but it is instilled in conjunction with the desirability of not being a troublemaker for neighbors.

To attain or maintain harmony, older children are taught to be kind and yielding, younger children to be compliant. The virtue of being *sunao* ("open-minded," "nonresistant," and "trustful") is inculcated as the most praiseworthy. Children are trained to restore harmony after a quarrel on their own initiative, without adult intervention, particularly when the conflict involves different families.

Role Conformity. Finally, the child is trained to conform to the norm governing the role he happens to be playing. The role is first defined by sex, age, and birth order. Generally, younger children are more indulged than older children, but each child is told to behave properly "like" a younger brother or "like" an older brother. While girls are more strictly disciplined, both sexes are encouraged to be "like" a male child or "like" a female child. The child may also be instructed to behave "like" the son of a farmer, a merchant, a doctor, and so forth.

Such role discipline increases when the child reaches school age. He is told that now that he is a schoolboy he must obey his teacher. The parents go so far as to undermine their own authority by stressing the schoolteacher's authority. The child learns his new role as a pupil in a rather abrupt way, and is motivated to concentrate his energy on performing the role. This parental attitude toward school education is not always commended. Ushijima, a psychologist, has observed:

> Parents feel relieved as soon as they put their children in school, confident that the school will educate them properly. Also, parents urge their children, when they are to enter school, to be mentally alert and to make special efforts [as pupils]. The parents will see their child off, telling him repeatedly that once in school he must listen to and obey his teacher. This sounds as if he does not have to obey his parents as strictly but must comply with whatever his teacher tells him to do. In other words, the authority of the school is stressed at the expense of that of the family. Teachers and schools in Japan, for their part, consider education to fall under their exclusive jurisdiction and do not like to have the parents interfere with school education, although they do not hesitate to make demands of the parents regarding home education (1961:50-51).

The Japanese child is thus encouraged to develop a strong sense of belongingness and total commitment to the group to which he happens to belong, and is inculcated with the motivation for status identification and role performance.

Method of Discipline

When we turn from the content to the method and style of discipline, we become more convinced of the existence of cultural differences. Particularly the emphasis on social harmony is revealed more clearly in the "how" than in the "what" of discipline.

Material and Physical Sanctions. Japanese parents are no different from parents in other cultures in manipulating the pleasure and pain directly felt by their children. The child is rewarded materially (with candies, toys, etc.) for good conduct and is punished materially (by being deprived of them) for misbehavior. Physical punishment is also used, such as pinching and light hitting. The main difference may be in the relative emphasis on reward or punishment (the Japanese seem more reward-oriented than, say, the Americans) and in the severity of punishment (the Japanese seem less severe). Japanese mothers, unlike their neighbors in Korea and China, seldom beat their children.

In speaking about severity in physical punishment, a word is in order with regard to the use of moxa, a type of inflammable grass. Moxacautery is a folk therapy for illness, organic and mental, used with adults and children. It also serves as a severe means of disciplining children. The noncompliant, unruly child who has tantrums too often may be subjected to this treatment. "Putting a moxa on [someone]" is a metaphorical expression meaning "punishing someone with utmost severity." A pellet of moxa the size of a rice grain is placed on a certain spot on the body and burned, leaving a permanent scar on the skin. Usually the mother first takes the child to a professional moxa therapist, who locates the efficacious points for burning. With the scars thus made, the mother herself can treat the child thereafter. The use of moxa has declined as medical therapy is increasingly available through national medical insurance. The decline of moxacautery, however, owes not so much to a disbelief in its effectiveness as to a concern not to disfigure the skin.

Verbal Sanctions. Beside material and physical sanctions, verbal approval and disapproval are also used for disciplining children. It is through verbal sanction that social relationships and social values are manipulated and reinforced. The following styles of discipline are particularly suggestive of the social focus of child-training among Japanese.

First, the child who has done wrong is often punished by the threat of abandonment. The mother may tell him that she is going away, far, far away, leaving him behind so that he will never see her again. She may threaten to give him away to someone and to adopt someone else's child in his place; she may pretend to love someone else's child more than her own. When a visitor is around, she might say, "We don't need this boy, so please take him with you." The visitor would cooperate with her by saying, "Oh, good. We wanted to have another child. Now come with me, my child." Meanwhile the child is clinging to his mother, crying frantically. This pattern of threat was noted and well described by Benedict (1946:262-263).

The threat of kidnapping is also used. The child is told that if he, say, plays outside too late in the evening, a person (perhaps a beggar or an idiot if there is any known to the whole community[1]) or a monster or ghost will kidnap him. If his misbehavior calls for severe punishment, the mother may threaten to negotiate with the beggar or whatever to adopt him.

The mother may go so far as to lock the child out of the house, leaving him banging on the door. This struck American observers (Vogel and Vogel 1961) as being in contrast to American practice.

> One fairly severe form of punishment used in Japan is to lock the child out of the house and require him to apologize before he can come in. . . . A comparable American punishment would be to prevent the child from going out.

Similarly:

> Whereas American mothers sometimes have to go chasing after their children, if the Japanese mother is in a hurry and can't get the child to hurry, she will run ahead, and without question the child will chase after. (p. 165)

Another more subtle form of abandonment is to warn the child of the unavailability of the mother's help when he needs it. The mother tells the child that his father will get angry as soon as

---

1. Such a person used to be quite visible and familiar to everyone of a community in rural Japan.

he discovers his misconduct, but "I will not help you." Literally translated, she is saying, "I won't care," meaning that she will pay no attention to the child's plea for help. The child will thus be fully exposed to the anger and punishment of his father, elder brother, nursery-school teacher, or whomever.

Second, praise is the most common means of rewarding the child for good performance and encouraging him to repeat it. The praise may be directly addressed to the child by the family, a neighbor, or others. More often, however, communication is carried on in a triadic interaction, as when the mother brags about her child to her relatives or neighbors in front of him or when a neighbor praises the child to his family in front of him. The child's gratification is doubled in the latter case because he can feel his parents' pride and pleasure.

This pattern of reward is linked with the inclination of adult Japanese to have a child exhibit some ability or skill as a sign of his accomplishments. When a guest is invited, the child is encouraged by his family to demonstrate his ability to, say, identify the names of family members, give his home address, count from one to ten, sing, or dance. The guest usually enjoys such performances and is generous with words of praise; Japanese adults are an eager audience for children's performances.

The mother also can frustrate her child by praising another child, either a sibling or an outsider. He is told to be like that model child, words that generate jealousy but that can be effective as a means of discipline.

Third, while straightforward scolding is by no means absent in Japanese child-rearing, children are often subjected to teasing, ridicule, and embarrassment. The older child who insists on having his mother's breast is teased for being a little baby and told, "You are laughable," or "You should be embarrassed."

The threat of embarrassment usually refers to someone other than the caretaker. The mother tells the child that he will be laughed at or ridiculed by neighbors, his playmates, his relatives, or anyone whose opinion the child values most; or, she may just refer to "everybody," in front of whom the child will lose face. The upshot of this kind of discipline is likely to be that the child retains attachment and trust for his caretaker but develops a fear and mistrust of others, especially the outsiders with whose ridicule he has been threatened.

The third person thus plays a significant role in sensitizing the child to shame and embarrassment. The mother uses the third person not only as a verbal reference but as an audience present on the scene. The child learns the difference between the dyadic situation (with only himself and his caretaker) and the triadic situation (with a third person present as audience) in terms of freedom: he feels completely free in the dyad, inhibited in the triad. This may result in sensitizing the child more to outsiders' opinions than to those of intimate insiders, to the extent that his own family may not be able to discipline him.

Fourth, what seems to be distinctively Japanese is an appeal for empathy. The mother presents herself as a victim of her child's misbehavior and appeals to his capacity for feeling the pain she is going through. "If you don't stop doing that, it is I, your mother, who will suffer most. Try to put yourself in my place."

The child is thus trained in the vicarious sharing of another person's pleasure and displeasure so that he regards the possibility of hurting another person's feelings as frightening. The mother threatens her child by saying, "Your father will be displeased," which is a subtler and yet more effective way of dissuading the child from a wrongdoing than saying, "Your father will scold you."

Appeal for empathy is used in conjunction with embarrassment. It is not so much the child himself who is said to be the victim of embarrassment. It is the mother, father, or the family as a whole who will be laughed at by neighbors because of the child's misconduct. The mother tells the child that everybody will laugh at her; that his father will lose face at his company; or that the whole family will be disgraced. In this case, the child may be motivated to reform through guilt rather than shame as such.

MOTHER FIXATION

Throughout this volume, the mother appears to play a crucial role in the Japanese life cycle, to be a central Alter to Japanese Ego. Since the mother-child relationship is crystallized and stamped on the child's memory in the course of socialization, it may be appropriate to elaborate here upon the mother image as held or recalled by adult Japanese. This should be considered a supplement to the previous discussion of the mother-child relationship with reference to dependency (chapter 4). According to

Yoshiaki Yamamura, the Japanese mother is unique in that her influence over her child goes beyond his infancy and continues until the last day of his life (1971:1). Such mother fixation is pointed out by frequent newspaper articles in which someone attributes the motivation for his success or triumph to his mother. When something dishonorable is done, the offender is likely to be reminded of his mother's sorrow over his conduct. Rebellious left-wing students in prewar Japan are said to have been persuaded to renounce their ideology when the authorities strategically induced sympathy for their tearful mothers. The crucial significance of one's mother is realized particularly when one faces death. Mountain climbers threatened by disaster are reported to have left messages like "I wish I could see my mother once more"; "Forgive me, Mother" (Yamamura 1971:2).

What are the analytical components of mother fixation? We shall again rely upon Yamamura, who included in his study an analysis of a serialized radio program, *Haha o kataru* [Chats about my mother], in which hundreds of celebrities participated, including movie actors, comedians, singers, writers, poets, and baseball players. Yamamura saw several dominant themes in the celebrities' recollections of their mothers. First, the mother is characterized as having suffered hardships. Her suffering is associated with "endurance" and "dedication." This is illustrated by remarks like: "My father got involved with a mistress, but my mother endured quietly without making jealous accusations"; "She cared for Father and us children only, never for herself."

Derived from this is a second theme, a feeling of guilt toward the mother who has thus endured hardship and dedicated herself. For example, "Father used to beat us children, and Mother, trying to stop it, got hurt herself. One day, when Father threw a teapot at me, Mother caught it and burned herself. My eyes still smart at the memory of the white bandage she had to wear." Guilt feelings further stem from mother's indulgence and forgiveness of one's recalcitrance as a child.

Third, mother is recalled as having provided the moral support for one's pursuit of his goal. The young man who achieved fame by sailing alone in a small yacht across the Pacific to San Francisco in 1962 confessed that the thought of his mother and her hopes for his success sustained him while at sea. It was his mother who had helped with his dangerous plan while keeping it secret from his father. An actress declared that she felt she could survive in the rough world of show business thanks to the spiritual power coming from her mother.

Further, mother is a driving force that motivates one to achievement. A popular writer recalled the time he went home, before his success, ill and defeated. He was at a loss about his future, but his mother, poor though she was, decided to sell rice to earn money for a new start for him. Thus provided, he embarked again, telling her, "This time, I will not come back until I can give money back to you, mother. . . . Please wait until then." He pursued his career and became a first-rate writer. There is nothing strange, therefore, about the wish to display one's success to mother before anybody else. An actress wished her mother could have seen the play that brought her an award. (Yamamura 1971:101-125; also see DeVos 1960; DeVos and Wagatsuma 1959).

CHAPTER 9

Selfhood

INDIVIDUALITY

The preceding chapters have characterized the Japanese in terms of several aspects of social relativism, wherein priority goes to the maintenance or modification of social relationships. The Japanese concern for social relation is expressed in cultural elaboration of the manner of interaction as well as in the cultural desirability of social involvement. Solidarity, cooperation, and togetherness thus tend to be a dominant cultural theme. The previous chapter examined early socialization in an attempt to locate a genesis of this cultural theme in childhood experiences. Does this mean that the Japanese are indifferent to individuality and autonomy?

We know that Japanese are as concerned about maintaining the individual's independence and freedom as are other peoples. Doi reminds us that Japanese use the distinctive expressions *jibun ga aru* ("having the self") and *jibun ga nai* ("lacking the self"). The first refers to an individual's awareness of some independence from the group he belongs to, the second refers to the individual's total involvement in the group (Doi 1971:160-163). Indeed, Japanese often take pride in the freedom of *jibun* and its power to resist social pressure.

Suggestive in this respect is the study of value orientations by Caudill and Scarr (1962), who applied the theory of Kluckhohn and Strodtbeck to Japanese subjects. One of these value orientations was the "relational" orientation, which varies from "individualistic" to "collateral" to "lineal." The collateral orientation refers both to sibling relationships within the family and to a group orientation outside the family; likewise, the lineal orientation involves the parent-child relationship in the family setting and hierachical relationships outside the family. Caudill and Scarr elicited their subjects' relational orientations by asking their response to seven concrete problem situations. The following is one of them, having to do with seeking "help in case of misfortune" (1962:61).

> A man had a crop failure, or, let us say, had lost most of his cattle. He and his family had to have help from someone if they were going to get through the winter. There are different ways of getting help, as in the following.

> (Coll)   Would it be best if he depended on his brothers and sisters or other relatives all to help him out as much as each one could?

> (Ind)   Would it be best for him to try to raise money on his own, without depending upon anybody?

> (Lin)   Would it be best for him to go to a boss or to his head house (*honke*), and ask for help until things got better?

The other items on relational orientation referred to "bridge building," "family work relations," "choice of delegate," "wage work," "personal property inheritance," and "land inheritance." The subject was asked to rank-order the solutions according to his preference, rather than to choose one. There are six possible rank orders: I>C>L, I>L>C, L>I>C, L>C>I, C>L>I, and C>I>L. Given the high priority of solidarity and cooperation in the Japanese ethos, one might expect the Japanese to show an overwhelming preference for either L>C>I or C>L>I. The findings, however, show dominant value orientations of I>C>L in four items, C>I>L in two items, and C>L>I in one item. The individualistic orientation thus stands out as dominant or as competitive with the collateral orientation. How do we account for this?

Before attempting an explanation, we must face the basic question of the validity of this type of test for a group of people under the sway of social relativism. Unlike a subject whose culture is dictated by unilateral determinism, the Japanese subject is likely to be most concerned, apart from his real feelings toward test questions, with the relationships implied by the test. In other words, he tends to engage in what is called "metacommunication" (Watzlawick, Beavin, and Jackson 1967). Many respondents to Caudill and Scarr's test, well aware of postwar ideological change, may have chosen an individualistic orientation to meet the expectations of test givers or possible audiences.

With this reservation in mind, let us explore the Japanese concept of selfhood, which may give a clue to the individualistic value orientations thus expressed in a test situation.

SOCIAL MORATORIUM

We know that a cultural value is a source of strain as well as of pleasure. Social involvement, while strongly desired by the Japanese, is also felt to be a burden they often wish to unload. Belongingness, for instance, is an indispensable condition for enjoying life, but it puts one under pressure to comply with the will of the group against one's own will. The more internalized the value of solidarity, the more acute will be the sense of obligation to comply. Japanese find beauty in the ideas of *omoiyari*, *on*, and *giri*, but they do not fail to perceive the troubles and nuisances inherent in them. Acceptance of help generates the obligation to offer help in return. If one wants to avoid the latter, one should not indulge in the former. Empathetic kindness may deteriorate into a maddening meddlesomeness—a caution against its ready acceptance. Vertical alliance with a superior, necessary for one's status elevation, may involve virtual slavery. The same holds true for dependency.

All this indicates that individuality for the Japanese is at the opposite pole from social involvement. The autonomy of an individual is assured and protected only in social isolation, only when a social moratorium is declared. Individuality lies not in society but away from it. It is not surprising, then, that the same Japanese who complain about loneliness often wish to be alone. Also understandable is the fact that Japanese cultural heroes include the *rōnin*, masterless, homeless samurai, and the traveling gangster who leads a lonely but free life. The popularity in the early 1970s of Kogarashi Monjiro (a fictitious hero in novels by Saho Sasazawa), who is noted for his abstention from social affairs, derives from the very bedrock of Japanese culture. Social moratorium in this sense takes two forms: introspection and emotional anarchism.

Introspection

The Japanese find their individuality in self-reflection, which can be fully enjoyed only in isolation. This may be one explanation for the Japanese habit of keeping a diary, which is a written testimony of one's introspection and assurance of having *jibun*. Perhaps Caudill and Scarr's test situation induced self-reflection in the subjects and that is why the individualistic orientation is so prominent in their findings.

Introspection leads the individual into his inner world and its center, *kokoro* ("heart"). His routine life, saturated in social involvement and preoccupation, is thus punctuated by an occasional confrontation with his *kokoro*. He expects to discover and rediscover his *kokoro* to be intact and autonomous from external pressures. When he is swept away by social demands to the point of "losing *jibun*," his friends are likely to advise him to recover his *jibun* and *kokoro*. Moral integrity for the Japanese often turns out to be supported by a habit of introspection.

Confrontation with the self under social moratorium conditions presupposes and reinforces a clear distinction between the external, social world and the inner, asocial world, as well as an awareness of this duality of existence. In Japanese parlance, the inner self is symbolized not only by the heart (*kokoro*) but by the belly (*hara*), whereas the outer self is located in the face or mouth. Since what is inside the *kokoro* or *hara* is faithful to the self, what appears on the face or what comes out of the mouth, namely, words, tends to be distrusted. (For a detailed discourse on the symbolism of *hara*, see Durckheim 1962.) One is advised not to trust people with smooth tongues. The following proverbs, taken from Fischer and Yoshida (1968), reflect this:

> *Kuchi wa motte kuubeshi, motte iu bekarazu.*
> "Mouths are to eat with, not to speak with."
> *Kuchi kara umarete, kuchi kara hateru.*
> "Born mouth first, he perishes by his mouth."
> *Kuchi ni mitsu ari, hara ni ken ari.*
> "Honey in his mouth, a sword in his belly."

With a sharp awareness of the duality between the heart-belly sphere and the face-mouth sphere, the individual occasionally succumbs to an irresistible temptation for masochistic self-exposure. Confession is a common style of writing used in the so-called I-novels (Hibbet 1966). In the same vein, the Japanese, while compulsive in ritual behavior, cannot resist ridiculing someone who is excessively circumspect in maintaining a front; they cynically point out what is going on behind the mask, particularly with reference to the person's physiological functions. Self-ridicule, too, is a common phenomenon. A writer, for example, gives a detailed description of the constipation he suffered during his visit to Paris and of the painful but ludicrous difficulty he had telling a pharmacist in French what his trouble was (Yamada 1971). A popular series of essays by Shusaku Endo (1972) show a similar obsession.

If the truth is hidden within the *hara*, people must search each other's *hara* (*hara o saguru*) for information. When two persons talk frankly, they "disclose" or "split" their *hara* (*hara o miseru* or *hara o waru*); perfect solidarity is reached by "attaching" one *hara* to another (*hara to hara o awaseru*). Needless to say, these are all figurative expressions, yet they indicate the importance of *hara* as the repository of truth, in contrast to the externally visible or audible aspect of self, which is prone to deceitfulness.

Emotional Anarchism

Introspection, carried to an extreme, produces an awareness of one's immediate feelings and emotions unperturbed by social norms. The Japanese cherish and dignify *jikkan*, "real and direct feelings," and revere the person who is attuned to his own *jikkan*. "Pure" Japanese literature, as distinguished from popular literature, is filled with expressions of *jikkan*, with all its variations and subtleties, which are so subjective that their meanings tend to be beyond the comprehension of a reader who has no personal knowledge of the writer. Whatever comes in the way of such emotional experiences must be played down; cool reasoning and goal-oriented calculation, as well as the social facade of ritualism, are discredited from this standpoint. *Jikkan*-ism, then, may lead to emotional anarchism. It has been asserted that some students who fought the police at Haneda Airport (in protest over the prime minister's overseas trips) in 1967 did so not to accomplish a rational objective but simply to find out how they would feel when face to face with armed authority (Noguchi et al. 1968).

This emotionalism further leads to an indulgence in sentimental desires (*ninjō*) and tolerance of such indulgence in others. Romantic love stories have always appealed strongly to Japanese readers. *Ninjō* was glorified in the townsman (*chōnin*) literature of feudal times by such writers as Chikamatsu Monzaemon and Ihara Saikaku, in contradistinction to the samurai virtue of control over emotion. Tolerance of *ninjō* in others seems to derive from the naturalistic belief that no one can put out the fire of passion once it is ignited. Despite the pull of *ninjō*, it is realized that passions are transient and reflect nothing more than the ephemerality of the "floating world." And when *ninjō* comes into conflict with *giri*, it is *ninjō* that must give way.

MENTAL EXORCISM

Introspection, together with emotional subjectivism, sensitizes one to the truth of one's inner world. For the Japanese, truth is associated with what might be called mental exorcism, whereby one is supposed to eradicate all the inner pollutions that are clouding the true self.

The pollution-free *kokoro* or *ki* (a term used as often as *kokoro*, meaning mind, spirit, *kokoro*, or a diffuse mixture of these) is described by such adjectives as clear, clean, transparent, fresh, bright, unclouded, weightless, bouncy, free, empty, and so forth. Self-identity for a Japanese may ultimately derive from confidence in the purity of his inner self.

Emotional Purity

Inner purity is manifested variously. It can be allied with emotionalism to justify an action as motivated by "pure" emotions, even when the external consequences of the action violate a major cultural norm. Many Japanese adults, while retaining the traditional bias toward gerontocracy, tolerate and sympathize with adolescents and students who rebel against the established order out of *junjō* ("pure emotions"). Even violence and homicide, if proved to be motivated by *junjō*, are forgiven. Cold, rational calculation is regarded as indicative of inner pollution.

Moral Purity

The exaltation of *junjō* relates to the moral significance of inner purity. The pure self is identified, morally, as sincere, selfless, altruistic, while the impure self is identified with calculation and pursuit of self-interest. Lacking a dogma to serve as the ultimate value standard, the Japanese make moral judgments in accordance with the presence or absence of such pure, sincere motives. Purity boils down to egolessness (*muga*). Unlike the Greeks, Indians, Jews, or Chinese, "the Japanese seem to have identified the truthfulness of the human being with the clean, bright *kokoro* that is devoid of 'I' " (Watsuji 1962:298). *Magokoro*, "true heartedness," signifies such an "I-less" state of mind.

When mental exorcism takes this direction, the self comes into perfect harmony with social relativism. Indeed, the Japanese sense of obligation is supported by the morality of *magokoro*. But the emotional anarchism mentioned above is also supported by the culturally recognized correlation between pure emotion and selflessness and between rationality and self-interest.

Contentment

There is another quality involved in inner purity. Mental exorcism is not complete unless it eradicates all inner tensions, frustrations, and preoccupations, which are another sign of pollution. In this sense, purity is associated with self-contentment, serenity, and tranquillity, and ultimately leads to the Buddhist ideal of the empty, detached self.

Both emotional purity and moral purity are supposed ultimately to raise themselves to this last sense of purity. Pure romantic love, which is unconsummated and thus frustrating, should ideally be transformed into serenity, not necessarily resignation, and moral dedication should generate self-contentment. The Japanese are indeed concerned with maintenance of the contented, serene, happy, mentally healthy self, and confident that this state of self can be attained through self-dedication. It was interesting to find that many of the subjects in my sentence-completion test indicated autistic satisfaction as a result of social dedication. Autistic satisfaction, generated by one's having given a kindness (Appendix, Table 3) or practiced filial piety (Table 4), was expressed as self-contentment, weightlessness, bounciness, brightness, happiness, joyfulness, serenity, and inner richness.

Eradication of frustrations is synonymous with fusion between the self and the objective world, or between body and soul. Acceptance of nature as it is, then, underlies the ultimate form of purity. The term *hara* is sometimes used to express a mental state at this level, as when someone is described as "having his *hara* ready," or "having accomplished his *hara*."

Mental exorcism in the sense above may be traced to the beliefs and rituals of Shinto, centering on defilement and purification, both physical and spiritual.

POTENCY

The self that emerges in introspection and exorcism is thought to be the source of great potency. The Japanese are confident of the inexhaustibility of energy emanating from the inner core of the self or *hara*, the vital center of the body. Many a Japanese finds his satisfaction in work deriving from energy expenditure, attaches moral significance to a steady flow of physical or mental energy, namely, perseverance and endurance to the point of masochism, and holds an optimistic belief in what one can accomplish through single-minded effort.

A common type of religious discipline involves a simple, monotonous, repetitive action, for example, the repeated incantation of a magical phrase, or prolonged, motionless sitting, or an endurance walk. These are thought to test and foster the ability to concentrate mental and physical energy. The underlying belief is that through such concentration one can achieve anything one undertakes. Familiar proverbs say that "A shaft can pierce a rock if pushed by a concentrated mind" and "Single-minded faith can reach heaven." In prewar Japan, this faith in the unlimited potency of spiritual concentration culminated in the nationalistic glorification of *Yamato damashii* (the spiritual power of the Yamato race). During the war with the United States, which all Japanese knew far surpassed Japan in material power, *Yamato damashii* was mobilized as the Japanese version of the most invincible weapon.

Hara, as the origin of potency both physical and spiritual, assures stability and peculiar autonomy for man. The person who has a *hara* at all (*hara ga aru*), who has a large *hara*, or whose *hara* is well settled, is able to remain detached and serene in face of a situation that would be upsetting to one who has no such *hara*.

Potency of the inner self is not something that emerges overnight. One must train, improve, and polish oneself in order to develop a strong, mature character. The Japanese are interested in this developmental, maturational process, as was shown in many responses to my sentence-completion test. Perseverance and suffering were also appreciated for their contribution to character development (Appendix, Table 1: categories 2 and 3; Table 2: categories 3b and 4).

Ultimate potency is derived from a perfect union of body and spirit. Traditional cults in swordmanship, archery, and karate, and other arts all stress this union as necessary for successful performance. The principle of body-spirit unity goes further to promote one's bodily power as an end value; hence the Japanese *tairyoku shugi* ("body-power principle") and *taiatari shugi* ("principle of direct body attack"). These terms refer to a quasi-religious faith in the direct exposure of the live self to a hazardous situation without external help. The rise of kamikaze pilots in World War II would have been unthinkable without wide acceptance of *taiatari shugi*. This principle also implies a mistrust of civilization, which, by interposing machines and a complex social organization between man and nature, increasingly denies man real bodily experiences. Even today Japanese movies depict the samurai swordman more than the modern soldier equipped with firearms. Ideally, even the sword should be dispensed with: *taiatari shugi* and *tairyoku shugi* are best manifested in weaponless fighting, such as karate or judo. Kogarashi Monjiro only used a toothpick! Better still, a real hero can defeat an enemy without moving a finger, merely by seizing him in a frightening stare that reveals his unlimited *hara* potency.

Physical potency is sometimes thought to be the core of self-identity. Middle-aged men particularly seem openly concerned with maintenance of their virility and receptive to any medicinal treatment promising sexual rejuvenation. A large portion of television advertising goes to a fantastic variety of so-called virility pills (*seiryokuzai*), and men discuss the relative effectiveness of different brands. Nor are women bashful about discussing sexual problems with friends or calling their husbands' attentions to them. It may be said that the Japanese have a general preoccupation with their bodies that is a natural outcome of their introspective nature.

COSMIC IDENTITY

Fatalism

Finally, the Japanese individual finds his self-identity anchored in a cosmic law, be it called fate, destiny, karma, or *innen* imbedded in the Buddhist belief system. According to fatalism, everything in the world is predestined to occur by an endless chain of causes and effects from the unknown past, through the present, to the future, the sequence of which is beyond human control. The Japanese refer to fate (*un*) as an explanation for success or failure. The successful person is described as a man of good *un*, strong *un*, or simply as a man with *un*, whereas the unsuccessful person receives sympathy and condolence with such a statement as, "You just had no *un*," or "Yours was a bad *un*." While faith in good *un* may lead one to success, much in accordance with W. I. Thomas' principle of "self-fulfilling prophecy," faith in bad *un* puts one in a state of *akirame* ("resignation").

In addition to *un*, the Japanese have assimilated, whether they are declared Buddhists or not, the idea of *innen* or *en*, *innen* being the combination of *in* and *en*. In Buddhist doctrine, *in* refers to the inner, direct cause, and *en* to the outer, indirect, facilitating cause, that produces an effect (Nakamura 1962). The average Japanese, unconcerned with formal Buddhist doctrine, seems to identify these ideas with a mysterious power underlying predestination, transmigration, and reincarnation. *En*, in particular, seems to be associated with social relationships. *Fushigi na en*, "mysterious *en*," is a common expression for some unexpected, or unaccountable, encounter or affinity of two persons in a certain situation. Two strangers become friends or spouses by an *en*, or they may remain strangers if there is no *en*. A marriage proposal is called *endan* ("*en* talk"), and marriage itself *engumi* ("*en* match"). Likewise, the person who must give up a certain goal (such as marrying the girl of his choice) is likely to be told by an elder, "Be resigned since there was no *en* [that could have led you to success]." Suffering and hardship must be accepted with resignation, one may be consoled, because one has been loaded with such *innen* since one's previous life.

Fatalism is linked with the futility of making an effort to control what has happened or is going to happen. Things are considered irreversible once they have taken place. It is silly, therefore, to regret that things have turned out as they have because no amount of regret can reverse the course of events. Belief in such fatalistic irreversibility seems to have a realistic basis in the status mobility structure of Japanese society. To get good employment one must be from a good university, to get into a good university one must study at a first-rate high school, and so on. At a certain point, the course of these events does indeed appear irreversible. (Note the contrast with Americans, who seem to be compulsive believers in the reversibility of one's lot throughout life.) The point is that the sense of irreversibility may make a person resigned to what has happened but it may also motivate him to plan his life as early as possible before it is too late.

It is my hypothesis that fatalism is necessary for a culture that encourages achievement as a moral obligation and regards achieved status as one's entire being. Since not everyone can be successful, and no one can be successful always, readiness for resignation must be learned as an important part of culture. Resignation is facilitated by the ideas of *un* and *en*, which liberate the unsuccessful person from self-blame and a sense of inadequacy.

Universal Impermanence

Resignation, encouraged by fatalism, is also supported by the Buddhist idea of universal impermanence, evanescence, and ephemerality. The belief that nothing in this world lasts forever but that everything is short-lived is well reflected in many proverbs: "Life is more fragile than the morning dew"; "Yesterday's lovely flower is but a dream today"; "When the moon is full, it begins to wane." The Japanese sense of beauty itself is so closely associated with universal evanescence that esthetic pleasure is sometimes found only in things short-lived. Japanese love cherry blossoms for this reason and have compared young, brave soldiers who willingly died in battle to beautiful, short-lived cherry blossoms. Likewise, romantic love is regarded as beautiful, not only because it involves motivational purity but also because it is destined to be short-lived. (Romantic love thus is clearly separated from marriage, which entails permanent obligations and, above all, the perpetuation of the household.)

The belief in universal impermanence leads to the idea that the future state of things is unpredictable and uncertain. In one proverb the unpredictability of human life is compared to that of the flow of water. The sequence of events is determined entirely by chance, such that planning and commitment to goals will prove futile. What is sensible in this world of chance and randomness is resignation.

The unpredictability and randomness of future events engender pessimism and a negative view of happiness. There seems to be a culturally conditioned conviction that happiness is necessarily followed by unhappiness, "Pleasure is the seed of pain." In the same vein, "Meeting is the beginning of parting." One would be better off, to avoid the subsequent unhappiness, not to be too happy at all. Pessimistic anticipation after a great happy event is such that Japanese seem to find a defense mechanism in their taste for mild depression and distaste for smugness. The beauty accorded "unfulfilled love" is explainable in this context, too.

Pessimism is only one side of the philosophical coin of universal impermanence, however. If happiness does not last long, neither does misfortune. If pleasure is the seed of pain, pain is the seed of pleasure. There is thus a mutual cancellation of pessimism and optimism. The proverb "Fortune and misfortune are like the twisted strands of a rope" suggests that good luck and bad luck befall one alternately. The Japanese are thus furnished with a cushion protecting (or preventing) them both from faith in an absolutely bright future and from despair over anticipated doom. The combination of mild pessimism and optimism based on belief in the alternation of fortune and misfortune seems a significant factor in inducing one to resignation.

Cosmic self-identity thus turns out to be primarily oriented toward resignation. Resignation is a mechanism that reduces tension by abating motivational energy or commitment for changing unfavorable conditions. If one is unsuccessful in his career or in developing a desirable social relationship, he is advised to accept what has happened as inevitable. *Akirame*, "resignation," is often urged, and *shikata ga nai* ("cannot be helped") is often said, when things have irreversibly gone against one's wishes. One's capacity for *akirame* is often taken as proof of maturity and wisdom. The Buddhist concept of *satori*, "enlightenment," is closely associated with the attainment of *akirame* for Japanese.

The Japanese concept of self-identity, no matter how it emerges, seems ultimately either complementary to or compatible with social relativism. The autonomy of the self is assured only in social isolation and in self-reflection. The emotionally and morally pure self is associated with selflessness, which in turn is thought to bring self-contentment and to eliminate the boundary between self and environment. Faith in the potency of the self serves culturally sanctioned ends. The self, anchored in fatalism and the belief in impermanence, may seek solace in resignation whenever it is frustrated by social dilemma or conflict.

CHAPTER 10

Organized Delinquency:
Yakuza as a Cultural Example

Up to this point we have been concerned primarily with normative patterns of behavior that most Japanese share and regard as desirable or normal. Now we shall delve into behavior that is not commonly shared and is looked upon as deviant or pathological.

The general significance of studying deviancy to understand a culture is obvious. As deviancy is either the opposite or the complement of the dominant cultural configuration, knowing what behavior is considered deviant and is avoided or enjoined by a culture will throw the culture's normative patterns into relief. Indeed, the dominant values and norms often are recognized only after they have been violated. My concern with deviancy goes beyond this obvious significance, however. If there is any deviancy that is peculiarly Japanese, it may be considered a result of the strain and pressure built in Japanese culture. Deviancy then can be viewed as a product of cultural strains or as an extreme expression of dominant values, rather than as a contrast to normative culture. This and the following four chapters will delineate some cases of deviancy, pathology, and treatment characterized as Japanese, under the assumption that they represent an oversimplified, selectively exaggerated picture of Japanese culture.

Yakuza as Deviant Groups

Culturally representative of organized deviancy in Japan are the *yakuza*, a general term for violent, antisocial groups and their members (Hiroaki Iwai 1966). Most Japanese regard the *yakuza* as deviant and strongly disapprove or fear any involvement with them. Nonetheless, some aspects of *yakuza* behavior are considered beautiful and morally valid and are still glorified in popular literature and films despite the strenuous police effort to exterminate *yakuza* organizations. Many culture heroes have been *yakuza* leaders. The following discussion is based primarily upon Hiroaki Iwai's voluminous study of "pathological groups" (1963) and my personal interview in 1973 with a *yakuza* in Eastern City.

Yakuza include such groups as *bakuto* (organized gamblers), *tekiya* (organized operators of street stalls or those who live on the protection money extorted from street-stall traders), and *gurentai* (gangs of violent hooligans) (Iwai 1966). In the narrow sense of the word, however, *"yakuza"* refers to gamblers alone, and "real" *yakuza*, in their pride and with regard for their honor, despise *gurentai* and exclude them from the *yakuza* category. Here we shall focus on gamblers, although much of the following should hold for other groups as well.

Yakuza organizations are said to have been established during the Tokugawa regime (1603-1867). In spite of punitive campaigns by the Tokugawa government, and even more stringent governmental measures after 1868, *yakuza* organizations survived to become incorporated in the ultra-right-wing movements, militarism, and imperialistic expansionism of the Shōwa period prior to 1945. The nationalistic bent of the *yakuza*, incidentally, is clear from their religion: as guardian gods they worship Shinto deities such as Amaterasu, Hachiman, Kasuga, as well as emperors.

After the war, there were many large-scale arrests and imprisonments of *yakuza* members, which seemed to reduce the *yakuza* population. Besides vigilance by the police, other factors have made it increasingly difficult for the *yakuza* to recruit new members. Among them are the legalization of some types of gambling, such as pinball games, bicycle races, and horse races. Furthermore, the internal control system of *yakuza* organizations has deteriorated to the point that internal friction tends to flare up in acts of open violence and self-destruction. If Japanese society as a whole has moved toward democratization, so have the *yakuza*, to their detriment. All this does not mean that *yakuza* no longer exist or that there is no nostalgia for the good old *yakuza* days. According to an investigation by the Detective Bureau of the Police Agency in 1970, there were 3,517 *bōryokudan* ("violent groups") with a total membership of 139,417. These are broken down into *bakuto*, *tekiya*, and deliquent gangs, and the *bakuto*, representing the most typical *yakuza*, constituted the largest subcategory (Keisatsuchō Keijikyoku 1970:145-146).

How do the *yakuza* recruit? Potential recruits are likely to congregate in certain places—areas of entertainment, amusement, prostitution, and the like. Occasional outbreaks of quarreling and fist-fighting in such places provide the chance for recruiters to discover promising candidates. Those who demonstrate the most skill and strength in fighting are most likely to be picked up. Such a candidate often turns out to be a runaway from home or an ex-convict. He is likely to be alienated from his family because of parental discord, father's death, disaffection from a stepmother, poverty, and the like. He is probably a school dropout and was involved in a *gurentai* gang. The candidate need not take a passive role in recruitment, but may actively seek membership in a *yakuza* group. The latter course is followed especially when the individual needs the protection of the group against people seeking revenge for past injuries or betrayals. Iwai mentions many instances of *yakuza* recruitment on such grounds.

Yakuza behavior is deviant, illegitimate, or outright criminal for reasons known to everybody. First, a *yakuza* engages in and lives on the proceeds from illegal occupations, such as gambling, pimping, and smuggling guns, narcotics, and other contraband items. Second, a major source of his income is in the illegitimate manipulation of power, such as blackmail and fraud. Third, he readily resorts to physical violence as the most reliable and effective means for solving a problem or putting an end to intragroup or intergroup conflicts. The status of a member of a *yakuza* group is derived from his invincibility in fights and from the length and frequency of his having been "fed with prison food." Thus, *yakuza* groups are associated with bloodshed and, in the eyes of the general population, violate the very basic norms of society, namely, maintenance of peace and an orderly, market-controlled circulation of money.

Given such clear illegitimacy, it is no small wonder that *yakuza* groups are secret organizations, with all the characteristics of secret societies as described by Simmel (Wolff 1950:pt. 4, chap.

4). One means of maintaining secrecy is through a secret language. *Yakuza* organizations have developed their own language, verbal and nonverbal, to control the flow of information to the outside and to establish and signify the *yakuza* identity of their members. A systematic analysis of that language is impossible, partly because it varies regionally as well as from one *yakuza* group to another. However, Iwai's analysis is enlightening. Among others, he mentions the following as *yakuza* linguistic devices: reversal of the segments of a word (*santaku* for *takusan* meaning "much," *bita* for *tabi*, "travel," *kuya* for *yaku*, "misfortune"); abbreviation (*satsu* for *keisatsu*, "police," *bai* for *shōbai*, "trade"); sinicized pronunciation of native Japanese words (*gan* for *me*, "eyes," *jin* for *hito*, "people"); dissolution of a Chinese character into its strokes, part meanings, or sounds (*yagi* for *kome*, "rice," *guniya* for *shichiya*, "pawnshop") (1963:316).

SIMULATED KINSHIP AND IE ORGANIZATION

Before going into *yakuza* behavior per se, let us examine the social organization of a *yakuza* group. A *yakuza* group is organized along lines of simulated kinship, modeled after the *ie*, "house," the basic unit of Japanese social structure. A group may be identified with the surname of its founder, such as Shimizu or Yamaguchi, or with the name of the district under its control, together with a word for house, *ikka*, and thus referred to as Shimizu *ikka*, Yamaguchi *ikka*, and so forth. For public presentation, *ikka* may be replaced by more common words such as *kumi* ("group") or *kai* ("association"), and the founder's name may give way to an impersonal name. Regardless of its "official" name, the *yakuza* organization simulates a household.

Because an *ie* is based on a cluster of kinship roles, real or fictive, its solidifying principle is farthest from that of a modern bureaucracy. However, the *ie* is foremost a corporation perpetuating itself as a unit independent of its constituent members and functioning to attain its goals. Biological kinship must be sacrificed, if necessary, in the interest of the corporation.

These two principles of *ie* seem synthesized in the system of kin-status terminology used by *yakuza*. The smallest *yakuza* unit consists of one *oyabun* and several *kobun*. These terms aptly imply a mixture of kinship ties and corporate primacy in that they refer to the occupants of kin-based parts of the corporation. *Kobun* are related to one another as siblings, as *aniki-bun* or simply *aniki* ("elder brother") and *ototo-bun* or *shatei* ("younger brother"), depending upon seniority. These terms indicate that *yakuza* are related to one another with intimacy and emotional attachment as in an ideal family, and at the same time are functionally organized by status and role as in a typical corporation.

In addition to this kin-status terminology, succession takes place just as in the ordinary *ie*. One of the *kobun* is chosen as the successor to the *oyabun* so that the *yakuza* house will perpetuate itself. My *yakuza* informant, whom I will call Mr. Yamato, identified himself as "about the fifth-generation *oyabun*" of his *ikka*. I understood his uncertainty about the number of generations when he said that the genealogy of *oyabun* had been handed down only orally, not in written form. Nonetheless, the perpetuation of the *yakuza* house through the smooth succession to *oyabun* status is regarded as most important, and the *shumei-hiro* (ceremony for introducing the successor) traditionally called for an extravagant banquet to which a large number of people, both outside and inside the house, are invited.

As befits the interests of such a corporation, the successor is probably chosen on the basis of leadership ability, including skill in the use of violence and "occupational" skill in the gambling business. If the *oyabun* favors as his successor a candidate of whom the majority of the group does not approve, the *oyabun* will have to relinquish his choice, despite his absolute authority in other matters. If he did not, the group might be torn by dissension. Yamato was apparently chosen unanimously as successor by "recommenders" appointed from the "relatives" of the incumbent *oyabun*.

It should be further noted that biological kinsmen are rarely involved in an *oyabun-kobun* relationship or in succession. To have one's own child as heir apparent goes against the *yakuza* code of conduct. Asked why, my informant answered that one would be accused of favoritism and of bypassing the "real" *kobun* who had been loyal.

In this sense, the *kobun*, including the successor, are all "adopted." But "adoption" is misleading, too. First, the *kobun* retains his original name and remains known by that name, although he is identified to *yakuza* of other *ie* by a combination of his name and the name of his *ie*. Second, the word "adoption" is reserved for the recruitment of someone other than a *kobun* of the retiring *oyabun* as the successor to the *oyabun*. Should the designated real *kobun* not want to succeed to *oyabun* status, he may "adopt" a "son" to take over his succession right. Often that person is his *oyabun*'s "brother." Despite the strangeness of this situation, in which the *kobun* adopts his "uncle" as his "son," it was by no means unknown in legitimate prewar Japanese society. In case an *oyabun*'s natural child enters the *yakuza* world and proves himself as a candidate for succession, the problem of favoritism can be resolved by the *oyabun*'s choosing a symbolic child as his successor, who would then retire early to give way to the natural son.

Once succession takes place, the retired *oyabun* may have to rely upon his successor for financial help unless he has an independent source of income. The new *oyabun* is in a position to create his own *kobun*. Yamato has thirty "pure" *kobun*, who entirely depend upon the "house" business, and about seventy others who, although holding "straight" jobs, have come under his influence in one way or another.

The elevation of a *kobun* to *oyabun* status naturally creates tensions between him and his "brothers," the latter now having to pay respect to their former brother. The tension may be reduced through a kind of branch-house (*bunke*) system. The *oyabun* allows *kobun* other than his successor to branch out, to establish their own independent *ikka*, and become *oyabun* of them. If the *oyabun* has many *kobun* who have thus established *ikka* of their own, he is called *sōchō*, president (a bureaucratic title), which signifies that he is the supreme head of a complex organization comprising many semi-independent units. Theoretically there remains a hierarchical relationship between the *honke* ("main house") *oyabun* and the *bunke oyabun*, similar to the relationship between *honke* and *bunke* in ordinary society. Yamato dismissed the *honke-bunke* analogy as applicable only to *tekiya*, not *bakuto*.

Another way of solving the rivalry tension that illustrates the *ie* system is for the successor to retire as soon as possible so that his rival brother can become his successor. Iwai notes that for this reason one *yakuza* house has many retired *oyabun* who are close to each other in age and yet are titularly separated by a "generation," such as first generation, second generation, third generation . . . down to "previous" generation. This has happened in ordinary Japanese society, the imperial household being no exception.

Unlike a household in ordinary society, a *yakuza* household does not necessarily involve the co-residence of its members. Instead, each member has his own natural family, and low-ranking members tend to rely upon their wives for the livelihood of the family. Many members, both *oyabun* and *kobun*, hold outside jobs that are totally unrelated to the "house" business (Kanehiro Hoshino 1970:26-27). Such a dual life may be a basis for maintaining the solvency of the *yakuza* house. The *oyabun*'s wife plays a crucial role in looking after the *kobun*'s families, is identified as elder sister or mother, and is adored or sometimes feared by *kobun* as the real power-holder behind the *oyabun*.

Another peculiarity of the *yakuza* household is that the lack of natural kinship ties is compensated for by the ritual consecration of fictive kinship roles. While in ordinary society a child is gradually socialized by his parent to develop his kinship identity, a *yakuza* inductee traditionally "became" a *kobun* to an *oyabun* by taking an oath in a solemn rite of passage. In front of a Shinto altar the *oyabun* and the new *kobun* drink ceremonially from the same sake cup. As in a wedding, this act symbolizes the creation or confirmation of a permanent, sacred tie between the two parties. To "receive a sake cup" from an *oyabun* means to be formally accepted as a *kobun*, and to "exchange a sake cup" means to establish an unbreakable tie. The two principals are attended in the ceremony by a witness and someone designated responsible for the novice's future conduct, and all members of the *ie*. The ceremony is dignified by the presence of invited guests, including *oyabun* of other groups who are either "relatives" or intimate friends of the *oyabun*. All this shows the seriousness of the "parent-child" sake-cup ceremony.

According to my informant, the recent trend is away from the formal sake-cup ceremony for the initiation of a *kobun*, and an oral commitment now suffices. When he was initiated as a *kobun*, Yamato went before the *oyabun* alone and said, "Although I am not worth much, please look after me from now on." The *oyabun* responded, saying "The business you are getting involved in is not a good one, but try hard to do your best." That was all. However, the sake-cup ceremony is still important for formalizing sibling ties and for marking the succession of a new *oyabun*. Retiring and incoming *oyabun* exchange sake cups, and then the *kobun* take oaths of loyalty to the new *oyabun*. The importance and drama of this ceremony imply the intensity of the rivalry surrounding succession and the need to solidify the new order immediately. Following the ceremony, a large banquet introduces the new *oyabun* to the *yakuza* world. Yamato pointed out that succession festivities are analogous to wedding festivities in ordinary society: the latter consist of a ceremonial exchange of sake cups between the bride and groom presided over by a Shinto priest in the presence of the go-betweens and close relatives only, followed by a banquet to introduce the new couple to a larger group of invited guests.

BEHAVIOR PATTERNS

Conditioned by the social organization just described, *yakuza* behavior can be characterized in terms of (1) loyalty to *oyabun* and *ikka*, (2) hierarchical orientation, (3) ritual expression of humility, (4) sensitivity to face, (5) intergroup courtesy and exclusion, and (6) body symbolism.

Loyalty to *Oyabun* and *Ikka*

A *yakuza* is trained to be absolutely loyal to the house to which he belongs and to carry out the obligation of filial piety to his *oyabun*. In the sake-cup ceremony to consecrate the parent-child bond, the novice is told: "Once you receive this cup, your duty is to be loyal to the *ikka* and to demonstrate your filial piety to your parent (*oya*). If necessary, you must let your wife and children starve and sacrifice your life on behalf of your *oyabun*." (Iwai 1963:151). The *kobun* is expected to be ready to "jump through fire or into water for the sake of the *oyabun*." Self-sacrifice is institutionalized by the common practice of *migawari*, "substitution," whereby a *kobun* may be killed or put in jail as a substitute for his *oyabun*. Needless to say, one cannot change one's *oyabun* or *ikka*.

Such intense dedication to the *oyabun* and *ikka* is coupled with absolute obedience to the *oyabun*. The *kobun* is told to believe whatever the *oyabun* says, "even if he says black is white." Furthermore, the *oyabun-kobun* bond is expected to run so deep that the *oyabun*'s wishes can be communicated to the *kobun* nonverbally. The *kobun* is supposed to feel the *oyabun*'s command from his body, not just from his voice, to make quick moves according to the *oyabun*'s facial expressions. You cannot be a *yakuza* if you wait until your *oyabun* tells you to kill so-and-so. You must be able immediately to judge from his eye motion alone that he means "Kill!" and instantly take action (Iwai 1963:164).

Loyalty to the *oyabun* takes dramatic form if he is wounded or killed or, worse yet, ridiculed by his enemy, usually another *yakuza*. The *kobun* takes revenge at the expense of his life, and many *yakuza* stories glorify the "beautiful" relationship between *oyabun* and *kobun*. In ordinary society as well, to take revenge not for oneself but for one's master is considered praiseworthy, even though that action violates the law of the larger society. Witness the perennial popularity of the story of the forty-seven masterless samurai, who killed the slayer of their lord. They violated Tokugawa law by disturbing the peace and were put to death, and yet they have remained heroes for the Japanese audience.

That kind of total self-devotion may be explained in various ways. The *kobun* may have been alienated from his own parents, or his parents may be deceased, and thus he is susceptible to the authority of a substitute parent, the *oyabun*. It is also possible that once a person joins a *yakuza* group he has burned his bridges and cannot go back to ordinary society, and that he has no choice for his own survival but to follow his *oyabun* faithfully. My informant's explanation was that his society is in no way different from an ordinary family or a company in which ties between parent and child or boss and subordinate are strong. Asked if he, while a *kobun*, had ever wanted to leave his *oyabun* when reproached by him, as an ordinary child might try to run away from home when scolded, he said, "Well, even if I wanted to, I would not have left him. I would have been ridiculed [by other *yakuza*] for lacking perseverance." This remark suggests that loyalty may be maintained by the external pressure of *yakuza* society as a whole.

There are other motives underlying the *oyabun-kobun* ties. The *oyabun* is regarded as an *on* donor to whom the *kobun* feels indebted. First of all, the *kobun* was picked by the *oyabun* and may have been fed, housed, and otherwise looked after by the *oyabun*. The *oyabun* may even have done a great favor such as saving the *kobun* candidate from a heavy debt that had driven him to the point of suicide. Such *on* would generate the resolution to do anything for the *oyabun*, even to die. On the other hand, showing loyalty may be understood as an investment for a future reward. Iwai says that the *kobun* is ready to act for the sake of the *ikka* and *oyabun* because the displayed loyalty will bring him a promotion. Formal designation as *kobun* alone involves a promotion; a new recruit must first demonstrate his qualifications to the *oyabun*. Sometimes it takes years, during which the candidate does not even see the *oyabun*, to attract the *oyabun*'s attention and "receive a sake cup" from him. After becoming a *kobun* the follower moves up the status ladder by risking his life to show his dedication and ability. The greatest reward is to be selected as the heir apparent to *oyabun* status. Preclusion of one's natural son as a successor may be partly because such natural succession would remove incentives and frustrate the expectations of the *kobun*.

In all these ways, the relationship between *oyabun* and *kobun* is a copy of the reciprocal obligation between a feudal lord and vassal. That is why *yakuza* society, though illegitimate, is thought to represent the moral values of traditional Japan. Just as old-timers complain about moral degeneration in postwar Japan, so do senior *yakuza* leaders complain about postwar *kobun* who do not know their duty to the *oyabun*.

In a recently conducted psychological study of the *oyabun-kobun* relationship (Kanehiro Hoshino 1970), it was pointed out that the sampled members of violent groups tended to regard this relationship more in terms of mutual aid and protection-dependence than as a master-slave relationship. This implies that the strict discipline and compliance described above are based on interdependence and voluntary commitment rather than on coercion. The same study showed that the *kobun* was willing to obey his *oyabun* because he was awed by the great personality of the *oyabun* or because obedience was to his advantage, not because of his fear of the *oyabun*.

What has been said about the *oyabun-kobun* relationship applies, if with less intensity, to *yakuza* siblings. If one's *aniki* ("elder brother") gets involved in a life-or-death fight, one is supposed to go to his aid. There may be intimate pairs of *yakuza* brothers. One would fight to the death to protect or avenge his special brother. Such special brotherhood may arise not only within an *ikka*, but also between members of different groups, as when prison inmates, formerly unknown to each other, become close friends. Since intergroup brotherhood is potentially threatening to the solidarity of a group, designating such a friend a "brother" requires the *oyabun*'s permission.

The filiative and fraternal bonds in the *yakuza* world are claimed to be the ultimate manifestation of *giri* and *ninjō*: the ideal *yakuza* is supposed to be firm in carrying out his obligations and to be vulnerable and empathetic as regards human feelings. Yamato, while stressing the imperatives of devotion and loyalty and the severity of sanctions against the unfaithful, characterizes the *yakuza* world as sustained by overwhelming *ninjō*. For example, "When you have just got out of prison, you are destitute. But your *aniki* rushes over to see you and throws a party to celebrate your release. Donations are taken, and if each person gives ¥100,000, you will receive ¥1 million from only ten people." Yamato was referring to his own experience as the receiver of such help after serving a prison term. The *yakuza* world is unequalled, he declares, in the abundance of such *ninjō*. This does not mean that betrayal is unknown in that world. "Yes, there is a lot of that, probably more than exists outside. But an immoral man is destined to perish even in the *yakuza* world."

Hierarchical Orientation

As is shown by the suffix *bun* attached to kinship terms, *yakuza* are extremely sensitive to status and are expected to behave in exact accordance with status distance. Such expectations are a reflection of the rigid hierarchical structure of *yakuza* society. There is a clear superordination-subordination between *oyabun* and *kobun*. The siblings are also hierarchically graded in a strikingly elaborate system based on seniority. One is a junior brother or a senior brother vis-à-vis every other brother, unless the two happen to have entered the group at the same time. The amount of inequality is numerically expressed by a combination of two unequal fractional numbers whose sum is one. Thus, two brothers are described as 4/10 to 6/10, 3/10 to 7/10, or 2/10 to 8/10, increasing in status distance in that order. Equal brothers are called 5/10 brothers and address each other *kyōdai* ("brother"), instead of as *aniki* or *shatei*. The almost but not quite equal relationship is described as "below 5/100," meaning 55/100 to 45/100 (Iwai 1963:135).

Status difference, so elaborately graded, can be detected by subtle verbal and nonverbal cues, as well as by more explicit social devices. Even among independent *oyabun*, remnants of a hierarchical relationship can be detected, for example, by their reference terms for each other. The superior is referred to as the person of such-and-such district, while the inferior is identified merely by the name of his district, without "the person of." Another cue is the position of their hands while they are seated on the floor, talking to each other: the inferior places his hands on the floor, which makes him appear to be bowing, and the superior places his hands on his knees (Iwai 1963:136). In a ceremony, the status hierarchy is clearly and dramatically symbolized in the seating arrangement.

Status is associated not only with ritual expression, but also with the distribution of roles played in the gambling business. Each member of a *yakuza* group performs a necessary role. At the top of the hierarchy is the *oyabun*, who, interestingly enough, does not play a significant role in the business; he only makes a brief, ritual appearance to greet the customers, even though he sponsors the gambling. A special effort seems to be made to hide the *oyabun* from public exposure. Although the reason is that the *oyabun*'s safety is crucial to the survival of the group, it is interesting to note in this rituallstic headship the same taboo of status we have seen in legitimate organization (chapter 5). Below the *oyabun* is his deputy, who in fact supervises the entire gambling business. Next to the deputy is the person who actually gambles with customers, and below him is an assistant gambler, who plays minor, secondary games. Next are a bunch of *wakamono* ("young fellows"), whose roles range from custodians of the gambling room, the stairway, and customers' shoes, to the doorkeeper, customer-solicitor, and the person who sees customers off. At the bottom is the watchman ouside the building.

The hierarchical orientation of the *yakuza* world is basically unstable and contradictory, however: movement, both upward and downward, is frequent. Unlike an established bureaucracy, *yakuza* society is governed by the "ability principle," whereby a strong, clever man can attain top status over weaker and less clever rivals. His ability will be inevitably recognized by the rest of the *yakuza* and an implicit consensus will develop that he should succeed to *oyabun* status. The ability principle goes directly against the principle of seniority, the very basis of the hierarchical orientation. The apparent conflict is resolved by the *yakuza* code of humility.

Ritual Humility

To be recognized as a leader, one must show humility, particularly ritual humility and politeness. Arrogance and rudeness will invite immediate sanctions from other *yakuza*, no matter how able one may be. The person who has acquired leadership through his ability should continue to pay respect to his *sempai* who have lost power or have been superseded. Otherwise, people will lose confidence in him. On the other hand, the *sempai*, too, should readily admit their inferiority in ability, concede their power to the junior upstart, and show respect for him as a new *oyabun*. Humility should be ritually expressed especially at a formal gathering. A *kōhai* should acknowledge the superiority of a *sempai* in seniority, and, conversely, a senior should concede real *sempai* status to an able junior, by, for example, taking a seat farther away from the higher-status side of the room.

The code of mutual concession and humility is crystallized in what is called *jingi. Jingi* refers to a set of abstract standards of justice followed by *yakuza* members. More specifically, it denotes a set of concrete rules of speech and manners used when two *yakuza* of different *ikka* introduce each other.

In the extremely formalized style of *jingi* speech, the person is supposed to inform the stranger of his name, birthplace, the *ikka* he belongs to, and the name of his *oyabun*. Before this introduction starts, the two parties should know their status relative to each other. If one is the *oyabun* of a group and the other a *kobun* of another group, the hierarchy is quite easily established. When the parties greet each other, the *oyabun* may indicate his status by revealing his thumb, and the *kobun* may hide his thumb behind the other four fingers. If both happen to be *oyabun* or *kobun*, they may be uncertain as to their relative status and will try to offer and take cues about their seniority. The *jingi* ritual, however, demands that both parties take an inferior position to each other, expressing humility and respect. In the self-introduction, humility is expressed by introducing oneself before the other party does. One will say, "Please wait and let me introduce myself first because I am lower." The other party is expected to refuse, saying "No, I shall start first." The first one would then say, "I am still young and immature, in no position to be allowed to wait. Please let me start." This kind of competition in humility goes back and forth about three times before the issue is finally settled. Even when it is settled, the person who accepts a superior position by waiting is supposed to ask the other person to forgive him in case he is making an error.

In the course of the *jingi* performance, humility is constantly expressed by such statements as: "I am young," "I am still disciplining myself," "I am good-for-nothing," "I am a nobody." Help and support are asked of the other party. As this is going on, one's hands are supposed to be put forward to make one's head lower. At the end of the ceremony, both parties again start to argue about who is to withdraw his hand first. The inferior is supposed to urge the other to withdraw first. (Iwai 1963:261-267). All this is performed in the highly stylized *yakuza* language, which sounds as if one were reading the lines of a traditional stage play.

Yakuza ritualism also involves the ritual performance of fixed obligations that bind together the members of one *ikka* and that foster good will between different *ikka*. Among such obligations are regular visits, with appropriate gifts, to a superior or someone with whom one is supposed to maintain ritual ties. Neglect of such obligations would be taken as a sign of hostility, arrogance, or disobedience.

Sensitivity to Face

The concern for ritual control over visible behavior is linked with sensitivity to face (*kao*—like the English term "face" in both literal and figuative senses). We know that the average Japanese is concerned about face, but the behavior of *yakuza* shows that they have an exaggerated face sensitivity. With *yakuza*, as with society at large, preserving face takes both defensive and aggressive forms. Defensively, the dignity must be kept from injury, destruction, or pollution. Ritualism, discussed above, may aid the mutual, cooperative defense of face. The *yakuza*, being extremely defensive about his dignity, overreacts to the feeling that face has been "smeared with mud," "wounded," or "crushed." Any act slighting his status may trigger such feelings—the act may range from a minor, accidental ritual error to malicious mockery in public. The average Japanese, when humiliated, would conceal his emotion, punish himself with shame, or patiently postpone retaliation until the opportune moment. The humiliated *yakuza*, however, would impulsively jump at the offender, risking bloodshed. Impulsive, violent action in such a circumstance is approved as "masculine" in the *yakuza* world, masculinity being a crucial component of dignity. *Yakuza* impetuousness is quite a contrast to the ritualistic conformity also characteristic of *yakuza* behavior. The exaggerated sense of personal dignity is another apparent contradiction to the exaggerated humility described above.

The aggressive aspect of preserving face refers to ensuring that the prestige, power, or influence of a *yakuza* is recognized by fellow *yakuza* and even by the outside world. A powerful, influential *yakuza* is described as *ii kao* ("having a good face"), *kao ga hiroi* ("having a widely recognized face"), or *kao ga kiku* ("having an effective face").

Face in this sense is to be imposed and utilized, instead of being protected, to get things done. An influential *oyabun* will have to resort to violence less than an average *oyabun* to carry out his wishes. Face, then, operates as a nonviolent means of settling a dispute. An influential *oyabun* is thus often asked to arbitrate a conflict between two parties in different *yakuza* groups. His success in arbitration will attest to the reputed "effectiveness" of his face and further enhance his status. His failure, on the other hand, will "pollute" his face. The arbiter, therefore, asks each party to make peace with the other party for the sake of his, the arbiter's, face. The two parties can then concede without losing face themselves.

Used thus to solve a problem, face becomes a sort of transferable commodity. Among the *yakuza*, loaning or borrowing face is part of daily life. "Loan me your *kao*" means "use your influence for me." Furthermore, face can translate into credit, permitting one to purchase things without cash payment. It is interesting to see this bipolarity of power in the *yakuza* world: on the one hand, power is based on the sheer exercise of physical might, or on the number of "kills"; on the other hand it is based on the credibility or trust placed in a person, which obviates the use of violence. These two aspects, of course, do not contradict each other because the *yakuza* cannot build up a creditable face without demonstrating competence in violence.

Intergroup Courtesy and Exclusion

As was alluded above, a network of communication and control cuts across different *yakuza* groups, as much as is necessary for their survival. The interaction between groups is generally characterized by extreme courtesy, similar to the hospitality shown by ordinary Japanese to guests. The *jingi* ritual described above applies particularly to a stranger recognized as a *yakuza*. Intergroup courtesy is necessitated by, and in turn enables, the practice of itinerancy from group to group, province to province. As in ordinary society of traditional Japan so in the *yakuza* world, traveling was one of the disciplines required to make a creditable *yakuza*. The idea was that in the absense of a formal educational system the best way of learning a trade was to apprentice oneself to a professional, who was often a stranger. A journeyman *yakuza* was treated as a "guest *kobun*" by the *oyabun* of the house he stayed at temporarily. According to the *jingi* code governing the *yakuza* world, the itinerant *yakuza* was accepted and provided with shelter and food only if he identified himself by name, residence, *ikka*, and *oyabun*. Identification was made through the *jingi* ritual, which was conducted at the entrance of the host house.

Discipline may have been only a nominal motive for frequent travel. It is likely that *yakuza* resorted to itinerancy to hide from the police or to avoid struggle and rivalry within or between *yakuza* groups. According to my informant, both itinerancy and the *jingi* ritual are out of practice today.

In any event, in popular literature and the mass media the itinerant *yakuza* is romanticized, modeled after the wandering masterless samurai, as a man of justice who exposes and punishes a local *yakuza oyabun* who is exploiting poor peasants. His freedom, rootlessness, and loneliness, coupled with selflessness, give him the aura of a hero.

The point is that there exists, or existed, a code of courtesy governing intergroup interaction. On the other hand, *yakuza* behavior is characterized by a strong sense of belongingness to one's own house and by the mutual exclusiveness of groups. Exclusiveness is indicated by the word *nawabari*, literally "rope stretch," which means a clearly bounded territory over which a group claims exclusive control, much as a feudal lord did over his territory. Each *yakuza* group claims possession of a *nawabari* and is vigilant in protecting it from invasion by enemy *yakuza* groups. Small wonder, therefore, that a *yakuza* group or its *oyabun* is identified by the name of the district in which its *nawabari* is located. The territorial claim is incorporated into the succession ritual so that the successor formally inherits a *nawabari* from the retiring *oyabun*. According to my informant, the succession ritual includes a transference from the retiring to the newly nominated *oyabun* of a charter prescribing that "So-and-so (the name of the successor) be in charge of such-and-such area for protection from such day of such month on."

A *nawabari* is a taboo to outsiders: to enter it is to provoke violent retaliation. Nonetheless, *yakuza* groups are typically desirous of expanding their *nawabari*, and the *oyabun* of each group tries to "widen his face." The result is constant intergroup struggle and fighting over territorial jurisdiction.

This is additional evidence that *yakuza* behavior is an exaggerated expression of Japanese culture and behavior in general, which is characterized by high sensitivity to the group's boundary and behavioral differentiation according to whether one is addressing himself to the outside or the inside of his group. Two extreme patterns emerge: ritual hospitality toward outsiders on the one hand, and an intense sense of in-group belongingness coupled with exclusive, anomic behavior toward outsiders, on the other.

Body Symbolism

In previous chapters we have emphasized the special meanings attached to the body in the Japanese thinking. We noted body preoccupation, the social significance of sickness and death, the cultural accommodativeness to bodily desires and needs, and body contact. The body seems to be fully used as a means of communication.

Among *yakuza*, the body seems to play an especially important role, perhaps because the body is the most crucial capital and resource for a group so reliant on violence. A *yakuza* establishes his identity by a visible mutilation of the body, tattooing. Besides displaying *yakuza* identity, tattoos may indicate a sibling or parent-child bond: two persons may have the same pattern of tattoo as proof of permanent commitment. The unerasability of the tattoo makes *yakuza* identity irreversible. Because of the pain involved in acquiring it, the tattoo is also taken as evidence of masculinity, not only of the violent, aggressive type but of the quiet, enduring type. For this reason, the painful manual tattoo is considered more prestigious than the painless machine tattoo. A tattoo is also useful in intimidating people (Iwai 1963: Mugishima, Hoshino, and Kiyonaga 1971). My informant gave another reason: he got his arms and back tattooed because he thought it would make him look "snappy," as a future *oyabun* should—he was determined at the outset to become an *oyabun*. He was "foolish," he added.

Research by Mugishima, Hoshino, and Kiyonaga (1971) indicates that a large number of *yakuza* (73 percent of the sampled members of violent groups) are still undergoing the tattoo operation. The content may be words or pictures. Examples of words are "Man Alone," the name of a mistress, a nickname, "Cherry," "Honor to the Wonderful Law of the Lotus Sutra," "Buddha," "Endurance"; pictures include animals (snake, dragon, carp, hawk, fox, tiger), plants (cherry, rose), and inanimate natural phenomena (moon, clouds, waves).

Finger-chopping is another type of body symbolism among *yakuza*. It is used to chastise a deviant member, to apologize to another *yakuza* group against which a wrong has been done, to solve group conflict, and to demonstrate one's sincerity (Mugishima, Hoshino, and Kiyonaga 1971). The last purpose seems the most common. When he has violated a code, a *yakuza* might show his sincere repentance by cutting off a finger, and the amount of pain is considered to correspond with the intensity of his sincerity. Compared with such body communication, verbal repentance would seem to have little persuasive power. Self-mutilation as a proof of *magokoro* ("true-heartedness") is not far from the dominant value patterns of Japanese culture.

The brotherhood bond is said to have been established in olden days only after the ceremonial drinking of each other's blood. The present sake-cup ceremony may be a symbolic substitute for such a blood ceremony.

If these are extreme, literal cases of body symbolism, the body is also used figuratively. "To bet one's body on something" (*karada o kakeru*) refers to a single-minded determination to carry out a goal. Risking one's body seems to be the ultimate expression of strong will. In the *yakuza* world the principle of direct body attack (*taiatari shugi*) is routinely invoked.

Other bodily figures of speech commonly use *hara*, "belly." The union of everyone's *hara* is emphasized as crucial for effective teamwork. In the sake-cup ceremony, the *oyabun* and the novice pledge themselves to unite their *hara*. This oath is visually represented by the presence of two whole fish on the Shinto altar. Initially placed back to back, after the ceremony they are re-arranged to face each other, the two *hara* touching.

MOTIVATION AND RATIONALIZATION

Finally, we shall venture into the inner world of an individual *yakuza* and try to learn what induced him to join a *yakuza* group and to continue in it despite the obvious drawbacks. By what motivation or rationalization would a *yakuza* himself explain his illegitimate involvement?

Oyabun Yamato repeatedly emphasized that he had always been aware of the evils of *yakuza* life, that *yakuza* were "antisocial groups" that really should be put out of existence. Unlike many other boys, who joined on impulse or for no other reason than to secure "a piece of bread," he thought it over a long time before finally deciding to "enter the *yakuza* world." In his school days, he would not have dreamed of having anything to do with *yakuza*.

He was born the fourth son of a fisherman in a small fishing village. Although the family was poor—so poor that his mother had to visit her natal family to "borrow a basketful of rice"—it was decided that at least one son should be well educated and should rise in the world. My informant, with his good mind and school record, was chosen to be the one. After successfully passing the difficult entrance examination, he became a middle-school student, a status enjoyed by few boys in the village under the old academic system. He was determined to succeed and fulfill the expectations of his family, above all to please his mother, who had suffered so.

This determination for success, bolstered by his mother-attachment, collapsed when Japan's position in the war began to look desperate. Yamato felt that schoolwork was pointless now that Japan was in a life-and-death struggle with Western powers. If the world had been in peace, he mused, he would have stayed on course and become a doctor or lawyer. Instead, his personal goal became the national goal—to win the war. Being "pure-hearted" and burning with patriotic zeal, he resolved to dedicate his life to the country, to save it from disaster.

Then, his mother died. His school performance declined from bad to worse. After graduation without distinction, he joined the army, where he was trained as a cadet while preparing to be a kamikaze pilot.

Yamato calls that his first wrong step. A worse one came later, after Japan's surrender. Many of his friends, released from the military, went back to school and entered college, which he, too, should have done. Instead, having taken the national cause too seriously, he was now entirely alienated and convinced that Japan was going to be a slave to America. He was too ignorant, he admits, to have foreseen that Americans would behave as "gentlemanly" as they did in Japan, or that Japan would be democratized and quickly recover from near catastrophe. Goal-less, he started to help his father with the fishing business, but it went bankrupt. In despair he drifted into a circle of *yakuza* in the neighborhood; his father, who had kept warning him against having such friends, died. He decided to become a *yakuza*. He summarily owes this decision to his resignation (*akirame*) that had accumulated from renouncing his ambitions for "status and fame," Japan's defeat, and the death of his mother, for whose sake he once aspired to success.

He thus regards himself as a victim of the war. But how could an event that ended twenty-seven years ago have sustained his participation? He has no intention of retiring soon. What keeps Yamato committed to the *yakuza* world or how does he rationalize his present life? He draws an analogy between society and a living organism: "In order for an organism to live, it must always be supplied with clean blood; to keep its blood clean, it has to eliminate waste such as feces and urine. These wastes are necessary, no matter how useless or filthy they are." He means that society, in order to survive, has to put up with such undesirable elements as robbers, prostitutes, and *yakuza*. In the same vein he refers to capitalism: "If you want to keep capitalist society pure and as profitable to capitalists as possible, you must allow the existence of the victims of that system." He goes on, "People who were born near the top of Mount Fuji are able to reach the top without trying," whereas those born at the foot have a long way to go. One cannot judge the latter's actions in the eyes of the former. His conclusion is that no matter what measures the government and police take, they will be unable to eradicate *yakuza* and other antisocial groups. If he dissolved his own group, Yamato contends, another group would immediately spring up; if he retired, another man would take over.

In short, Yamato rationalizes his *yakuza* involvement by the idea of "necessary evil," combining two kinds of self-image. On the one hand, with overtones of self-pity and self-denigration, he regards himself as a victim of his time, the war, society, and especially capitalist society. On the other hand, he claims, with a tone of moral righteousness and indignation, that he has sacrificed his personal goal to save the country and society; that society needs "evil" people for its own survival despite its claim to the otherwise; and that even "good" society is riddled with injustice. Listening to him, I came to realize that these two self-images merge into one through the use of the Japanese word *gisei*, which means both "victim" and "sacrifice." Yamato tends to see himself as a *gisei*—in both senses—of forces beyond his control. Here we see a Japanese version of moral masochism, and we recall that Yamato saw the embodiment of moral masochism in his mother when he was a child.

CHAPTER 11

Suicide

LEGITIMACY OF VOLUNTARY DEATH

While the last chapter examined a cultural example of deviancy that is directed against society, this chapter calls attention to another form of deviancy directed against the deviant himself, namely suicide. As it is for other peoples of the world, suicide is an extraordinary occurrence for Japanese; when someone takes his life, his family is likely to want to cover it up, fearing disgrace if it is known. For this reason, suicide is considered deviant behavior.

Nonetheless, it is a widely acknowledged fact that in Japan a heroic, romantic, esthetic, and moral aura surrounds death in general, and voluntary death in particular. This may be traced to the samurai tradition, in which the code of honor, *bushidō*, was equated to readiness for death, and it was considered honorable to kill oneself to prevent being killed or captured by an enemy. The sanction of voluntary death may also have been reinforced by the legalization, under the Tokugawa regime, of *seppuku* or *harakiri*, ceremonial self-immolation by disembowelment. The dramatic effect of this ritual form of suicide, with its religious setting and elaborate procedure (described by Seward 1968), is indicative of a cultural investment in death. It is true that *seppuku* was used not only for voluntary death, but also as a penalty. But this penalty was a privilege accorded to the samurai class that saved the offender from the disgrace of being put to death by an executioner. *Seppuku* is thus associated with the honor of the ruling class and the elitism of feudal Japan.

Institutionalized suicide reached a climax during World War II, when the military leaders instructed the Japanese people, soldiers and civilians alike, to commit suicide rather than be captured. Indeed, troops did commit *gyokusai* (literally, "beautifully crushed to pieces like a jewel"), a euphemism for mass suicide, rather than surrender. A more aggressive form of suicide was inaugurated with kamikaze attacks. People were led to venerate kamikaze pilots as saints. In the kamikaze mission, the suicidal act attained such perfect legitimacy that it was not conceived as suicidal. In fact, many of the pilots themselves did not think of their action as suicidal, as is shown in their wills. The following is an example:

> Dear Mother:
> I have been selfish and have caused you worry, and I find myself without words to express my apologies. But I have now made up my mind to be a good member of the great Japanese navy. I am your son, Mother. As a male representative of this divine country, I am going to accomplish what a true man should. I have done my best since childhood, with the conviction that though born in a poor family I shall be second to none in self-dedication. It will make me happy only if I can serve my country as an instrument for smashing the enemy. With this heavy responsibility on my shoulders, I shall smile in defeating our foe. I am determined to live for good in the Pacific, and to persevere until the day of final victory. (Quoted by Ohara 1970:75-76)

Referring to *raiden* (suicide submarines), another wartime invention, Masaaki Kato states that *raiden* operators "regarded their behavior as other-destructive, not self-destructive," and that they believed in immortality (1969:291).

The legitimation of voluntary death is further based upon the culturally idealized state of self, namely, the clean, pure self. The purity of *hara*, the vital center of the body, can be disclosed through disembowelment. According to Nitobe, a staunch partisan of Japanese culture, a sort of "mental physiology" underlies the custom of *seppuku* in that the person committing *seppuku* is virtually saying, "I will open the seat of my soul and show you how it fares with it. See for yourself whether it is polluted or clean" (1969:114). Aside from such "physiology," we can say that suicide is supported by the cultural concept of self insofar as self-destruction is an unequivocal expression of selflessness (*muga*). Benedict observed:

> Suicide, properly done, will, according to their [Japanese] tenets, clear his name and reinstate his memory. American condemnation of suicide makes self-destruction only a desperate submission to despair, but the Japanese respect for it allows it to be an honorable and purposeful act. In certain situations it is the most honorable course to take in *giri* to one's name. The defaulting debtor on New Year's Day, the official who kills himself to acknowledge that he assumes responsibility for some unfortunate occurrence, the lovers who seal their hopeless love in a double suicide, the patriot who protests the government's postponement of war with China are all, like the boy who fails in an examination or the soldier avoiding capture, turning upon themselves a final violation (1946:166).

Given the cultural approbation of suicide, the Japanese "play up suicide as Americans play up crime and they have the same vicarious enjoyment of it" (Benedict 1946:167). Japan had one of the highest suicide rates in the world prior to 1960 (DeVos n.d.).

The idea of death is associated further with the final resolution to a crisis situation. If a person cannot kill himself, he at least can put himself in the imagined state of being dead (*shinda tsumori*), which arouses the courage and resoluteness in him. A man in despair will be told, "If you become ready to die, you will be able to accomplish anything undertaken." The courage to live often derives from such a state of death. Furthermore, readiness for death can indicate a state of perfect happiness or contentment.

MOTIVATIONS AND FUNCTIONS

Several attempts have been made to interpret Japanese suicide using Durkheim's typology (1951) as a point of departure (DeVos n.d.; Masaaki Kato 1969; Iga 1961, 1967; Iga and Ohara 1967). While drawing upon these studies, I shall offer an alternative view of Japanese suicide in light of the motives or goals of those who attempt it.

Communication

Accounts of suicide cases suggest that people resort to suicide often to break through a blocked communication channel. The frustration of not being able to communicate with or persuade someone may drive one to this drastic means of getting heard. Two cultural factors enter in. First, communicational frustration ties in with the culturally shared mistrust of words and the alleged ineffectiveness of verbal communication. Second, the Japanese sense of guilt, generated by an empathetic understanding of another person's suffering, is maximized in the face of this extreme form of masochism, suicide. These two factors make one sensitive and vulnerable to whatever message is implied in another's suicide. The person to whom the suicide victim has tried to communicate, at the expense of his life, is likely to succumb to the victim's appeal, either out of guilt or under pressure from other sympathizers.

This type of suicide is likely to be accompanied by a suicide note and a dramatic suicidal act, even *seppuku*. A recent example was the *seppuku* suicide in 1970 of Yukio Mishima, the world-famous novelist, in front of a large number of witnesses. The majority of Japanese were shocked at Mishima's "madness," but this did not prevent a group of right-wing radicals from deifying him. In contrast to this open, extroverted dramatization is the introverted, passive method, often used by women, of poisoning oneself in a closet or back room at night. In dramatic effect, this method is just as devastating to the family member who opens the closet door the next morning as the extroverted method. Overall, however, there is not much difference between sexes in the methods of suicide employed. Both sexes most commonly use hanging, followed by poisoning.

The suicidal message, whether implied in the act of suicide or expressed in a suicide note, involves either an extrapunitive or an intropunitive motive. An extrapunitive message ranges in degree of punitiveness from instruction or advice to remonstration or protest. An extremely punitive message is implied in a suicide committed out of rancor, resentment, or revenge.

Kanshi, "remonstration suicide," has been committed against a superior who erred in his conduct (Seward 1968:38; Chamberlain 1971:219). Hearn noted that a wife remonstrated with her husband by committing suicide:

> Perhaps the most touching instance occurred in 1892, at the time of the district elections in Nagano prefecture. A rich voter named Ishijima, after having publicly pledged himself to aid in the election of a certain candidate, transferred his support to the rival candidate. On learning of this breach of promise, the wife of Ishijima robed herself in white and performed *jigai* [suicide] after the old samurai manner. (1904:318)

A superior may commit suicide to dissuade his subordinates from recalcitrance. A general sent to Manchuria at the end of World War II to persuade the Manchurian Japanese forces to surrender found them resistant. He "had his pilot take off from the airstrip and crash the craft in front of the entire body of assembled troops" and thus secured their compliance (DeVos n.d.). Modern Japanese history abounds with incidents of suicide committed to rally protests against the government. A corporal of the First Regiment in Tokyo committed *seppuku* in 1880 to demand the establishment of a parliament (Seward 1968:97). Political assassinations were often followed by the assassin's suicide, which served not only to expiate his guilt but to make his protest or demand more persuasive. Mishima's suicide was supposedly meant "to castigate the Japanese 'self-defense forces' for their lack of patriotism," and "to bring about a military coup by inducing in others a sense of rededication to Japan" (DeVos n.d.).

Kambe (1972) advises us to pay more attention to the retaliatory motive of suicide, particularly among Japanese youth. They tend to blame other people, Kambe claims, for forcing hardships upon them and want to let others know of their responsibility and to punish them by committing suicide. "Many a Japanese youth resorts to suicide as a most effective means of upsetting another person or causing him to lose face, and thus of 'taking revenge' upon him" (p. 43).

Cutting across these examples of extrapunitive messages is the sender's wish to arouse guilt in the receiver and the audience that will trigger a desired action, change of attitude, or repentance in them. Similar persuasions may be attained through the threat of suicide, which is a masochistic version of blackmailing.

Intropunitive communication, on the other hand, is intended when a person has made a serious error or has failed in performance and takes his life to demonstrate the sincerity of his repentance and apology. A suicide note in this case is likely to contain a statement like *Shinde owabi suru* ("I apologize by dying"). Suicidal apology may be considered an extension of the practice of self-mutilation, for example, finger-chopping, to prove the sincerity of the apology.

The ultimate objective of the intropunitive message is expiation of guilt. By proving his sincerity in repenting and apologizing, the suicide can expect to expiate his guilt and to be forgiven by the victim of his misconduct. Ego's guilt is believed to be canceled by the guilt aroused in Alter as a result of Ego's suicide. Thus, intropunitive and extrapunitive suicides, although quite different in original motive, are similar in effect: the empathetic guilt induced by the suicide serves as leverage to eliminate the communication barrier and assure the compliance or forgiveness of the receiver of the message.

Social Cohesion

Suicide further relates to the value of belongingness, especially interpersonal cohesion based upon loyalty, esteem, love, or a simple desire for togetherness. Ego may find suicide tempting because it will culminate his cohesion with Alter or because it will put an end to his frustration at a lack of cohesion. Underlying the suicidal tendency here are, positively, compulsive feelings of inseparability and fusion between Ego and Alter, and, negatively, loneliness and discontent at the lack of solidarity.

The classic type is *junshi*, suicide of loyalty or devotion committed to follow one's lord, master, or superior in death. The same term is used for a nonvoluntary, forced suicide, either to continue to serve the deceased master or to prove loyalty. Death for a cause may also be called *junshi*. Here let us focus on voluntary *junshi* following a superior's death. One of the most famous instances of *junshi* in modern times was committed by General Maresuke Nogi and his wife following the death of Emperor Meiji in 1912. The emotional basis for suicidal loyalty of this sort may range from the sense of *on* indebtedness and obligation to repay to the realization that the death of a benefactor has left one's life meaningless and worthless. Both feelings appear to have been active in General Nogi's case.

Shinjū is another type of suicide motivated by or aimed at social cohesion. This word literally means "inside" or "at the center of" *kokoro* and implies a self-sacrificing action to show *magokoro*. Although it has had additional meanings in the past, today *shinjū* refers to (1) double suicide by lovers and (2) any suicide involving the death of more than one person.

Double suicide in its "pure" form involves a man and woman committing suicide together out of love, often physically binding themselves to insure a perfect union in the hereafter. The theme of inseparability stands out not only in the motivation or goal, but also in the method. Historically, 'such a love suicide is a legacy of the feudal system where marriage based on free choice was prohibited. Also, the Buddhist idea of reincarnation probably made the lovers, without hope in this life, hopeful of a final union in the next life.

Closer examination reveals a greater variety of causal factors in double suicide. According to the sociologist Yasuma Takada, the causes of love suicide can be classified as "(1) the hopelessness of bringing love to the final consummation [marriage]; (2) one party feels inseparable from the other because of love when the latter, for some other reason, has no choice but to die; (3) both parties, unable to live for their respective reasons, choose to die together since they happen to be in love; (4) one party, facing an unavoidable death, forces the other, with whom the former has had a love affair, to die with him or her" (quoted by Ohara 1965:189). Except for the first, love is only partially or peripherally involved in these causes. The last type, commonly called "forced double suicide," is distinctive because it involves one party's dying against his or her will, or homicide by the other party.

What cuts across these subtypes of *shinjū* is a refusal to be separated by one or both parties. Sharing death appears to be the culmination of togetherness. Being outlived by a person to whom one is attached seems as unbearable as outliving the person. Sometimes the possibility of sharing death triggers or facilitates suicide: someone in despair but unable to commit suicide alone may acquire the courage to take his life when he finds a suicidal companion.

This leads us to the broader meaning of *shinjū*, namely, any suicide involving more than one person. It includes parent-child suicide, mother-child suicide, and suicide by the whole family. Where an infant or young child is involved, the "suicide" is actually homicide, specifically infanticide, followed by the parent's suicide. It has been noted that the children most often victimized by parent-child suicide are under ten years of age, most frequently of preschool age (Takiuchi 1972:50).

Whereas love suicides have decreased since the legitimation of marriage based upon free choice, family suicides have not decreased. The reason for this relates to another question: Why is infanticide by the mother so common in Japan, where the mother-child bond and mother's sacrifice for the child are extol-led? Strange as it may sound, it is this very bond or inseparability between mother and child that necessitates the infanticide-suicide *shinjū*. According to the native logic, the desperate parent cannot bear to leave the child alive alone; she would rather kill the child because she feels that nobody in the world will look after him, that the family would be better off if they depart together.

Takiuchi postulates that this feeling of *ittaikan* ("oneness") between parent and child has intensified as a result of the break-down of the "community," where children belonged to a wider circle and had fictive parents along with their real parents. Today, children, particularly preschool children, belong to their parents alone or are believed to be solely under parental jurisdiction. This helps explain the high frequency of parent-children suicide in recent years (Takiuchi 1972).

That both suicide and homicide are subsumed in the term *shinjū* is suggestive of the Japanese attitude toward death in gen-eral. What matters is not whether one dies by suicide or homicide but whether one shares death with another or dies alone. Co-dying appears as a lesser evil, if not a salvation, in comparison with a lonely death or life. The concept of *shinjū* obscures the differ-ence between voluntary and forced death or the question of whose will is responsible for death, and throws into relief the cohesiveness experienced or expressed by those involved.

"Cohesive suicide" takes a negative form when one takes his life because of interpersonal disharmony or loneliness. Suicide by a lonely old person falls under this category. He may not only want to be free from his present state of friction or isolation, but also may hope to regain lost cohesion by joining his departed spouse or ancestors.

Such a negative form of suicide occurs in *shinjū* as well. A man may decide to commit double suicide on discovering that his mistress is attracted to another man. Many forced double suicides are a result of a triangular entanglement. Likewise, family suicide often is regarded as the final solution to a lack of cohesion in the family.

There is another variant, which we shall call vicarious or sacrificial suicide. This takes place when Ego, strongly identifying with Alter, takes his life to save Alter from losing his life, or to help Alter attain his goal. After a revolt of young army officers in 1936, a lieutenant was upset that his closest friend had been involved as one of the rebels. He was also afraid that the incident might generate internal strife in the imperial military forces. He reached the conclusion that he could bring the conflict to an end by committing suicide. Leaving a note, he disemboweled himself, and was followed by his wife, who agreed to share this vicarious death (Ohara 1970:61). The above-mentioned instance of suicide by the wife who wished to remonstrate with her husband may also be considered a vicarious suicide committed on behalf of the guilty person. In both cases, role vicariism is in full play. Similar to this is the sacrificial suicide in which Ego removes himself, realizing that he is in the way of the goal-attainment of Alter, to whom he is attached (DeVos n.d.).

Status-Role Commitment

A third major type is suicide committed through compulsive identification with or commitment to the status and role to which one holds or aspires. This corresponds with what DeVos calls "role narcissism," "an intense identification of one's self with one's professional or occupational self" (n.d.). Role narcissism compels one toward suicide when a serious error is made in role performance by oneself or by another for whom one is responsible.

The suicide committed out of guilt for having caused others trouble through a failure in role performance combines intropunitive communication—apology—with role commitment. The suicide committed out of shame for having denigrated one's status through a failure in role performance may have elements of "self-assertion" or "self-inflation" (Iga 1966, 1967) and may be considered an expression of self-centered mortification. Guilt and shame, apology and mortification, both are likely to be present in one suicide except when the error committed is a ritual one that hurts only the pride of the status holder.

Not only a committed error but an anticipated error or failure may induce suicidal anxiety. That anxiety corresponds to the intensity of Ego's awareness of the expectation held by significant Alters and onlookers about his successful performance, and of the likely sanctions by them in case he fails. Anticipation of an error or failure is intensified when one is in transition from an old to a new role or when one has just assumed a new role. A freshman student, a new employee, or a new appointee, whose role performance has not been tested, is a likely victim of such anxiety. On the basis of casual personal comments by Japanese colleagues, I am inclined to view the recent (1972) suicide of Yasunari Kawabata in that light. Japan's first Nobel prizewinner in literature, Kawabata was driven to suicide, in my opinion, because his new world renown became a burden too heavy to carry.

What is more noteworthy on a nationwide scale is the extent of suicides by young Japanese facing an actual or anticipated failure in schoolwork, especially in entrance examinations. A seventeen-year-old girl who attempted suicide was reported to have been filled with anxiety that her school grades would not be good enough for her to qualify for the college entrance examinations (Ohara 1965:149). She would lose sleep and appetite whenever she faced a test and would be unable to concentrate on her studies. Finally on one test she could not even read the questions. She began to cut her school classes and a month later she attempted suicide by strangling.

The suicidal tendency rooted in status-role commitment is only aggravated in a society where everyone is under pressure to elevate his status through academic and occupational achievements. In this respect, too, Japanese culture tends to drive young "status-dropouts"—both actual and anticipated—toward feelings of hopelessness and self-destruction.

As serious as an error or failure in performance is the deprivation of role and status because of illness or old age. The individual may suddenly find himself roleless or statusless, pushed out of the seat he used to occupy, his status taken over by another person. Role deprivation of this sort may be conducive to suicide, particularly in a culture that places primary emphasis, as the Japanese culture does, on the occupancy of a proper place or *bun* in society. Outliving one's *bun* is to expose one's shame and to become a troublesome burden on society. One would rather die voluntarily than cause *meiwaku* to other people by living too long.

As implicitly noted, the three types of suicide delineated above are far from mutually exclusive. One suicide may be understood from all three points of view. An aged person's suicide, for example, may imply an extrapunitive message (communication) directed at a living person guilty of having abandoned or disobeyed him; may be an escape from loneliness (cohesion); or may indicate frustration over and an inability to perform a useful role or maintain a status (status-role commitment). A suicide attempt by a student can be attributed not only to concern over school performance (status-role commitment), but also to a desire for retaliation (communication) against his teachers, school, the examination system as a whole, or his family for forcing him into this academic slavery, and to a feeling of aloneness in a world of competition and rivalry (cohesion).

General Nogi's suicide also turns out to be more complicated than a simple *junshi* to follow the emperor in death (cohesion). His suicide note reveals that he had been waiting for a proper time to take his life since 1877, when he lost the regimental colors, a serious military offense, during a civil war. Furthermore, he felt too old to be useful again (Sumiya 1966:460-461). The emperor's death in 1912 provided the opportune moment. Thus, shame and a sense of uselessness (status-role commitment) also contributed to his suicidal wish. Both Mishima's suicide, interpreted above as reproach (communication), and Kawabata's, interpreted as role-commitment, may also relate to social cohesion when it is remembered that suicide by distinguished authors is a part of Japanese literary tradition. Mishima and Kawabata may have been tempted to join their professional ancestors in death.

The above typology may serve as a clue to understanding Japanese suicide, especially its epidemiological characteristics. Specialists have pointed out that Japan has a distinctively high suicide rate among young and old, forming a bimodal curve, and a higher rate among women than do other societies. I suggest that communicational frustrations apply to the young, old, and female alike because of their relative powerless positions, and that they also keenly feel frustrations over social cohesion because of their dependency and socioemotional sensitivity. Role-status frustrations may also affect young and old people most.

Overall, the high suicide rate in Japan—at least in the past—points up the cultural appeal of masochistic behavior. Indeed, most suicide notes end with a statement of self-accusation and apology for causing trouble or for being unfilial. This doubly insures the empathetic appeal of the suicide victim.

CHAPTER 12

Culturally Based Moral Rehabilitation: The Naikan Method

Now that we have examined some manifestations of culture-based strain and deviancy, let us turn to the treatment of deviants or patients. Naturally, methods of rehabilitation vary according to one's philosophy of human behavior. The rehabilitation method that to me best elucidates the core values of Japanese culture is a moralistic type of therapy called Naikan.

A culture inclines toward one of two polar patterns of morality. At one extreme, moral values may be "asocial" in that they are conceived to be more or less independent of social matrices. A moral principle of this type may reside within an individual self, within a transcendental being whose message may be transcribed in scripture, or within nature itself. Morality derives from something beyond social relationships and interaction. In a culture dominated by morality of this type, the moral reformation of a prisoner may cause him to question the validity of the culture's whole system of law from the moral standpoint. He could rationalize his criminal commitment by attributing it to social ills outside his own control. The society, rather than the criminal, may come under attack.

The other extreme is socially contingent morality, morality imbedded in the social matrices. Moral judgment of an action is based upon its social effect, such as whether it hurts others. Here morality tends to support social conformity.

Japanese culture inclines to the latter position more than to the former. Thus, moral reformation of criminals and delinquents in Japan—through Naikan and other culturally based methods—is likely to induce moral conviction and willingness for social conformity simultaneously. John Kitsuse, who first introduced Naikan to English readers (1962, 1965), contends that its objective is to produce "conformance" through reformation.[1]

BACKGROUND

Naikan (*naikanhō*, literally, "method of inner observation") was developed by Inobu Yoshimoto, a devout Buddhist and former businessman, from the idea of *mishirabe*, an ascetic method of self-examination, which he had learned from the Shin sect of Buddhism. Although of Buddhist origin, Naikan tenets are devoid of religious elements and are claimed to be a purely secular method of moral rehabilitation. Yoshimoto himself emphatically denies the idea of supernatural intervention and dissuades prospective clients from anticipating miraculous salvation. This does not mean that Yoshimoto is no longer religious or that the Naikan practice does not involve religious or other-worldly sentiments. It came to my attention that the residence of Yoshimoto and his family in Yamato-Kōriyama, Nara Prefecture, consists of two sections, the Naikan school (*naikan kenshūjo*), and the Naikan temple (*naikanji*). Yoshimoto admits to calling himself *jūshoku* (chief priest of a temple), and occasionally refers, during a Naikan session, to the "Karma destiny carried over from the previous life." Nonetheless, his primary job is as a teacher and counselor in Naikan treatment, and he carefully distinguishes his two roles, secular and religious.

The Naikan method was first applied by Yoshimoto in 1954 to inmates of penitentiaries and reformatories and later came to be used for treating patients with mental and physical ills. Naikan was later extended to aid in the moral and spiritual training of normal adults and children. Ordinary members of society who

---

1. For information on Naikan, I was able in 1973 to interview Inobu Yoshimoto (1916-   ), the creator of Naikan, and to observe him counseling his clients. With his approval and cooperation, I interviewed three clients as they were undergoing Naikan treatment. Further information was provided by about forty tape recordings of Naikan lectures, sessions, and clients' statements obtained from Yoshimoto. The following studies were also consulted: Sato 1972; Okumura, Sato, and Yamamoto 1972; Yoshimoto 1965; Murase 1971; Suwaki, Yokoyama, and Takezaki 1969; Rokuro Ishida 1968.

have a marital, occupational, or other problem are welcome at Yoshimoto's Naikan school. Some public schools are adopting the Naikan method for moral education. Naikan has also attracted the attention of some company executives for use in the orientation of new employees. There are companies, Yoshimoto claims, in which every person, from president on down through the rank and file, has undergone Naikan treatment. Some people return for repeated treatment: one of the clients I interviewed was back for the seventh time, another for the sixth time.

A successful outcome is naturally the best advertisement, and word of Naikan has spread widely through networks of kinship and friendship. One or more relatives of all the clients I interviewed had been Naikan clients. The actual extent of the use of this method is not known, but it is safe to say that Naikan has been increasingly recognized as a valid rehabilitation method among professionals, particularly psychiatrists, psychologists, and correctional officers. As regards its use in correctional institutions, it was officially reported that[1] six reformatories and fourteen penitentiaries had made use of the Naikan rehabilitation method as of 1960 (Takeda 1972:199).

The Naikan client, whether he is a normal person, patient, or convict, must be self-recruited; without voluntary, self-motivated readiness for the treatment, he cannot hope for successful results. Asked what type of person would be difficult to treat, Yoshimoto readily replied, someone who comes solely because he was told to do so by somebody else. How to motivate prison inmates to volunteer, therefore, is an important problem. As for Naikan counselors, Yoshimoto declares that the only necessary qualification is the experience of Naikan as a client. Today there are a number of unofficial mini-Naikan schools, each led by a former client and disciple of Yoshimoto.

THE NAIKAN METHOD

Naikan treatment involves a specified period of intense, guided self-reflection in isolation from all external stimuli.

Segregation and Immobility

The physical setting for Naikan treatment is one of maximal segregation and immobility of the client. A solitary prison cell is ideal for confining the client and insulating him from external stimuli. One room per client is not always possible, however.

Yoshimoto uses three adjacent rooms in his house, placing a client in a corner of a room screened from other clients by a folding partition. Twelve corners being available in the three rooms, maximally twelve clients can be treated at a time.

In this secluded corner, three by three feet in size, the client is supposed to sit all day from 5:30 A.M. to 9:00 P.M. and to sleep at night. Except to go to the bathroom, he is not allowed to leave his corner. Every meal, prepared by Mrs. Yoshimoto, is brought to him.

Physical segregation is accompanied by segregation from people and information. The client may not receive any visitors or read or listen to anything from the outside—newspapers, radio, letters, or telephone. His only contact is with the counselor, who comes every hour or so to ask what the client has thought about in the past hour, what questions he has, to suggest what he should reflect on during the next hour, and to give advice and encouragement.

No less important is the injunction against interaction and conversation among the clients, which would be easy to violate since they are separated only by paper screens. A violator of this rule may be asked to discontinue Naikan and leave. To prevent irrelevant communication, a set of rules of conduct are announced to the Naikan client at the outset. They include taking a bath according to a prearranged schedule, leaving slippers outside the latrine as a sign that it is vacant, and placing one's dishes by the screen after a meal so that the cook will know how much one can eat.

The client does not have to sit in formal, rigid style; he may lie down if necessary, postural stiffness being far from the Naikan ideal. He may have his eyes open or closed. But he is cautioned not to fall asleep. All this is to create optimal conditions whereby the Naikan client can concentrate on himself in total privacy.

Normally, one week of the isolated introspection is considered long enough, but this does not mean "graduation" from the Naikan school—there is no graduation at all. Yoshimoto advises the client to continue "dispersed" if not "concentrated" Naikan by himself at home.

Specific References for Self-Reflection

Naikan introspection should lead one to "discover" or "grasp" his true self (*jibun*) (Suwaki, Yokoyama, and Takezaki

1969) through recollections of his past. Unlike free association in psychoanalysis, the recollection of one's past in Naikan must not be free, arbitrary, or diffuse but guided by specific, predetermined codes.

First, there are two points of reference for conceptualization of self: temporal and social. The temporal reference locates the self in a sequence of specified periods in one's past. What periods those are depends upon the client's age, experiences, problem at hand, and other factors. They may range from remote to recent past, from preschool to school age to adulthood. The duration of a period, too, ranges from a few years to decades, which are further broken down, for sequential reflection, into smaller units of appropriate intervals: the interval varies from several years to a few months. For example, the client may be asked to start by reflecting on what he was when he was twenty to twenty-five years old, when he was in the first year of elementary school, or in January and February of a particular year. After he completes that reflection, he will be asked to move on to the next interval, namely, age twenty-six to thirty, the second year of elementary school, or March and April, and so on.

Coupled with the time reference is the social reference. The self is recalled in a specified period *in relation to* a series of significant others. The social reference, too, varies from case to case depending upon the client and upon the period selected. In one's childhood, the most significant other is likely to be one's parent, grandparent, other kin, or schoolteacher; significant others in adulthood will be one's spouse, in-law, child, colleague, employer, or employee. The client may be told to reflect upon his self in the relationship with his mother the year he entered high school. When this task is completed, he may be asked to reflect either upon the same relationship the next year or upon the same year in relation to another significant person, such as his father.

Table 1 depicts these variations in matrix form. The columns refer to a series of significant others from 1 to n, and the rows refer to intervals of a period, also ranging from 1 to n. The Naikan client begins reflection by locating his self in the cell of the first column (SO1, e.g., his mother) and the first row (T1, e.g., his first school year). His next step is to move horizontally or vertically. Horizontally, he moves along the arrow of H1 to place himself in the second column, that is, in relation to a second significant other, such as his grandmother, while remaining in the

Table 1. Matrix of References for Naikan Introspection

Time	Significant Other					
	SO1	SO2	SO3	SO4	SO5	SOn
T1	Self	— — —	— — —	— — — —	— — →	(H1)
T2		— — — — —	— — — —	— — — —	— — — →	(H2)
T3		— — — — —	— — — —	— — — —	— — — →	(H3)
T4						
T5	↓	↓	↓			
Tn	(V1)	(V2)	(V3)			

interval T1. When the first row is completed, technically, a similar sequence is followed along H2. Yoshimoto once called this procedure "horizontal Naikan." The other possibility is "vertical Naikan" where the significant other is fixed while the time reference moves from T1 to T2 to T3 and so on, and then from V1 to V2.

Though this matrix gives an overview of all possible combinations of references for self-reflection, in actual cases only certain cells are chosen for the client. Furthermore, the counselor tends to have a bias for a certain period and a certain significant other, regardless of the client's individual age, experiences, and need. Yoshimoto has recently concluded that the most revealing period is one's elementary school years. That is because every person is more dependent on parental care at that time than in later years; the preschool period is too remote to recall unless the client is very young; and more recent experiences would involve too much self-interest to be amenable to objective recollection. As for the social reference, Yoshimoto singles out mother as the most crucial Alter. The standard beginning for Naikan, then, is to reflect upon how Ego related to his mother when he was in the first year of elementary school. The next step is to move to T2, namely, the second school year, with the mother fixed as the social reference. After that the client is encouraged to proceed to other temporal and social references that might be more relevant to his situation. I am inclined to label the mother/elementary school combination "the primary reference." Needless to say, this general rule does not apply to a person whose mother died early, was remarried, or is otherwise impossible to recall. In that case father, grandmother, aunt, or other surrogate would replace mother as the primary reference.

Given these specific references, the client is further guided in the content of his reflection. This thematic reference consists of three questions the client should ask himself: (a) What care (*sewa*) have I received? (b) What have I done to repay (*okaeshi*)? (c) What troubles (*meiwaku*) or worries (*shimpai*) have I caused (the caretaker)? The client is asked to reflect upon what *sewa* he received from his mother, for example, when he was a schoolboy, what *okaeshi* he did for her, and what *meiwaku* he imposed upon her. Of the three points of the thematic reference, the last is stressed. Yoshimoto allocates reflection time for (a), (b), and (c) in the ratio of 2:2:6.

It is clear that Naikan is far from abstract speculation or meditation on universal, philosophical topics such as What is true? but is reflection guided by specific rules and oriented to concrete events and experiences (Takeda 1972:173-174).

Outcome

The ultimate objective of Naikan is for the client to transform himself through a radical reconceptualization of his past, recalled self. The reconceptualization is directed, as can be inferred from the Naikan method described above, toward an inculcation and reinforcement of some Japanese core values. First, one's past self is to be reconceptualized as totally dependent upon a series of persons, especially one's caretaker. If the client evinces any confidence that he is what he is because of his own capacity and character, this arrogance must be smashed. The counselor will ask, for example, how he would have been able to participate in special school-sponsored events without the support and cooperation of his family. The client may then remember how his mother took on extra work outside the house to earn money to buy him a new outfit for the beginning-of-school ceremony, or to pay his travel expenses for a school study-tour. He would further recall how his mother packed an elaborate lunch with special candies for his school picnic so that he would not lose face in front of competitive classmates. Sometimes the client is asked to calculate how much money it cost the family to bring him up. He would recall that whenever he was sick, he was wholly dependent upon his mother's care around the clock. Along with these specific kindnesses, the depth and intensity of parental indulgence and love are recalled: the client might remember how pleased his father was with his report card and take this as evidence of fatherly indulgence. One client spoke on tape of his marrying into a family without a son and thus becoming its heir. His mother could well have reproached him for having abdicated responsibility as the eldest son in his own family. Instead, she happily threw herself into wedding preparations, buying furniture for him to take to the bride's house, "as if he were a bride entering the husband's house." In recalling this, he could not hold back tears of gratitude. The client thus becomes aware of his absolute helplessness without others' indulgence and acknowledges to the counselor that he has indeed benefited from abundant *sewa* from particular persons.

Awareness of one's dependency upon another's caretaking and indulgence is accompanied by a sense of *on* debt and concern for repayment (*okaeshi*). Although itemization of *okaeshi* deeds is on the Naikan agenda, the client is expected ultimately to arrive at the conviction that either he did nothing in *okaeshi* or what he did amounted to nothing in comparison with what he received. Indeed, he might recall, he played around when his help was needed, as when his mother was ill.

That is not all. The debtor not only failed in repayment, but he imposed inexcusable *meiwaku* and *shimpai* upon his benefactor due to his thoughtlessness and lack of *omoiyari*. A high school girl speaking on tape confessed in tears that she had shown no sympathy for her mother, who, while working to support the family, spent extra time and resources to provide for the children's comfort and safety, neglecting her own well-being. When she was in the second year of elementary school, her mother told her to come home from school before dark. One day, in disregard of that warning, she stayed at school until dark, and her mother locked her out to teach her a lesson. Now she realizes that all this was because her mother worried about her, but at the time she was only resentful. A successful thirty-one-year-old businessman recalled on tape how his mother protected him, when there was an air raid during the war, by spreading her body over his. He also remembered resenting and retaliating against his paternal grandmother for mistreating his mother, at the time not realizing that it doubled his mother's hardships by aggravating her relations with her mother-in-law. In his early twenties he left home for Tokyo to achieve success and provide a better life for his mother. He was determined not to tell his family his new address until he succeeded in his goal. Meanwhile, his father became bedridden, and his mother had to work to support the whole family. She finally fell ill and died, which the son did not know until it was too late. Empathizing with the *shimpai* and hardships he had caused his mother, he sobbingly repented and apologized for his stupid, heartless refusal to let her know where he was.

For a convict, delinquent, or other "problem" client, this feeling of having done harm to others tends to be overwhelming. An alcoholic or gambler is encouraged to calculate how much monetary loss he incurred for his family. He then realizes how many people—his wife, parents, children, friends, boss, and so on—have been victimized by his aberration, and how much *meiwaku* they have suffered because of him.

This last point—reflection on the injury inflicted upon others—constitutes the most important part of Naikan. As in other parts, the client is supposed to recall concrete incidents and experiences that definitely and irreversibly establish his guilt, however trivial they may sound.

Before Naikan, clients, particularly the deviant, the handicapped, victims of a broken family, and the mentally or physically ill, tend to be bitter and resentful of parents, more fortunate persons, and the world as a whole, and filled with self-pity. Through Naikan, this resentment and self-pity are expected to be replaced by the realization of one's egocentric social insensitivity, an insurmountable sense of debt and gratitude to others, and a deep empathetic guilt toward those who have suffered because of one's heartless, ungrateful conduct. *Sumanai*, the word in which gratitude is mingled with guilt, is the final word of confession expressive of all these feelings.

What can one possibly do to redeem this guilt? The client is encouraged to resolve or reform himself (e.g., to abstain from alcohol, gambling, stealing, lying), to repay his debt, and to dedicate himself, worthless though he is, to the welfare of his victims and other people. A former gambler, asked by Yoshimoto if he was ready to give up gambling even if someone threatened to kill him, answered yes without hesitation. Indeed, the fear of death is not supposed to hinder a new resolution.

This process of transformation is schematized in Table 2, based on a reciprocity matrix adapted from W. L. Wallace (1969:33).

The rows stand for what Alter (a significant other) has given to Ego, which is divided into benefit, nothing, and injury (abbreviated, respectively, +, o, and −). Alter has benefited, done nothing for, or hurt Ego. The columns refer to what Ego has returned, similarly divided. Ego has repaid (+), done nothing (o), or hurt (−) Alter in return. Cells 1 and 9 represent symmetric reciprocity, where Ego has benefited Alter in return for Alter's beneficence (+/+) or Ego has injured Alter in retaliation against the latter's mistreatment (−/−). The central cell 5 (o/o) shows the

Table 2. Transformation by Naikan

Alter has given:	Ego has returned; will return:		
	Benefit (+)	Nothing (0)	Injury (−)
Benefit (+)	1 +/+ (b)	(d) 2 +/0	3 +/−) (c)
Nothing (0)	(a) 4 0/+	5 0/0	6 0/−
Injury (−)	7 −/+	8 −/0	9 −/−

absence of a reciprocal relationship. All the other cells represent asymmetric relationships, in which one party has overgiven or overreceived benefit or harm from the other. Extreme asymmetry is shown in cells 3 and 7: in 3, Alter has benefited Ego whereas Ego has injured Alter in return; conversely, in 7, Ego has been overly forgiving and generous toward Alter despite the latter's malice.

Prior to treatment, the Naikan client may place his past self in the bottom row, seeing himself a victim of Alter's malevolence. If he had no chance to retaliate, as in cell 9, and instead had to endure the hostility, his resentment toward Alter in particular and toward the world in general for permitting such unfairness would be maximal. Let us suppose that the pre-Naikan client does place himself in cell 7. Through Naikan he will come to realize that Alter, far from having injured Ego, has actually indulged or enormously benefited Ego. Ego moves toward cell 1, as indicated by arrow (a). Furthermore, when he reflects upon what he has returned to Alter, he finds himself in debt, having returned nothing to speak of. He moves along arrow (b). When he starts to enumerate what harm he has inflicted upon Alter, he will be overwhelmed by the extreme imbalance between the *sewa* of beneficent Alter and the *okaeshi* of ungrateful Ego. He now places himself in cell 3, the exact opposite from the starting point, thus completing his self-reconceptualization. When this stage is reached, the client is advised to reorient himself along arrow (d) and resolve to do his best to repay.

This is a simplified schema of Naikan "brainwashing." In actuality the transformation process is far from smooth. In the first few days, the client seems totally confounded, unable to recall anything. In some cases, reflection only serves to reinforce resentment against Alter, inducing Ego to complain about the mistreatment he has received. This phase is called *gaibatsu*, "outer punishment," as against *naibatsu*, "inner punishment"; the counselor reminds the client that what he is doing is *gaikan*, "outer examination," not *naikan*, "inner examination." In other cases, the client may be carried away by what *okaeshi* he has done for others, and start to boast. Speaking on tape, a priest expressed gratitude to his wife but launched into a long discourse on how in return he had saved her from near death through his prayers. The counselor rebuked the priest, saying that it sounded more as

if his wife had saved herself through her own spiritual enlightenment and that a true Naikan exercise would reveal the
client's repentance.

During this initial period, when the client is still unable to
respond as expected, he may be aided by listening to tapes of the
best examples of "confession." He will also be urged by the counselor to take his task seriously, to think of the kind intention with
which his parent, employer, or superior has recommended
Naikan treatment to him. He is told that his stay will cost his boss a
lot of money—room and board plus his salary without work. In
short, the pressure of reciprocal obligation in present social relationships is mobilized to facilitate one's recollection of debts accumulated in past social relationships.

On the third day or so, the client usually begins to emerge out
of confusion, becomes "awakened" to his "true" self, and finds
himself able to "confess" in response to the counselor's question:
"What have you thought about in the last hour?" When self-
reconceptualization is completed, or when cell 3 is reached, the
client, now guilt-ridden and sensitized to his worthlessness, may
have sunk into a state of depression. As Kitsuse has observed, he
may be seized by a temptation to commit suicide "as the only
means of redemption." The counselor then reminds him that

> as undeserving and miserable a person as he has realized himself to
> be, *even so* the society has fed, clothed, and housed him (*ikashite
> morau*). To commit suicide or to abandon hope would be the
> supreme act of ingratitude which would completely deprive his life
> of meaning. He is offered in its stead the opportunity to redeem
> himself by "living as though he were dead" (*shinda tsumoride*), i.e.,
> without regard to one's own egotistic desires. In so living he might
> devote himself to the task of repaying others with a lifetime of
> selfless good works. (Kitsuse 1965:15)

Thus, depression is replaced by hope and joy, and emotional
turmoil by tranquility.

The phases of Naikan may be summarized as: initial confusion or resistance; "awakening"; self-repulsion and depression;
hopefulness and tranquility.

If the "conversion" lasts, the deviant client becomes morally
upright and the ill client may be cured. Yoshimoto frankly admits
that physical cures occur only rarely, but taped confessions reveal
successful cures of arthritis, cirrhosis of the liver, stomach disease,
stuttering, and many symptoms of neurosis. Recognized as a

unique method of psychotherapy, Naikan is widely studied and has been adapted for use by some psychiatrists (for example, R. Ishida 1969). During my interview with Yoshimoto, a new client showed up with a letter of introduction from a psychiatrist who apparently, after an unsuccessful attempt to cure the patient, had sent him to Yoshimoto. General therapeutic results have been noted by professional observers as well as by clients themselves: "One feels one's whole body vitalized and lightened; does not get tired; does not need as much time for sleeping; does not become ill; recovers soon if one gets ill; most chronic diseases are cured before long." "Frustrations and anxiety diminish, while vital energy is heightened; interpersonal relations improve, the feeling of happiness increases, and self-control is strengthened" (Takeda 1972:227).

COUNSELOR-CLIENT INTERACTION

Naikan makes one recall the individuals who have played a significant role in shaping one's life but who have been relegated to the periphery of one's memory. The counselor, or more accurately, the interaction between the counselor and client, is crucial in stimulating, steering, facilitating, and otherwise affecting that recollection.

The first thing that strikes the new client and the observer alike is the unusual humility exhibited by the counselor. Although addressed as *sensei* ("teacher"), Yoshimoto appears never to impose himself in an authoritarian way. The hourly Naikan session is begun and ended with a deep bow from the *sensei* to the client across the screen. This must seem particularly impressive to those who are accustomed to nothing but arrogance or hostility from other people. One can imagine how disarming this gestural humility and politeness might be to a prison inmate.

During the session, the *sensei* listens carefully to what the client has to say, makes short comments for encouragement, correction, suggestion, and at the end thanks the client for his cooperation. He never gives an order but requests or begs the client in the humblest possible language to reflect as he should for "true" Naikan. Humility is further noted in the tapes, where a client's confession is occasionally interrupted by the *sensei*'s comment, addressed to the tape audience, admitting that, to his embarrassment, his client is more advanced than he is in Naikan discipline. He refuses to be considered a specially endowed leader and stresses that Naikan is conducted by the client, that the counselor only has to listen.

His humble behavior, however, does not reduce Yoshimoto's charismatic appeal to many clients, who are apparently awed by his personality or saintly disposition. It may be that charismatic leadership for Japanese is inseparable from the leader's humility, rather than his air of self-imposing righteousness. The persuasive power of such a leader seems to lie in his exemplary role as a model of humility. Indeed, the clients I interviewed were all strikingly humble in behavior and speech. Humility, thus learned from the leader, is likely to make the follower susceptible to persuasion.

Seemingly paradoxical is the other dominant characteristic of the *sensei*'s behavior, his disciplinarian approach. Without being authoritarian or arrogant, Yoshimoto appears rather strict in training and correcting the client. He does not allow the client to deviate from the Naikan rules but admonishes him for not doing a "true" Naikan, for only telling a nice-sounding story, or for a pretentious confession. If for more than three or four days the client fails to produce an expected confession, he may even be told to quit and leave. On tape Yoshimoto told a priest's wife, "Maybe you should quit; you are beyond my capacity." Frightened by this suggestion of abandonment, she suddenly straightened around and began to make a serious confession. Humility and discipline seem to reinforce each other.

Mention should be made of the supportive role played by Yoshimoto's wife, who does all the clients' domestic chores, including cooking and serving meals, laundry, and preparing the hot bath. The woman I interviewed expressed her reverence for Mrs. Yoshimoto, describing her as a true Buddha. The inconspicuous yet heavy sacrifice made by this maternal figure must remind clients of their own mothers.

The sense of indebtedness and self-blame, emphasized in Naikan introspection, is transferred to the counselor-client relationship. The client begins to feel indebted to the counselor (and his wife) and to blame himself if he cannot respond as expected. A client I interviewed said that she felt *sumanai* toward the *sensei* for the first two days because in utter confusion she could not think of a single thing. This is easy to understand since the client is totally dependent upon the counselor and his wife for sustenance as well as counsel.

CHAPTER 13

Shinkeishitsu and Morita Therapy

If Naikan may be considered a folk therapy developed by an extraordinary layman, the topic of this chapter is part of professional psychiatry. Morita therapy is the theory and practice of psychotherapy developed by Dr. Shoma Morita (1874-1938) and refined by his disciples. Jikei Medical School is the academic heir to Morita's legacy, and it publishes a journal primarily dedicated to this therapy.

There is controversy over where to locate Morita therapy with respect to Western psychiatry, psychotherapy, and psychology.[1] Some specialists emphasize the continuity of Morita therapy, or aspects of it, with Western therapeutic tradition, pointing out that it prefigured the Western counterpart but owed an intellectual debt to Western predecessors. Many more characterize Morita therapy as being culturally embedded and discontinuous with Western theory and practice. In taking the latter position, one inclines either positively, to recognize the Japanese contribution to world psychiatry and psychotherapy, or negatively, to discredit the universal applicability of Morita therapy. (For the various arguments, see Jacobson and Berenberg 1952; Kondo 1953; Kumasaka, Levy, and DeVos in Kora 1965:641-645; Miura and Usa 1970; Nakao 1969; Nomura 1962*a*; Noonan 1969; and Veith 1971.)

---

1. For the literature on this subject, I am indebted to Mikako Borden, who reviewed the available sources in her unpublished paper, "Morita Therapy" (1973).

For our purposes, let us view Morita therapy in light of its cultural implications and set aside the technical question of whether it is universally applicable or not. As an ethnotherapy, Morita therapy is closely linked with Buddhism, especially Zen Buddhism. Indeed, Morita and others, including Kondo (1953), Kora and Sato (1958), Miura and Usa (1970), Sato (1972), and Tomonori Suzuki (1970), have revealed this association in their minds by referring to Zen tenets or parables in their discussions of Morita therapy.

Shinkeishitsu

Morita therapy addresses itself to a particular type of neurosis called *shinkeishitsu* or *shinkeishitsu-shō*, which is considered relatively common among Japanese. *Shinkeishitsu* is translated as "nervosity" or "nervosis," which, accoding to a psychiatric dictionary (Hinsie and Campbell 1960), refers to "a wide variety of psychic manifestations that do not substantially handicap an individual in his daily activities, but which stamp him as temperamentally unstable, nervous, eccentric, etc."

Symptoms

While *shinkeishitsu* symptoms are so variable as to defy classification, Morita attempted a threefold classification that has been accepted largely intact by subsequent specialists. Kora, Morita's successor, provided an English version of this classificatory system:

> Type 1 is "ordinary" *shinkeishitsu*, which includes "insomnia, headache, heavy feeling in the head, beclouded feeling in the head, paraesthesia, inordinate feeling of fatigue, lowering of efficiency, feeling of lack of strength, gastrointestinal neurosis, inferiority feeling, timidity and over-anxiousness, sexual troubles, dizziness, writing cramp, ringing in the ear, tremor, loss of memory power, and distraction of attention."

> Type 2, called "obsession" or "phobia," includes such symptoms as "anthropophobia (including erythrophobia, morbid fear of inability to look straight in the eyes of another person, and morbid fear of one's facial expressions); mysophobia; pathophobia; morbid fear of not being able to be perfect, of inability to read properly, of fainting, of inability to go outside, of stammering, of doing something wrong and sinful, of omens, of desultory thoughts; aichmophobia; acrophobia; and inordinate inquisitiveness."

Type 3 is "paroxysmal neurosis" or "anxiety neurosis," whose symptoms are "palpitation seizures, anxiety fits, dyspneal seizures," and the like. (1965:612)

Etiology

These *shinkeishitsu* symptoms are etiologically attributed to two factors: a certain personality disposition called *shinkeishitsu* disposition, which, under an adverse circumstance, is triggered to give rise to a *shinkeishitsu* neurosis; and "psychic interaction," in the course of which a *shinkeishitsu* symptom develops, intensifies, and becomes irreversibly fixed.

The *shinkeishitsu* disposition, often identified with the hypochondriac temperament, is characterized foremost as self-reflective, introspective, or introvert. This self-focus drives one toward excessive self-consciousness, oversensitivity to and preoccupation with an actual or anticipated disturbance in one's mental or physical state. "These people are over-selfconscious and direct their attention to their mental and bodily conditions . . . and come to believe these conditions are unusual or maladjusted" (Kora and Sato 1958:220).

Coupled with introspectiveness is a conflict inherent in the hypochondriac temperament. As phenomenologically defined by Kondo (1966), the hypochondriac temperament involves three attitudes: (1) the subjective, idealistic attitude, which produces, and makes one preoccupied with, a mental image of what one wishes to be, (2) the egocentric attitude, which makes one so selfish that he will not compromise, cannot understand others' feelings, resents others, and indulges in self-pity, and (3) the perfectionist or "all-or-nothing" attitude, a futile wish to make the impossible possible. These attitudes combine to produce an irreconcilable conflict between what things ought to be and what they are, between one's ideal state and one's actual state. The inner conflict of a *shinkeishitsu* disposition was also underscored by Kawai and Kondo: "The characterisitic of the nervosity personality is rather of a complicated character in which both introvert and asthenic inclinations and extrovert and sthenic inclinations are repulsing each other" (1960:93-94). With a more sociological perspective, Fujita (1968) states that the *shinkeishitsu* patient is torn apart by strong anxiety, tenseness, and fear on the one hand, and by the desire to overcome these and to participate in human interaction, on the other. Though he wants to maintain the relaxed state of mind that is possible only within the family, he wants to go out and participate in social activities where one is constrained to be reserved and socially discreet.

The *shinkeishitsu* disposition, then, may be summarized as the propensity toward introvert overattention and autosuggestibility to a bodily or mental disturbance that reinforces and is reinforced by an exaggerated sense of discrepancy between an actual and an ideal state of body or mind, as well as an excessive concern for overcoming this deficiency.

Given this disposition, a person develops a neurotic symptom of types 1, 2, or 3 in the course of psychic interaction (*seishin kōgosayō*)—the second causal factor. Psychic interaction refers to "the process whereby, as concentrated attention is drawn to a sensation, the sensation becomes sharpened, which in turn calls for more attention, the result of which is an increasing intensification of sensation and attention through mutual stimulation" (S. Morita 1960:29). Simply put, psychic interaction refers to a vicious circle or positive feedback between sensation and attention involving autosuggestion.

PHOBIA OF INTERPERSONAL RELATIONS

The foregoing general characterization of *shinkeishitsu* alone is suggestive of a link between a *shinkeishitsu* patient and a normal Japanese with respect to selfhood, the former being only excessive, more conflict-ridden, and therefore morbid in introspective convolution. We find a more specific insight into Japanese culture in a particular *shinkeishitsu* syndrome called *taijin-kyōfu-shō*, anthropophobia or phobia of interpersonal relations. This belongs to type 2, obsessive neurosis, and comprises a variety of symptoms including erythrophobia, fear of eye-to-eye confrontation, fear of body odor, and stranger anxiety. Here we shall concentrate primarily on the fear of eye-to-eye confrontation as a typical example of *taijin-kyōfu-shō*, simply because fairly detailed studies have been done on this subject (Kasahara 1969, 1970).

Fear of eye-to-eye confrontation consists of two elements, often coexisting: fear of being stared at by others and fear of staring at others unintentionally. A typical patient suffering from this phobia would say:

In the presence of others, I get tense and feel ill at ease. I am self-conscious of being looked at by others. At the same time, I am embarrassed as to where to direct my eyes. I cannot decide whether I should look away from other people's eyes or not. I cannot tell to what extent I should stare into the others' eyes. Meanwhile, my looks lose their naturalness, and I end up by staring into others' eyes with piercing looks. Rather, it would be more accurate to say that my eyes become automatically glued to others' eyes. When this happens, rather than fear that I am being looked at, I feel that my own eyes stare at others in an unnatural manner. This is not merely an imagination, it is indeed a fact for me. The reason why I can insist on this is that I know this intuitively by the way others behave towards me. Others look away from me or become restless or make grimaces or leave their seats abruptly. It is psychologically so painful for me to embarrass people in this way, so that I end up by avoiding people as much as possible. (Kasahara 1970:3)

Judging from a sample of student patients, Kasahara estimates that this type of neurosis occurs more among Japanese patients than among patients in other countries. Assuming it to be "typically" Japanese, how do we relate it to Japanese culture and behavior?

Avoidance of Inadvertent Social Exposure

As Japanese behavior is sensitive to situational variation (see chapter 7), especially to the boundary between within and without the intimate situation, the actor is naturally cautious about his exposure to the outside world. More so than one whose culture places less stress on internal-external distinctions, the Japanese actor must control his behavior to conform to situationally prescribed codes of conduct. There are thus cultural grounds for a fear of being caught by unexpected witnesses. The eyes being the central organ for witnessing, one would be most concerned with the possible witness' eye. Inadvertent social exposure may subject one to embarrassment and loss of face. Precautions about unexpected exposure, then, are closely interlinked with Japanese orientation to face.

As we know, Japanese culture provides a set of face-saving mechanisms that are all intended to protect the person from direct, unexpected confrontation with others. These exist not only to defend one's own face but to protect others' face by empathetic discretion. According to the face-saving code of behavior, it is just as shameful to embarrass another person as to be embarrassed by one. Thus, it is interesting to note that the neurotic patients observed by Kasahara (1970:4) "clearly suffer more from the fear of unintentionally staring at people with strange looks than from the fear of being looked at by others." This was even more true of his severe cases of neurosis.

Face is to be protected only in the ritual situation, and therefore one is supposed to be on guard against inadvertent exposure only to those witnesses with whom one is obligated to maintain a ritual relationship. Within the intimate situational domain, one can afford to expose everything of oneself, and in the anomic domain one is indifferent to one's reputation. Japanese uninhibitedly express their strong curiosity about others when in a crowd or with strangers. This hypothesis is substantiated by Kasahara's observation that the patient with the phobia of eye-to-eye confrontation "does not experience any fear in the presence of his own relatives, with whom he is in intimate relationship, or of doctors and counselors. Conversely he never experiences the fear when he finds himself among total strangers in such places as a crowded street. Fear is induced in the presence of those who are neither particularly close nor totally strange . . . people of intermediate familiarity" (1970:4-5). Intermediate familiarity corresponds, in the terms we have used here, with ritual interaction.

Furthermore, one is vulnerable to embarrassment in a situation where the ritual code of behavior is not clearly defined, particularly where there is ambiguity or conflict between intimacy and expected ritual politeness. Such uncertainty arises in a triad more than in a dyad. This general pattern is again manifested in Kasahara's neurotic sample. The patient is unable to establish a triangular interaction pattern: `

> The patient feels relatively at home when talking tête-à-tête with any person whoever happens to be around. But if a third person enters this situation his presence upsets the patient, no matter who he happens to be. The patient automatically directs his sight to this third person. And the patient feels that his action is indeed repulsive, and hurts the other's feeling. (1970:5)

The tendency for a neurotic person to be thrown into ritual rigidity by the intrusion of a third person into his intimate dyad may be further grounded in the socialization process. The child is taught to be sensitive to the punishment of outsiders, such as neighbors, who constitute a nonintimate third party to the intimate dyad of the child and the caretaker. It is my contention that the third party plays an indispensable role in inducing shame among Japanese.

In this connection, Kasahara makes another interesting observation: "Some severe patients insist that they look from the sides of their eye-sockets and their look pierces the person sitting right next to them." They fear "side-glancing" more than looking people in the face. They complain that "their sight field is too expansive or that they can see sideways more than they want to." (1970:6) This seems to indicate the patient's concern about his ritual relationship with a third person who may be watching him without his knowledge and who thus becomes the focus of the patient's own glance.

Sensitivity to Social Approval

A person suffering from fear of eye-to-eye contact is oversensitive to others' opinions of him. He is concerned about how others respond to him, whether they approve or disapprove of him. The patient interprets the slightest motion by someone as an intended message for him. That the patients complain more about unintentionally looking at others than being looked at indicates that they suffer from the feeling that they are hurting and embarrassing others. This "altruistic" concern leads them to visualize themselves as rude, repulsive persons. Self-repulsion thus seems to be a major characteristic of this phobia.

This is not unrelated to the concern for one's own reputation—"egoistic" phobia, involving egoistic interest. As Kasahara rightly points out, both altruistic and egoistic phobias boil down to "the threat of public display of [one's] inadequacy and imperfection" (1970:8). Causing embarrassment to others by staring at them would prompt disapproval, compelling the aggressor himself to lose face as if he were being stared at.

How the patient is sensitized to social sanctions can also be seen by the way he determines that he is repulsive to others. He judges from the way people around him behave: "Others look away from me or become restless or grimace or leave their seat abruptly." Others' eye expressions may be the particular basis for such judgment, which fixes the patient's eyes on theirs all the more. Cooley's "looking-glass" theory seems to apply perfectly to this patient, except that his looking glass distorts reality.

This distortion effect is clearly demonstrated by another phobia of interpersonal relations, the phobia of body odor, which Kasahara also takes into account. The patient afflicted with this phobia is afraid that he emits an unpleasant smell. It is found, however, that this fear does not come from his own olfactory perception, that in fact he cannot smell himself at all. His fear is based on the observation of people around him. Because he sees people cover their nose, cough, and laugh, he concludes that he emits a bad smell. It is not hallucination but social reference that constitutes the basis of this phobia.

Friction among Equals

As a third link between the phobia of interpersonal relations and Japanese culture, we should mention the difficulty peers often have in relating to each other. It was argued with reference to status orientation (chapter 5) that Japanese relate better to people of higher or lower status than to people of the same status.

Whereas superior and inferior complement each other's expectations, a peer relationship evokes competition and jealousy. The reason is that one's social acceptability or prestige is judged by comparison with one's peer.

Kasahara notes that patients with the phobia of interpersonal relations find it most difficult to relate to those who share similar backgrounds. He finds additional significance in the fear of side-glancing in this context: patients fear glancing to the side, which is involved in a relationship with equals, more than the vertical movement of eyes up or down.

We have examined the fear of eye-to-eye confrontation as representative of the phobia of interpersonal relations, which psychiatrists have noted occurs often among Japanese patients. There are other manifestations of this general phobia. Recently some psychiatrists have called attention to *hitomishiri* as the native synonym for stranger anxiety. They say the *hitomishiri*, which usually refers to an infant who fears anybody unfamiliar, may also appear in adult behavior. Maeda (1969) observed adult *hitomishiri* in a sensitivity training session for ten student counselors under the guidance of a psychiatrist. The trainees were instructed to talk freely and express how they felt then and there, which turned out to be the most difficult thing to do. They were reserved, circumspect, concerned about what others would think, and remained silent, sometimes for as long as eight minutes. Talk was initiated and almost monopolized by "elder" participants, who acted as if they were responsible for keeping the participants congenial, while the "rank and file" members appeared dependent on them and chose to be as inconspicuous as possible. The author contrasts this reticence in the Japanese trainees with the behavior of their foreign counterparts, who lose no time in venting their anxiety, excitement, anger, in insisting on their egoistic point of view, attacking the trainer, and in competing for leadership. The author attributes the Japanese *hitomishiri*, as exhibited by these sensitivity-trainees, to two kinds of pressure: (1) worry about causing discomfort to others, hurting them, and consequently being ignored by them and losing their love, and (2) worry about being judged as odd, being laughed at, and as a result losing self-respect. (For more on *hitomishiri*, see *Seishin Bunseki Kenkyū* 1969.)

If this is a characteristic of normal Japanese, the neurotic Japanese suffering from stranger anxiety would be expected to exhibit such reserve or inhibition in an extreme form or to be obsessed with it and carry it over into a situation where such behavior is totally out of place. *Hitomishiri* as a phobic neurosis becomes allied with the fear of eye-to-eye confrontation, erythrophobia, and other phobias of interpersonal relations.

THEORY OF MORITA THERAPY—*Arugamama*

Morita therapy has been considered by its founder and his followers to be best suited for *shinkeishitsu* patients, including those with anthropophobia. Let us briefly look at the theory behind it. The main tenet of Morita therapeutic philosophy is the imperative of accepting things *arugamama*, "as they are." "Let nature take its course" would be an apt slogan. The therapy aims at persuading the patient to abandon his unnatural, "artificial" attitude toward his mental and bodily condition, to renounce his will to keep them under the control of his ego. The patient instead is urged to experience the "natural" motion and processes of mind and body and to get rid of all his presumptions about them (Kondo 1966). All things should be accepted as they are, including one's mental or physical disorder. "The patient must accept the sufferings and worries just as they are, must become 'open-minded,' and avoid any kind of repulsive tendency" (Kora and Sato 1958:221). Morita himself says:

> The main principle of therapy lies . . . in "You *may* leave it as arugamama; you have *no other means* than acceptance of arugamama; you *must* accept it as arugamama." . . . The patient should not try to escape from his pain or fear or overcome and deny his problem. Otherwise, the shinkeishitsu patient will become even more obsessed with his pain, more anxious over his inner conflict, and thus his symptoms will become more complicated. (S. Morita 1953:32; italics added)

The patient is persuaded to accept the *arugamama* philosophy in three ways. First, he is advised to submit to the symptom in defeat and resignation. Second, he is told to "unite" with his illness instead of repelling it. To put it metaphorically, "You do not feel your saliva filthy as long as it stays in your mouth because it is in unity with yourself; once it is spat out, it becomes a filth too repulsive to be swallowed back" (Kora 1964:7). Both the first and second exhortations involve an injunction against resisting, rationalizing away, or denying the fact of suffering and illness. The patient is even encouraged to convince himself of the hopelessness of his problem, instead of trying to fight and overcome it.

The third way may be called a paradoxical confrontation. The patient is brought closer to a straightforward recognition of his problem by being made to enact or produce it. If he has erythrophobia, he will not only be assured that blushing is a natural thing but will be encouraged to blush as often as he can. Someone with insomnia may be encouraged not to sleep at all instead of fearing the anticipated sleeplessness.

Considering the nature of the hypochondriac temperament and psychic interaction, acceptance of *arugamama* by these means appears to be effective in stopping the vicious circle. The patient may learn to take his illness for granted, which may emancipate him from self-repulsion.

Metaphysically, the *arugamama* principle endorses the union of the human self with the external, natural universe, in accordance with the Buddhist ideal. One should submit oneself to nature, be one with it, and face its reality. "Attempting to control yourself by an artificial means is like throwing dice and expecting them to turn up precisely as desired or like pushing the flow of the Kamo River upward. . . . Nature dictates summer to be hot, winter to be cold. It would be artificial to try not to feel heat or not to be sensitized to cold. One should naturally subjugate oneself to and endure the given temperature" (S. Morita 1960:86).

The following aspects of the theory behind Morita therapy are either derivatives or components of the *arugamama* principle: disregard of the past, realization through bodily experience, and emphasis on facts.

Disregard of the Past

Arugamama acceptance implies disregard of one's past. The self is what is to be forgotten rather than recalled and ruminated on. This is where Morita therapy comes into direct opposition to Freudian therapy. While Freudian psychoanalysis compels the patient to recall his remote past, which has been repressed, Morita therapy makes it a virtue to consign the patient's past to oblivion. The one digs up the past, like an archaeologist; the other buries it, like an undertaker. This contrast stems from the different importance placed on the unconscious in the two therapies. While Freudian therapy aims at bringing the unconscious into the conscious sphere, Morita therapy tries to reduce the excessive consciousness to a normal level. This is because *shinkeishitsu* is attributed to the overconsciousness of self and of the gap between the ideal and actual state of affairs. In Morita therapy, the patient's whole trouble is in the conscious, whereas Freudians impute a psychic aberration to the operation of the unconscious.

This further relates to the belief among Morita therapists that *shinkeishitsu* patients intellectualize too much about themselves and their experiences and that this intellectualism should also be banished. In contrast, Freudian treatment not only tries to arouse and maximize rationality in the patient but relies upon his rationality as therapeutic leverage.

In emphasizing forgetfulness of the past, Morita therapy also differs from Naikan therapy. But the latter encourages the client's memory retrieval in a highly selective, prescribed manner, unlike free association in Freudian therapy.

Taitoku Realization

Another contrast with Freudian theory is the "no-questions" policy in Morita therapy. The therapist pays no attention to the patient's questions and discourages him from asking questions. This policy is based on the belief that questioning and answering only increase the patient's preoccupation with his illness and aggravate the hypochondriac disposition through psychic interaction. Thus, therapy does not depend upon an exchange of words between the therapist and the patient. It depends upon the patient's own *taitoku*, literally, "realization through bodily experience." The patient is expected to come to a realization and acceptance of things as they are through his own experience rather than through the therapist's suggestions or instructions.

The stress on *taitoku* realization reflects the Japanese distrust of words, as pointed out by Doi (Morita Ryōhō 1966:727). More importance is attached to nonverbal person-to-person interaction between the therapist and patient than to verbal persuasion and verbal recollection; the therapist's personality and "conviction" are considered more persuasive than his outer "performance" (Aizawa et al. 1968; Sakaguchi 1967). Furthermore, it is "situational" or "chance" experiences and confrontation, rather than systematic reasoning, that offer a therapeutic key.

Jijitsu Principle

Reliance on one's own experience rather than verbal communication derives also from the philosophical position of Morita therapy called *jijitsu-hon'i*, which may be translated "factual principle." The patient is to learn to confront himself directly with the world of facts and to accept them as they are. Counter to the *jijitsu* principle are intellectual thinking and judgment by means of words. So are emotions and moods. One must liberate oneself from those detrimental activities of the mind.

The *jijitsu* principle is supported by the conviction that facts, and facts alone, can be relied upon, and that whatever operates within the mind, whether intellectual or emotional, changes constantly, never stays fixed even for a moment (Kondo 1966). It is interesting to note the contrast between this view and the Platonic realism underlying Western dualistic ontology. In the latter, it is the mind that is capable of permanence and is thus reliable, whereas matter constitutes the constantly changing "appearance" of reality. In Morita therapy, one is told to look to what does exist instead of wasting time conjecturing about what should exist. Likewise, what one does is a fact and therefore important, but what one thinks or feels is irrelevant. The *jijitsu* principle thus links Morita therapy with a sort of behaviorism, as suggested by Nakao (1969).

METHOD OF TREATMENT

Effective Morita therapy requires placing the patient in an environment that will induce his commitment to treatment. Hospitalization is thus essential, as Dr. Tomonori Suzuki, a practicing Morita therapist, found from trying to cure outpatients (T. Suzuki 1970:37). Morita believed about 40 days to be enough for treatment; Suzuki estimates that 90 to 120 days are necessary for a complete cure (1970:40). The following is a brief sketch of the therapeutic method that Morita used for a hospitalized patient. Modifications have been introduced since Morita's time (Ohara and Reynolds 1968), and the method may vary with the therapist, but the procedures followed in the Morita hospital I visited in Kyoto in 1971 seemed fairly close to the "original."

Bed Rest

Morita therapy consists of two major periods of treatment: bed rest and work. The first is a five-to-seven day period of absolute bed rest in total isolation.

> During this absolute bed rest period, [the patient] is denied any form of stimuli, as much as possible. He is made to lie in bed in a room allotted only to himself and is told to lie without doing anything. He is permitted to leave his bed only for meals, for washing his face in the morning, and for answering his physiological needs. He is forbidden to engage in any kind of distraction, including reading, meeting his friends and relatives, listening to radio or watching TV, smoking, or writing. (Kora 1965:625)

This reminds us of the isolation and immobility of Naikan treatment. The difference is that bed rest in Morita therapy leaves the patient entirely to himself whereas Naikan imposes specific tasks upon the client during his isolation. The result of such bed rest seems devastating. The patient is confronted, Kondo declares (1966), with the maximal conflict between what he wishes to be and what he actually is. This generates self-repulsion even more than experienced before treatment began, and the patient's *shinkeishitsu* symptoms are likely to intensify. Left to wallow in his suffering, the patient is told, "If you are worried about your symptoms and conditions, go ahead and worry. If you are suffering from them, suffer to your heart's content" (Kora 1965:625).

Through the experience of extreme despair and hopelessness, the patient learns how to live *with* his sufferings and worries, attains self-acceptance, and relaxes from his idealistic-perfectionistic tensions (Kondo 1966). "The patient may toss about in bed but the more severe the pain, the more likely he is to achieve a cure" (Kondo 1962:16).

Work

After the period of bed rest the patient is put to work. Work therapy is divided into three stages, based on the work load: light, moderate, and heavy. Each stage lasts for five to ten days. During the period of light work, "the patient is greedy for stimuli, the outer world has a fresh charm. Patients are to experience pleasure as pleasure, displeasure as displeasure" (M. Kato 1959). Picking up dead leaves in the yard and scrubbing the floor are typical light jobs. Kondo (1966) stresses that at this stage the patient is supposed to work spontaneously, not because he is forced to.

In the moderate-work stage, tasks are assigned that demand more effort, endurance, and persistence. By this time the patient is expected to accept a difficult task as a challenge. Involvement in work is expected to liberate the patient from self-consciousness and to confer self-confidence through the demonstration of the patient's ability to complete a task. This leads him to *taitoku* realization of his energy and competence.

In the last work stage, the patient learns to do whatever work is necessary in daily life. This is a period for training the patient in the *jijitsu* principle: he is disciplined to take up any task simply because it is necessary, not because he wants to. The practical necessity of work is stressed at this stage. This is to prepare the patient for ordinary life outside the hospital. He is allowed to go out and make contact with the outside world as long as his purpose is "practical," such as shopping.

Fujita has analyzed the two parts of Morita therapy from a sociocultural perspective (1968). Bed rest in isolation forces the patient to look into himself in relation to others, to realize his existence as a part of group life. Work therapy involves the patient's participation in group life, assumption of a social role, and awareness that others depend on him and that he is useful to others.

What stands out in these therapeutic periods, bed rest and work, is their exlusiveness. One is either supposed to be totally immobile or constantly working. No time is allowed for play, recreation, or diversion. This may well follow from the *jijitsu* principle.

The work discussed above is primarily manual work. Even though it discredits intellectual activity, Morita therapy does not prohibit reading and writing. In the last stage of work, reading is permitted. However, books are limited to factual treatises, in accordance with the *jijitsu* principle. Natural science, history, and biographies are allowed, but literature and philosophy are prohibited. The point is that reading as such is not encouraged but only tolerated, the major component of work therapy being physical work. The patient is not to be bothered by his lack of comprehension or inability to memorize what he reads.

Keeping a diary is also allowed—in some hospitals required—after the rest period. The therapist reads the diary and gives comments. If the patient complains in his diary about some fault, such as forgetfulness, the therapist would write a comment like "Why not?" If the patient writes about the hopelessness of his case, the therapist may express his agreement. Here too the patient is prohibited from indulging in emotional fantasies and moods or intellectual thinking and imagination. He is encouraged to write down facts and what he has done, not what he has thought.

Apart from its relevance to the *jijitsu* principle, communication between the patient and therapist through a diary is interesting to those who know that, for Japanese, writing is an important means of self-expression and communication, since direct communication is often considered undesirable or inappropriate. This is an important reason why Freudian psychoanalysis, which depends heavily upon the patient's voluntary, vocal self-expression in the presence of the therapist, does not work well in Japan.

Communal Interaction

Another characteristic of Morita therapy is its gemeinschaft-like community composed of patients, the therapist, and his family. In Morita's original plan, the therapist's own home was to be used as a hospital, and patients were to undergo "home therapy" as members of the "family." Unlike psychoanalysis, in which the therapist listens to the patient for an hour or so at a time in a secluded room on a contractual basis, Morita therapists and patients ideally should "live" together in the same "house" around the clock. This ideal is still in practice at the Kyoto hospital I visited. If the Freudian therapist must put up with the pain of sharing patients' personal secrets, the Morita therapist must subject himself to constant exposure to his patients. For him, therapeutic occasions crop up unexpectedly and at any moment, not just during the session.

Intimacy develops between the therapist and the patients to such an extent that they may bathe together. The reader will recall that bathing is regarded as a social pleasure not simply a hygienic necessity. The patient may scrub the *sensei*'s back or give him a massage. Physical contact is emphasized here again. Given the possibility of such physical intimacy, along with constant exposure to the patients, the therapist's character is as important as his therapeutic skills.

Intimacy occurs not only between the patients and the therapist but extends to the latter's family, particularly his wife. This family-involving relationship often survives the patient's release from the "hospital." The wife of a Morita therapist is quoted as saying:

> To me the patient is like my own child. I attach "chan" [a suffix of endearment] to his personal name. And the patient comes to me whenever he is happy or sad. Such relationships last for decades, and after leaving the hospital patients come to consult on such matters as employment, marriage, and failing in entrance examinations. (Aizawa et al. 1968:812)

Given the Japanese tendency to stranger anxiety, this kind of intimate setting would work better than the typical hospital situation, where bureaucratic impersonality prevails. The homelike intimacy can also be taken advantage of for group therapy, for which Japanese patients would otherwise not be suited because of their stranger anxiety. In fact, Suzuki does use group therapy in his community, along with diary guidance, lectures, round-table discussions, and asking questions of patients in the presence of one another as in a classroom. In diary guidance, he asks the patients in turn to read aloud to the assembled group what they had written on the previous day; he then comments on each. A housewife, for instance, read: "The 13th day in the hospital. Woke up feeling great this morning. Was delighted to feel that on a day like this I could work with full energy." Suzuki commented:

> That sounds very good, but you still have a long way to go. It was all right to work with full energy because you felt good. But if you fall apart and have to go to bed because your mood is not good, that would be called "being at the mercy of your moods." The most important thing in overcoming *shinkeishitsu* is to do whatever you ought to even when your mood is bad. (1970:49)

Side-by-side with intimacy, discipline prevails between therapist-teacher and patient-pupil. In Morita therapy, scolding the patient-pupil is considered beneficial, as indulgence of him with praise is not (Sakaguchi 1967).

Morita therapy provides a clue to Japanese culture in two ways. First, it tries to counter the extremes of cultural preoccupations, such as convoluted introspectiveness and face-orientation. Second, it reinforces cultural values, such as naturalism.

Let us conclude with a comparison of Morita therapy and Naikan therapy. Naikan was originally developed to rehabilitate a social deviant and turn him into a morally upright person, while Morita therapy was developed to transform a mentally disturbed person into a healthy being. Because of this original difference in purposes, there is naturally a gap between the two in ideology and method. Consider the concept of the self alone. Through Naikan, the prison inmate is expected to reconceptualize his self as being deeply indebted to others, totally dependent upon others, and something to be ashamed of. The whole purpose is to build a moral constraint, based on an overwhelming sense of obligation, into his personality. Morita therapy, conversely, aims at liberating the patient from over-self-constraint, enabling him to live naturally and to accept things as they are. If Naikan therapy is a tension-creating process, Morita therapy aims more at tension reduction. How the tension is created or reduced, however, seems based on the common cultural belief that the individual self is not an autonomous, separate entity, and that ideally it should be submerged in nature or the society of which it is only a part.

CHAPTER 14

Spirit Possession:
The "Salvation Cult"

Now we turn to religious behavior, particularly that in which man not only communicates with a supernatural being but assumes a supernatural role through spirit possession. Spirit possession may be considered a manifestation of mental aberration in its dissociation from "natural reality." Or, it may be considered a nonmedical therapy if it heals or alleviates suffering. Which of these is the more accurate description is beyond the scope of this chapter. What concerns us is whether and how spirit possession, either as a pathological phenomenon or as a therapeutic technique, gives us a clue to Japanese cultural values. Spirit possession has been anthropologically studied in the light of Japanese social structure (T. Yoshida 1967, 1972). My focus is on role-taking behavior. The data derive from my fieldwork in 1970 and 1971 among members of the healing-oriented Salvation Cult (my term) in Eastern City.

THEORY OF SPIRIT POSSESSION

The person who assumes a supernatural role must have some awareness of playing that role. Otherwise, he would be incapable of assuming it. This suggests the theory of self developed by G. H.

This chapter is a revised version of the paper, "Taking the Role of the Supernatural 'Other': Spirit Possession in a Japanese Healing Cult" that appears in *Culture-bound Syndromes, Ethnopsychiatry, and Alternate Therapies*, vol. 4 of Mental Health Research in Asia and the Pacific, edited by W. P. Lebra. Honolulu: The University Press of Hawaii, 1976. (For more detailed information on the same cult, see Lebra 1973*b*, 1974).

Mead that the individual is not a self unless he is an object to himself (1967:142). Such a reflexive self develops through one's taking the role of other individuals and responding to it. The role of other persons, thus vicariously assumed, becomes internalized and constitutes "me" as distinct from "I," the subjective side of self. "I" and "me" together make up the whole self.

Mead's concept of self fits the phenomenon of spirit possession remarkably well. Indeed, Yap used it for his interpretation of the possession syndrome. He attributed possession to "a disturbance in the balance of what Mead calls the 'I' and the 'me,' " to "the unusual predominance, temporarily, of one phase of the Self at the expense of the other; of a certain portion of the 'me' at the expense of the 'I' " (1960:126-127).

I shall take Yap's position as my point of departure. While Yap stressed the pathological imbalance of "I" and "me" in possession, I would like to delineate a variety of roles that the possessed can take voluntarily—which is not necessarily pathological. Taking the role of a supernatural other enables one to overcome, however temporarily, role deprivation being suffered in the "real" world, and this may trigger a healing change in the behavior system.

A role that is part of a social system can be taken and played only if other roles in the system are complementarily played. The "central role" to be played by Ego must be complemented by a "counter-role" played by Alter. This requirement of "complementarity" (Bateson 1935, 1971; Watzlawick, Beavin, and Jackson 1967) is no less compelling in the assumption of a supernatural role, no matter how arbitary that role may appear. The complementary role may be played by Ego himself or by other persons. The satisfactory performance of a supernatural role requires Ego or other persons to accept the complementary role willingly. Thus, the complementary role should be as desirable as the supernatural role. This is a big constraint on the repertoire of supernatural roles, and it precludes the randomness of possession behavior. In actuality, however, the problem is not great because internalization of a role through socialization entails internalization of its complementary role; to learn how to play a dominant role, for instance, one must simultaneously learn how to play a submissive role (Bateson 1972:91).

I shall apply these assumptions to the possession behavior

observed in the Salvation Cult. The social-psychological interpretation of possession seems particularly relevant to the Japanese case because Japanese culture sensitizes the individual to role gratification and role frustration as the primary source of his pleasure and pain.

THE CULT

The Salvation Cult was established in 1929 and has continued to flourish, since its founder's death in 1948, under the postwar freedom of religion in Japan. In 1969, membership was estimated at more than 168,000 (Bunkacho 1970). Doctrinally, the Salvation Cult traces its ancestry to Shugendō, the mystic mountain sect, which made the earliest attempt to amalgamate the indigenous Shinto with imported Buddhism and Taoism. This syncretism is at the heart of the Salvation Cult, which reveres all deities and spirits without discrimination, although it recognizes loose rank orders among them. The Shinto pantheon of *kami* ("gods") is worshipped side by side with buddhas of Hindu origin, and supernatural status is conferred upon ancestors and the departed. While "qualified" members study abstract doctrines that were developed by the founder and his successors and that typically involve interpretations of Chinese characters, the rank and file are led to believe in the ubiquity of supernatural beings, including animal spirits.

The difference between leading members and the rank and file is not limited to the beliefs; the difference is also apparent in the places for religious action. Important members operate primarily in the two centers of the cult. One is the "spiritual" center, a shrine complex, which is the most sacred place for members to visit as pilgrims or as religious trainees; the other is the cult's "headquarters," from which the organization is administered. These centers not only take leadership in religious teaching but run "health schools," treating sick members "medically" and prescribing "natural foods," which can be purchased at the cult's store. Ordinary members engage in cult activities most regularly in local branches controlled by local leaders. There were over 300 local branches as of 1971.

My fieldwork during the summers of 1970 and 1971 covered, intensively, two ward branches in Eastern City and, more superficially, three more peripheral branches. I also observed activities at the two centers.

The two ward branches together claim roughly 200 members, although the number of regularly active members is much smaller. Each branch is headed by a woman in her seventies, one a widow, the other a divorcée. In formal membership, the sex ratio is about 2 to 1 in favor of female members, but active members are overwhelmingly female, the ratio being approximately 5 to 1. (This gap between formal and active membership owes partly to the Japanese inclination to register in the name of the head of the household.) In age, the members seemed concentrated in the forties through the sixties.

Cult activities in local branches vary from regular, collective services to more private, informal ones. Collectively, periodic ceremonies are conducted at the branch leader's residence, involving a long, standardized ritual in front of an altar and a lecture by a teacher sent from the headquarters. In addition, as part of regular activities, group visits are made to local shrines, cemeteries, and other supernaturally affected places. The branch is always open to casual visitors (both registered and prospective members) for personal consultation and informal religious services. It is during such casual visits that interaction between a member and the leader is maximally intensified.

I interviewed sixteen members, fourteen females and two males, and made observations of rituals and personal religious services at the branches. The latter were always followed by relaxed conversation and the sharing of the food that had been placed on the altar. The sixteen informants ranged in age from thirty-eight to seventy-eight; a few of them had been members for more than thirty years. Occupationally, they included storekeepers, entertainment-business operators, and school teachers, among others.

SITUATIONS AND BEHAVIOR PATTERNS OF POSSESSION

Possession takes place in different situations. The most "sacred" possession is associated with a ritual called "Five Laws" that is deliberately performed to induce supernatural visitation. The leader takes the role of *chūkaisha* ("mediator") between the visiting spirit and the human host. The host, presented as *bontai* ("temporal body") for the spirit to enter, is a member who is suffering from illness, family friction, or the like, and who seeks a supernatural message that will explain this suffering. Note that the mediator and the host of the spirit are different persons, and that the receiver of the supernatural message is the same as the giver of the message. The *chūkaisha* and *bontai* sit side by side in front of the altar and go through a spirit-inviting ritual, invoking the names of deities and buddhas and repeatedly bowing to the altar. The spirit's arrival is signaled by the sudden rapid movement of the *bontai*'s folded hands in which a special charm is held. Unless unusually resistant, the spirit identifies itself and conveys its message through the *bontai*'s mouth or hands (by tracing letters on the floor) in response to requests and questions by the *chūkaisha*. The spirit is identified at least by sex and, if an ancestral spirit, by the number of generations by which it is separated from its descendant, the *bontai*. Beginners are said to be poor hosts "because their souls are still polluted"; sometimes they are only able to cry or shake. It takes six months, I was told, for a convert to become qualified. During this time the convert is supposed to work at self-purification by means of a meditation ritual called "Secret Law." However, there are devices by which almost anyone can generate some information about the spirit and thus perform a supernatural role. The commonly observed resistance to verbalization is overcome by ritually defined signs of communication: the *bontai* indicates the sex of the spirit, for instance, by pointing to the left or right side of his own body; he indicates the number of ancestral generations by hitting his knee a certain number of times. Whenever the question-and-answer communication becomes deadlocked, the *chūkaisha* gives a binary choice of a yes or no answer. She would ask, "Are you an ancestor or a *kami*? If you are an ancestor, please stretch your hands straight forward. Otherwise, raise your hands over your head." After giving its message the spirit is thanked and asked to return to where it belongs. The spirit that refuses to leave the *bontai* invites reproach from the *chūkaisha*. The whole possession performance is observed by any other members who happen to be present, unless the *bontai* demands privacy. I observed five instances of this possession ritual, one of which was performed especially for my benefit. In addition, one of the branches kept a written record of the possession ritual for a time, and I was permitted to read accounts of sixty-five cases thus recorded.

While members consider this ritualized possession, which tends to be a dramaturgical performance, the most important and legitimate form, a more spontaneous, unstructured possession also takes place. Some informants have experienced "unexpected" possession during the purifying meditation or while chanting a sutra in front of the altar, praying at a local shrine, and the like. Some claimed that spirits had taken control of them while they slept or talked to a neighbor. Spontaneous possession usually does not manifest itself vocally but through gestural simulation of the possessing spirit. If the spirit was a fox, the possessed might jump around like a fox. The snake spirit might be simulated by crawling and wriggling. Walking with a limp would show possession by the spirit of a person who was lame. These experiences were not observed directly but were described in interviews or at branch gatherings.

SUPERNATURAL ROLES

The supernatural visitors relate to the human host, *bontai*, in a number of ways. Both my observations and the written account of possession rituals indicate that the visitor is most likely to be an ancestor or departed kin. Not only ascending generations but descending generations are recognized as supernatural: a living mother may be visited by her dead child or miscarried fetus.

If the spirit is of human origin but is not Ego's kin, it is likely to be the spirit of a person who committed suicide, was killed in warfare, or whose death was otherwise disastrous, in the place where Ego presently resides. A number of informants identified their residential lots as former battlefields where thousands of samurai were buried and whose spirits now disturb the welfare of the current residents. These are called land-related spirits.

Different from these is the animal spirit. The spirit of a fox, for example, is recognized either as the deity who was worshipped by Ego's ancestors generation after generation as the family protector, or as Ego's personal guardian deity.

The other spirits mentioned are more or less miscellaneous, but I am tempted to group some of them into another class called sex-related spirits. Examples are the spirit of Ego's former fiancée, of a divorced husband, of the raped maidservant of Ego's ancestor.

Now let us look at the supernatural roles that the *bontai* takes upon identifying with one of these spirits.

The Supplicant Role

In an overwhelming number of possession cases, the spirit is dependent and supplicant. It suffers from pain, floats about helplessly, and solicits human help for its salvation. The *bontai* discovers that it was this spirit that was causing trouble, most typically sickness, to himself or his family; that the spirit did so only to remind the *bontai* of its suffering and appeal for the *bontai*'s sympathy.

The spirit's suffering usually owes to some *tsumi* ("sin" or "pollution") committed when it was alive in the world. Most often mentioned are *tsumi* of suicide, homicide, adultery, rape, abortion, and miscarriage. They are all considered *tsumi* because a moral standard was violated or because the sanctity of life was breached. They are *tsumi* also because they involve pollution with blood at the site where the action took place. Being killed or dying in a natural disaster is as sinful, in the polluting sense, as killing. Commission of such *tsumi* infuriates the deity governing or residing in that particular location and the deity punishes the spirit by preventing its salvation. My informants frequently referred to "strange deaths" of hanging or drowning; women's "strange deaths" were love suicides in most cases.

The suffering of the spirit is compounded by its isolation from other spirits. Thus, most suffering spirits soliciting human help are also identified as *muen* ("lonely, affinity-less") spirits. A spirit is *muen* not only because of its *tsumi* but because it has been neglected or abandoned by human survivors. For this reason, too, the *muen* spirit must notify an appropriate living person of its loneliness by causing trouble. Salvation for the *muen* spirit means joining a group of its own kind: an ancestral *muen* spirit is anxious to join its own group of ancestors; a *muen* fox spirit should have a shrine specially built for it or be placed in an existing Inari shrine dedicated to the fox spirit.

The supplicant role of the suffering spirit must be complemented by an indulgent or empathetic role. The *bontai* is expected to play the latter role after the possession. It is believed that the spirit is not indiscriminate in choosing a target for its possession. The spirit prefers a person who is responsive, helpful, dependable, and experienced enough to solve its problem. Informants generally believe that blood ties are the strongest attraction for the spirit, and one male informant stressed that the spirit chooses its descendant in the direct line. The *bontai* promises to do his best to relieve the spirit of its suffering, to gratify and please the spirit.

The relationship between the supplicant spirit and the nurturant human is acted out in two rituals. One is *kuyō*, a propitiatory service offered to the spirit. An ancestral spirit, for instance, would ask the *bontai*, through the latter's mouth, to indulge it with *kuyō*. The *kuyō* takes several forms: the repeated incantation of sutras and prayers in front of a tablet that has the spirit's name on it; the repeated pouring of hydrangea tea, believed to be sacred and purifying, over the tablet or any other spot where the spirit resides; and the offering of food and drink that the spirit likes. The last form accentuates the maternal, nurturant role of the human feeder for the hungry, infantlike spirit. Indeed, the spirit quite often is a *muen* infant who solicits maternal help from the *bontai*, for example, by causing pain in the breast. Milk and baby food are then considered the most appropriate *kuyō* offering. Sometimes the spirit specifies what it wants to eat and where the food should be placed.

The other nurturant role performed by the *bontai* for the sake of the spirit is *owabi* ("apology") made to redeem the spirit's *tsumi*. The *bontai* is asked by the spirit to present *owabi* on its behalf, since the spirit is incapable of doing so, at the shrine of the deity against whom the *tsumi* was committed. The spirit tells which shrine is to be visited, how many visits must be made (sometimes every day for a month), the kind of offering that should be taken, and so on. Usually *owabi* is presented at a local Shinto shrine, but if, for example, the *tsumi* has to do with water pollution, the *bontai* will have to visit the shrine of a water deity. A standard statement of apology is given "on behalf of such-and-such spirit."

Many informants told me they had to go to present *owabi* before dawn every morning even in winter. Presentation of *owabi* includes a ritual endurance walk back and forth, in front of the shrine, a hundred times. This is supposed to prove the sincerity of the one making the apology.

Owabi thus involves a substantial sacrifice by the human helper for the sake of the sinful spirit. Some informants stressed that unless *owabi* is completed, the spirit is not permitted to receive *kuyō* and that *owabi* should precede everything else to save the spirit. This sequence is not always followed, however. Nurturance in the performance of *owabi* involves empathetic role substitution: the human helper apologizes to the deity as a substitute for the sinful spirit. We are again reminded of the human's motherlike role as a complement to the infantlike role of the spirit. Indeed, in one recorded case, the spirit of a suffering girl begged its young female *bontai* to search for its missing mother and, if the mother could not be found, for the *bontai* herself to become a surrogate mother.

The two mutually complementary roles, supplicant and nurturant, or *amaeru* and *amayakasu*, are taken sequentially by Ego—the supplicant role during possession, and the nurturant role after possession. During possession, the nurturant role is played by the *chūkaisha*, leader-mediator, in communicating with the spirit. The *chūkaisha*'s role thus involves temporary substitution for the *bontai*, who is busy playing the supernatural role. It is the *chūkaisha* who asks the spirit what it wants and promises to carry out *kuyō* and *owabi* so that the spirit will be perfectly satisfied; the spirit demands food and drink as if from the *chūkaisha*. Being fully aware of this role substitution, the spirit sometimes openly addresses itself to the *chūkaisha*, asking her to do something in its behalf. In one of the ward branches whose activities I observed, the *chūkaisha*, the branch leader, is a grandmotherly woman whom the members indeed call Grandma, as well as *sensei* and *shibu-chō* ("branch head"). She takes a nurturant, indulgent role vis-à-vis the possessed member. Even after possession, she helps the member offer *kuyō* and *owabi*, often accompanying the member to the shrine.

Whether the complementary role is performed by the *bontai* or the *chūkaisha*, it is evident that both the nurturant and succorant roles are well cathected by my informants.

The Reciprocal Role

Though supernatural roles are predominantly of the supplicant type, other role types are seen.

When the suffering of the spirit has been relieved through the *owabi* and *kuyō* offered by the human helper, the spirit is obligated to return the favor. The spirit that appears in possession rituals after the *bontai* has performed such services typically expresses gratitude and promises to repay the debt. If the *bontai* happens to be ill, a cure is promised; a bankrupt man can expect to recover his losses and prosper in business; a single girl is guaranteed to meet a good prospect for a husband. Thus, the supernatural being, like its human counterpart, incurs an *on* debt and is obligated to repay it.

Complementary to the reciprocally obligated role is the role of benefactor—the receiver of gratitude—obviously a desirable role. Not only the *bontai*, but also the *chūkaisha* and the audience at the possession ritual, often receive the spirit's gratitude and promises of repayment since they have helped the *bontai*. General gratitude is expressed to "every member" of the branch and to the cult as a whole.

A widow said that when she was possessed it was always by her deceased mother-in-law. One day the mother-in-law appeared to tell the daughter-in-law, "You are troubled with your husband [the spirit's son], so I shall take him with me." Shortly after this, the informant found her good-for-nothing husband dead, which she seemed to take as a clear indication of her mother-in-law's gratitude.

The Disciplinarian Role

Some ancestors and personal guardian spirits scold the *bontai* harshly. Here the supernatural assumes a disciplinarian role. In a commanding tone using a masculine style of speech, the spirit berates the *bontai*, expressing displeasure with his lack of discipline, sincerity, and devotion. Such a punitive role may be played out not merely verbally, but also physically: in one of the cases I observed, a woman possessed by an ancestor kept saying, "I am displeased," shaking her head disapprovingly and striking her chest violently.

The complementary role taken by the *chūkaisha* during possession is dual. On the one hand, she serves as arbiter, trying to restore harmony between the spirit and the *bontai*. She tries to appease the spirit by assuring it that she will transmit its message to the *bontai* and oversee the latter's self-improvement. On the other hand, the *chūkaisha* occasionally slips into the complementary role to be played by the *bontai*, namely, an apologetic, self-accusatory, docile role. What takes place then is a temporary status reversal between leader and follower, the latter playing an authoritarian role and the former a submissive role. Status normalization follows as soon as possession is over, when the *chūkaisha*, now as the leader, reproves the *bontai* for displeasing the spirit. Comparing the two branches whose activities I observed, the spirit's assumption of a disciplinarian role took place more often in the branch that is headed by a woman of a more disciplinarian character. (The other branch, headed by the indulgent grandmotherly woman, shows a stronger inclination toward the supplicant role.)

Possession can thus gratify the wish to be both dominant and submissive. Also implied in this role is a disguised confession of guilt on the part of the *bontai* for neglecting his spiritual and social obligations. Finally, this role provides an opportunity for a member to demonstrate to others that he has a rigorous standard for religious devotion that keeps him discontented with what he is.

The Retaliatory Role

Similar to the disciplinarian role is the retaliatory role. The difference between the two is that, while the disciplinarian role is activated by a benevolent intention, the retaliatory role is activated by a malevolent one. According to my informants, the malevolence includes anger, curse, and, most commonly, a grudge.

Many instances of possession by animal spirits involved assumption of the retaliatory role. A fox spirit was often angry with the *bontai*'s ancestors for having abandoned it though they owed it so much for protecting their house. Usually these ancestors were samurai who moved from one battlefield to another, not taking the time to serve the house-protecting fox deity. Their worst offense was to destroy the shrine dedicated to the fox spirit. A woman discovered through possession the reason for her husband's neurosis: the fox spirit, angry at having been neglected by her husband's ancestors, decided to punish the descendants of the house.

Spirits of human origin also play a retaliatory role. A divorcée informant was possessed by the spirit of a maid who had served one of her ancestors. The master apparently had raped the maid, said the informant, for she became pregnant and was discharged. In despair, the maid drowned herself in a well, cursing all the descendants of the family. In no case did an ancestor or kin of the *bontai* play a retaliatory role.

The retaliatory role calls forth its complement, the role of the accused, obviously not a desirable one. The difficulty is resolved by expanding the dyadic role into a triad. The *bontai* does not take the role of the accused but of the innocent victim of the spirit's malevolence. The role of the accused is attributed to an ancestor of the *bontai* or of the *bontai*'s spouse. An ancestor angers a spirit, which takes revenge by punishing the wrongdoer's offspring. Such a triadic repercussion in punitive reciprocity is a common theme in Japanese culture; it reinforces the "lineal" focus of self-identity, coupled with the Buddhist idea of karma.

In this triad, the *bontai* is able to identify with the spirit to form an alliance against the sinful ancestor who has caused trouble for spirit and *bontai* alike. One might speculate that the aforementioned divorcée (who happened to be a geisha) may have perceived a parallel between the rapist ancestor and her former husband (or men in general) and between the raped maid and herself.

There are some exceptions to this triadic interchange. The retaliatory spirit sometimes is against the *bontai*, as in possession by a former fiancée or a divorced husband. In such a case, however, the retaliatory role is softened into a more supplicant role, which elicits a nurturant response from the *bontai*.

The retaliatory role merges with the supplicant role whenever the spirit faces the problem of its own salvation. However malevolent it is, a suffering and *muen* spirit depends upon the very person it is cursing for its salvation, calling forth a nurturant role from the *bontai*. A fox spirit will ask the *bontai* to restore its *kami* status by enshrining it, in addition to making *kuyō* offerings.

In triadic retaliation, the *bontai* performs two kinds of *owabi*. First, he assumes the role of the ancestor who was responsible for the spirit's malevolence and apologizes on his behalf to the angry spirit as well as to the deity of a local shrine; he then apologizes to the deity for the sin committed by the retaliatory spirit, that of holding a grudge. Role vicariism is thus doubly performed.

The Status-Demonstrative Role

The ancestral spirit tends to hold prestigious status, typically samurai status. A male informant was possessed many times by Taira Kiyomori, the first warrior-ruler of Japan in the early twelfth century, who identified himself as an ancestor of the *bontai* eighteen generations removed. This motivated the *bontai* to study his genealogical background.

The *bontai* can elevate his status through being possessed by prominent ancestors. In this case the main complementary role is played by the audience, who may be impressed by the disclosure of such distinguished ancestry. Many members do not question the credibility of such information and talk about it admiringly. Some individuals are singled out by leaders or fellow members as coming from a formerly eminent house that has declined.

Ancestors of high status are uniformly sinful, since there is perfect correlation in the members' eyes between power and moral deficiency. Such ancestors killed people, exploited poor commoners to enrich their own coffers, engaged in political trickery, indulged in sexual promiscuity, even seducing a reluctant virgin, and the like.

The *tsumi* committed by a high-status ancestor is certain to activate a retaliatory drive in its victim. This means that the status-demonstrative role and the retaliatory role are mutually complementary and reinforcing. Such complementarity may be responsible for the intimacy observed between a woman once possessed by a victim of her ancestor and a man possessed by his distinguished and sinful ancestor.

The status-demonstrative role also becomes a supplicant role. The ancestor asks the *bontai* to do *owabi* and *kuyō* for the ancestor's sake and for the sake of the victims of his *tsumi*. Taira Kiyomori, in the case mentioned above, asked the *bontai*, the direct descendant of the Taira family, to apologize for Taira Kiyomori's *tsumi* to the guardian deity of the family, and to save the spirits of those killed in warfare between the Taira and Minamoto clans, the two most powerful warrior clans of the time.

There is a variant type of status-demonstrative role. An animal spirit occasionally appears in possession to signify its wish to receive *shugyō* ("religious discipline") at the spiritual center of the cult. The *bontai* grants that wish by sending the spirit to the center from a local ward shrine, which means that the *bontai* goes to the shrine with offerings and "sees the spirit off." The *bontai* is accompanied by the branch leader and fellow members as helpers and witnesses. After several weeks of *shugyō*, the spirit returns to the local shrine, and its homecoming is marked by a ritual to "receive" the returning spirit. During the absence of the spirit, the *bontai* is supposed to undergo the same *shugyō*, as if he were accompanying the spirit. It involves such routine disciplines as getting up early, keeping the house clean, performing religious services regularly, and avoiding meat.

It is believed that the spirit raises its status to that of *kami* after the completion of *shugyō*. The status elevation of the guardian spirit means the status elevation of the *bontai*. Several months after joining the cult, many a member thus gets possessed by a guardian spirit who wants to undergo *shuygō* at the center.

Neither the role of *shugyo* candidate nor that of *shugyō* graduate can be played well unless fellow cult members play a complementary role. The *bontai* must be confident that fellow members will approve of his entering or completing *shugyō*. In an observed case of possession, the *bontai* was informed that her guardian spirit wanted to go to the spiritual center. Instead of willingly accepting its wish, the *bontai* let the spirit decide to postpone *shugyō* because it did not yet qualify. After possession, when the *chūkaisha* reprimanded her for not complying with the spirit's wish, the *bontai* confessed that there was criticism among fellow members about her being jealous of those who had already sent their spirits away for *shugyō*.

The Informant Role

Finally, the supernatural role can be that of an informant. Unlike the roles above, to which the role players are attached as an end, the informant role is an instrumental one used to facilitate communication. A person is able to express himself more freely by taking a supernatural role than by representing himself. The informant role, in other words, allows its player to make a statement to others that would be too embarrassing or audacious to make outside that role.

First, the spirit possessing the *bontai* praises the *bontai*, thanking him for sincerity, devotion, and religious accomplishment. A whole list of ancestors may be named as having been saved by the *bontai*. The spirit sometimes describes in detail what the *bontai* has done for his own self-discipline and for the salvation of many spirits. A young girl had the spirit of her kin praise her and declare that everyone was talking about her favorably.

Along with such self-praise, the *bontai* can express disapproval and hostility toward others. The spirit of a male cousin criticized many relatives of the *bontai*, including the mother, grandmother, and aunt, clearly indicating the *bontai*'s displeasure with them. Criticism is directed against selfishness, greediness, stubbornness, lack of faith, resistance to the cult, and so forth.

The spirit goes so far as to threaten that if the person continues this behavior, misfortune will follow.

The *bontai*'s wish is sometimes expressed in the form of a command by the spirit. If the *bontai* wants to have a new house built for his family, the spirit commands the family to start construction on a certain date. That command was efficacious in one instance, despite strong resistance by the male head of the household.

A credulous audience is a necessary complement to the informant role. The credulous person will be frightened if he is accused in this manner; even if the accused is skeptical, other credulous branch members may apply pressure to make him comply with the spirit's commands.

Cultural Implications

A review of the supernatural role types and their complementary roles leads me to believe that many of the cult members, although they do not form a separate group in socioeconomic status, were (or are) deprived in the social roles available to them; and that through possession they are able to surmount this role deprivation, at least temporarily.

Role-taking behavior through possession in the Salvation Cult can be linked to Japanese culture in two ways; one is explicit and direct, the other implicit and indirect. Some of the supernatural roles taken by the possessed are indicative of the roles Japanese are inclined to play. They epitomize cultural desirables in explicit, unambiguous form. An implicit, less obvious linkage lies in the fact that some supernatural roles seem to be called forth to remove a culturally imposed inhibition and gratify an individual's personal desire. These include the disciplinarian, status-demonstrative, retaliatory, and informant roles. Assumed under secular circumstances, they would be embarrassing or would provoke negative sanctions because the norms of Japanese culture emphasize humility, empathetic forgiveness, patience, self-blame, and subtle communication. Possession by a spirit legitimizes taking the roles suppressed or prohibited by the cultural norms. In short, possession behavior as observed in the Salvation Cult suggests both cultural desirables and cultural inhibitions.

What stands out in the variety of complementary roles is the supplicant-nurturant role pair, which appeared with overwhelming frequency, either singly or in combination with other roles. This might be attributed to the fact that the majority of the cult members are women of middle age and older. I believe, however, that Japanese in general, regardless of age and sex, tend to find gratification in playing a supplicant or nurturant role, or, more likely, both, as was discussed in chapter 4.

CHAPTER 15

Conclusion

To conclude the foregoing endeavor to analyze Japanese behavior, this chapter addresses itself to two major questions that may have occurred to the reader's mind: (1) Are there not any significant differences between two Japanese? and (2) Are the Japanese not changing?

CULTURE, THE INDIVIDUAL, AND ROLE CLUSTER

In the Introduction, a conceptual linkage was given between culture and behavior. Here we shall turn to the linkage between culture and the individual, the latter being the subject who carries culture and emits behavior. Whether or not an individual system—or personality—can be equated to a cultural system so that one may be deduced from the other and vice versa is no longer a vital issue in anthropology. If the equation were accepted, there would have to be uniformity between individuals participating in the same culture. In fact, wide variation is apparent between individuals, so the individual must be considered independent of the cultural system. As A. F. C. Wallace stresses, the relationship between culture and personality should be conceived not in terms of the "replication of uniformity" but of the "organization of diversity" (1970:22-24).

Replication of uniformity and organization of diversity are not necessarily logically opposed, however. The complementarity of two roles, such as male and female, would be impossible to establish or maintain if the two role players did not share an understanding of how a male and a female should behave toward each other, what each can expect from the other, and what sanctions one should be prepared for if one fails to perform the male or female role as expected. Of course, this shared understanding does not mean that male and female behave alike; on the contrary, each may display sexual difference, to maximize complementarity, by acting out the behavior code of his or her own sex while internalizing the code of the opposite sex. This is more easily seen in the superordinate-subordinate relationship, where Ego plays the role of superior toward Alter A and the role of inferior toward Alter B. In interacting with A, Ego exhibits only the behavior of a superior, suppressing the behavior of an inferior; behavior selection is reversed when Ego faces B, so he acts out an inferior's role. It is likely that Ego and the two Alters all share the knowledge of how a superior relates to an inferior and vice versa. G. H. Mead's "taking the role of the other" subsumes not only the complementarity but the shareability of role expectations between individuals (1967). This is not to say that there is perfect agreement between a superior and an inferior on the hierarchical system, nor that an inferior is always willing to play a submissive role without resentment. What is shared is the common basis for communication.

My argument is that uniformity and diversity between individuals are not mutually exclusive but, rather, mutually contingent. It follows that individuals, each being unique, nonetheless have partially overlapping orientations. Logically related to this argument is that the individual system and the cultural system are not completely discrete but are partially overlapping sets. I emphasize the partiality of overlaps because I agree with Wallace that cognitive nonuniformity or misunderstanding may be a "functional desideratum" for a society to sustain itself; "human societies may characteristically *require* the nonsharing of certain cognitive maps among participants in a variety of institutional arrangements" (1970:35).

Indeed it is not necessary, desirable, or possible for Ego to share the whole repertoire of behavior and attributes even with one Alter, let alone more, or to understand the "real" motives, obsessions, and other personal peculiarities of Alter with total accuracy. Sharing and understanding are necessary to the extent that Ego can play his role, if he is so inclined, as prescribed in response to Alter's expectation and predict the next step that Alter may take in response. Culture, then, may be conceived as a total complex of "partial overlaps" of orientations among individuals, cognitive and evaluative at various levels of generality. The overlaps are generated by, and in turn generate, social interaction; thus they occur around an infinite number of role clusters. The individual, too, may be characterized as a set of intraindividual overlaps occurring around a cluster of roles that he plays either serially or simultaneously. Viewed this way, the individual is associated more with "role-personality" or "status-personality" than with "basic personality" (Kardiner 1939; Linton 1945), modal personality, or national character. A more suitable term would be "role-cluster personality." Culture and the individual differ in that culture is incomparably greater in the magnitude, variety, and complexity of the overlaps impinging upon role clusters.

The foregoing view of culture and the individual implies that the two systems, cultural and individual, are linked by the social system, just as the social system and the individual are linked by culture. The social linkage of culture and the individual is especially significant in the Japanese case. The ethos of social relativism legitimizes and accentuates the contingency of the two systems and their relationships on social interlockings, and defies the concept of "core" personality as the locus of culture. In contrast, the individualistic or transcendentalistic ethos would tend to repress the social contingency of culture and personality in the mind of its bearer.

System Maintenance

In order to answer the second question (Are the Japanese not changing?), I shall take an indirect route by asking what mechanisms are conceivable to *maintain* a system. The directions of change will be then suggested with reference to a possible breakdown of system-maintaining mechanisms.

My consistent assumption has been that a culture is not a mere collection of elements distributed at random but a system whose components are at least in part interdependent. Though subjected to external influence as an open system, the culture maintains itself through self-imposed regulation and constraint. Even when it is changing, the direction of change is not random but within a limited range of options. There are two mechanisms of self-regulation: reinforcement and error-correction.

Reinforcement

Reinforcement is a mechanism whereby one element of the system is supported and strengthened by one or more other elements. The underlying assumption is that without support from other elements, single elements will not survive, ultimately resulting in the breakdown of the whole system. We have seen such reinforcement in Japanese culture. The propensity to dependency, for example, is supported and reinforced by the moral imperative of empathy, and vice versa. Likewise, culturally generalized "parenthood" (*oyabun*) is maintained by the equally generalized "filiality" (*kobun*). Status orientation is protected by ritual behavior patterns, and belongingness is reinforced by intimate behavior. Both ritual and intimate patterns of interaction benefit from the stress on empathy: Ego's empathy permits anticipatory communication and other forms of discretion to protect Alter's face, and the perfect, intuitive communication and unity sought in intimate interaction presuppose empathetic understanding. The concern for proper-place occupancy is based upon group belongingness; role commitment is inseparable from identification with the group goal. Role vicariism is made possible by a capacity for empathy and in turn makes "transitive reciprocity" acceptable. As a final example, the morality of *on* prescribing unilateral devotion and obligation in the name of reciprocity is built upon hierarchical orientations and vice versa.

Reinforcement, as illustrated in the foregoing list of arbitrarily selected examples, is based upon, first, the *complementarity* of two or more elements. Complementarity is primarily either social or logical. Social complementarity refers to the reciprocality of two roles—or two role players—such as "parent" and "child," nurturant and supplicant, the helpless and the empathetic, *sempai* and *kōhai*, benefactor-creditor and debtor-repayer, and achiever and admirer or vicarious achiever. Here two mutually supportive role orientations, rooted in cultural values, are respectively "specialized" by two actors. Self-regulation of the culture is attributed to social interlocking involving mutual expectations and sanctions between role incumbents. Reinforcement will occur as long as both sides of the role pairs have a balanced number of candidates.

Logical complementarity refers to the relationship between two or more cultural elements wherein one element is instrumental to another, one is a necessary condition for another to materialize, or one logically implies or presupposes another. Commitment to proper-place occupancy and, hence, role dedication presupposes a strong sense of group belongingness; hierarchical orientation is a necessary condition for acceptance of the generalized *on* debt, and vice versa; without a readiness to empathize it would be difficult to assume a vicarious role; and so on. This type of complementarity is congruent with the concept of culture as a configuration or syndrome in a logical sense. These two types of complementarity seem to operate together to reinforce parts of the culture, and ultimately the whole ethos.

Reinforcement takes another form when two or more elements, distinct in motivation, compound and stimulate one another to produce the same outcome. This I shall call *equifinality* in the sense of consequential equivalence. Some core values of Japanese culture evince the operation of equifinality. The orientation to achievement or success, for example, is derived from a striving for status elevation, from the urge, out of gratitude and guilt, to repay *on*, and from a dedication to the group, which benefits from a member's achievement directly or vicariously. *Enryo*, social self-restraint, is a product of the suppression of individuality under the pressure of group solidarity and conformity, empathetic considerations for Alter's convenience or comfort, concern to prevent Ego's own embarrassment, and the wish to maintain Ego's freedom by avoiding social involvement without hurting Alter. Both achievement and *enryo* contain two mutually opposed motivations, altruistic and egoistic; the same style of behavior, in other words, can satisfy two or more, often contradictory, desires. Such equifinality may be one of the factors that make intercultural communication difficult.

Let us examine more examples of core values reinforced through equifinality. Among the behavior patterns that have appeared again and again is the stress upon nonverbal communication, or mistrust of words. This cultural bias is supported, first, by the belief that one's *magokoro*, innermost sincerity, is incapable of being adequately expressed through the outer part of the body such as the mouth, which is inclined toward deception. Related to *magokoro* is the importance of the inner feeling of one's self as the mainstay of self-identity, for which words are again a poor substitute. Furthermore, nonverbal, intuitive communication is taken as a sign of solidarity, real understanding, and susceptibility to "social echo." In a group, the total belongingness, physical togetherness, conformity, and empathetic capacity of its members obviate an articulate exchange of messages. That is not all. The direct vocalization of Ego's state of mind may jeopardize Ego's own or Alter's face in ritual interaction by exposing irreversibly what should have been concealed. Thus, face-orientation also discredits verbal communication.

The cultural fixation on mother also has many roots. The total dependency on mother established and encouraged in early socialization keeps an adult Japanese attached to her as the person who is or was always helpful, reliable, and indulgent. This image is combined with that of mother as the ultimate embodiment of *gisei* (both sacrifice and victim), which, linked with the idea of *on* and the obligation of repayment, instills an everlasting guilt in the child. In other words, mother is the primary object of both dependency and empathy, and a cultural symbol of "moral masochism" and moral purity (*magokoro*). The perfect intimacy enjoyed in the mother-child dyad may also be recalled as an antidote to the ritually constraining and alienating world of one's adulthood. We have observed how this mother fixation has been mobilized in the Naikan technique for moral rehabilitation.

The foregoing are just a few manifestations of reinforcement through equifinality. If space permitted, we could similarly explain many more core patterns ranging from the general (e.g., nationalism; faddism) to the specific (e.g., diary-keeping; the popularity of the journeyman gangster hero).

Error-Correction

Whereas reinforcement is a system-maintaining mechanism by which parts of a system support and strengthen one another in a "positive" way, error-correction refers to a "negative" mechanism whereby the error or deviation of one element is controlled and minimized by another element so that the system as a whole can remain in equilibrium. This mechanism prevents one element from going too far at the expense of another thereby creating irreversible tension and instability in the system. One may well use the term "negative feedback."

Error-correction is performed, first, through a *compensatory alternative*. This allows the frustration or conflict generated by one cultural imperative to be reduced, neutralized, or made tolerable by access to a cultural alternative. For instance, the rigid decorum required in ritual behavior is compensated for by the total relaxation and social nudism encouraged in intimate interaction. The overwhelming cultural pressure for social saturation, which includes gregariousness, conformity, performance of obligations, and other forms of self-denial, can be periodically counteracted by the retrieval of the socially immune inner self through self-reflection in isolation. That *akirame*, "resignation," and self-contentment are regarded as wise and mature attitudes provides a tension-reducing alternative to the loser in a culture obsessed with success and status-elevation. Role orientation justifies or requires both commitment to a single role and versatility in performing various roles, which are compensatory for each other.

Similar to but logically distinct from compensatory alternative is a second mechanism, compensatory entrapment, or what might be called *price-payment*, which does not permit one to pursue or accept a cultural desirable without paying a price. What comes to mind immediately is the *on-giri* complex, where solicitation or acceptance of an *on* benefit incurs a *giri* constraint binding the *on* receiver to repayment or to the assumption of an inferior status vis-à-vis the *on* donor. By the same rule of reciprocity, dependency need is fulfilled only at a price. The dependency enjoyed by a protégé is bought by total compliance with his patron. The dependency of a superior upon an inferior attendant, necessary for preserving his status, incurs the superior's loss of freedom, often to the point where the status-attached power is usurped by the attendant. One cannot both accept *omoiyari* and reject meddlesomeness. One cannot eat one's cake and have it too: acquisition of one value goes hand in hand with renunciation of another.

After having paid such prices, often inflated ones, the individual comes to internalize the importance of suppressing his desire or rejecting a tempting offer. At the cultural level, Japanese culture, while endorsing interdependency, reciprocal obligation, benevolence, and kindness, provides safeguards against the easy or eager acceptance of favors, as well as against the unsolicited offer of favors. Hence, dominant values are kept from going to the extreme by the ambivalence articulated in the culture and internalized in the individual.

Third, errors are further checked or corrected by *contradiction* between dominant values. The highly stressed value of belongingness, involving cooperation and sharing, counteracts the pressure of competitiveness for status-elevation and one-upmanship. Likewise, the urge for status display counteracts the virtue of humility. The cult of belongingness underlies strong nationalism, which can turn into xenophobia, but prevalent snobbism is expressed in xenophilia, exalting things alien and disdaining things native. Compulsion for conformity to group norms, submission to a hierarchical order, a strong sense of obligation, and masochistic self-denial and sacrifice—all these are linked with their opposite, "emotional anarchism," which permits an individual any degree of aggressive deviance in the name of purity. At some point or other a compromise is reached, and a fully socialized adult Japanese seems receptive to such a compromise, acknowledging that the world does not run by reason (*rikutsu*) alone. This is facilitated by the cultural tolerance for logical contradiction and ambiguity.

These forms of error-correction may be most responsible for the many "but also's" that Benedict detected in Japanese culture.

SYSTEM INSTABILITY AND CHANGE

The foregoing analysis of system maintenance does not imply that Japanese culture has been or will be stable, immune from disruption and change. Cultural instability and crisis can be explained in terms of the ineffectiveness of the mechanisms of reinforcement and error-correction. Reinforcement will cease to work when one cultural element fails to receive support, complementary or equifinal, from another element. Benevolence and generosity, for instance, will become obsolete when they repeatedly fail to evoke gratitude and repayment of *on*, resulting in social alienation; the willingness for self-sacrifice will be diminished if it is not met by appreciation and admiration. It is not coincidental that the so-called generational discontinuity in Japan today is often attributed to the younger generation's lack of empathetic understanding and appreciation for the enormous sacrifice made by the older generation. The youths, who were brought up in peace and unprecedented affluence, "take everything for granted," rather than appreciate with a mixture of gratitude and guilt, others' sacrifices and hardships. To this complaint of the older generation, the younger generation would retort, "Who asked for sacrifice?" The mechanism of reinforcement then begins to operate in a negative direction toward mutual alienation and withdrawal of support between two cultural elements or two role-players.

System instability can be accounted for by a breakdown of the error-correcting mechanism. Preoccupation with success in the "war of status," if not controlled by a compensatory alternative such as fatalism, resignation, and contentment with one's place, will generate and intensify frustrations and tensions since there are no status winners without status losers. This is an instance of what Bateson calls "symmetric schismogenesis" (1967, 1972). The nationwide compulsion for higher education, accompanied by fierce competition for success in entrance examinations, seems responsible for many pathological phenomena, including truancy and delinquency. The situation will only be aggravated until a new set of compensatory alternatives becomes available. An alternative may be either a form of achievement other than passing an examination or an alternative to achievement itself.

Correction or prevention of errors through price-payment can also collapse. Pleasure will be sought without restraint if the pleasure-seeker is unaware of the price of pain involved; rights will be claimed without paying the price in obligations. Some adults criticize youth, particularly dissenting youth, as overly dependent or prone to *amae*. They say that youth exhibit the dependency wish without hesitation or ambivalence because they are neither aware of or prepared for the price to be paid—the price in freedom, autonomy, or dignity. On the contrary, youth demand freedom and equality at the same time. To these older people, the young rebels are trying to eat their cake and have it too. Meanwhile, there are victims of this transition who can neither eat nor have the cake. An analogy may be drawn of a market in which a system of pricing and exchange is breaking down.

The prevalence of contradictory values may magnify rather than correct errors. The value of sharing and that of getting ahead can stimulate each other and intensify value conflict instead of canceling or tempering each other. The complex of xenophobia and xenophilia is a good example of such "positive feedback," which has come to the fore whenever Japan has come into contact with a more advanced country or culture at a critical period in its history. That positive feedback seems to be at work today.

In what direction is Japanese culture as a system likely to change? If we are justified in labeling the traditional ethos as social relativism, change should be a departure from it, toward unilateral determinism. My research on the generation gap (1971b; also the Appendix) does suggest that the postwar generation, compared with the prewar, parental generation, is weaker in social relativism, less socially sensitive, and has a stronger bias toward unilateral egoism, altruism, and autism. Whether this is a function of economic-technological change; of postwar education; of exposure to TV culture, which precludes the interaction of role players "in the flesh"; or simply of age remains to be seen.

If this difference between generations is really a sign of culture change, Japan might be moving toward the Western model based on the complex of individuality, autonomy, equality, rationality, agression, and self-assertion, and away from the traditional complex of collectivism, interdependence, superordination-subordination, empathy, sentimentality, introspection, and self-denial. I am not ready to say whether this direction is probable or desirable, but I have a hunch that any immediate changes will be constrained or contaminated by the traditional system. The equalitarian value or resistance to authority, for example, may be inseparable from the collectivism-conformism complex, especially unconditional submission to peers' demands, and it would take a long time, if ever, to become locked with the individuality-autonomy complex. In the meantime, equalitarianism intensifies some traditional values. Furthermore, unless it is supported by a new pattern of universalistic, status-free, situation-free behavior and speech, equality is likely to be equated with status reversal or replacement of one status behavior by another. In reversal, an inferior would behave in a rude, arrogant manner and the superior would respond in a respectful, humble manner; in replacement, everyone, regardless of status, would behave as if he were a superior, possibly resulting in the extinction of the inferior's subculture. If neither is found acceptable, a likely alternative would be a cultural mutism, an exaggeration of the traditional mistrust of spoken words.

The speculations above are meant to show that culture change involves neither a total replacement of the old by a new culture nor a random selection. For the time being at least, some parts of the traditional system will be intensified or revitalized and thus will structurally constrain and guide the direction of change.

Generational Gaps in Moral Orientation

In 1970, I administered a sentence-completion test to a sample of adults and youths in Eastern City to study the relative positions of prewar and postwar generations on morality. The following tables show some of the findings. They are tabulations of the responses to eight of the twenty-nine sentence fragments that were given to the sample to complete.

The prewar generation in the sample (identified in the tables as A) was represented by 100 adults ranging in age from forty to seventy-nine; most were in their forties and fifties. The postwar generation (Y) was represented by 98 high school seniors. Each of the tables shows the responses (R) to one sentence fragment (S). The responses are grouped into numbered categories. Figures indicate percentages, except those in the bottom row, which denote total numbers of responses.

Table 1. Consummative Forms of Compensation for Perseverence

S1: If you persevere through all the hardships that you encounter ...

R1	Male		Female		Total	
	A	Y	A	Y	A	Y
1. Relaxation or gratification "You will have an easy life" "Happiness will follow" "There will be pleasure"	23.1	14.3	25.0	21.7	24.2	18.2
2. Functional utility "You will develop self-confidence" "It will be useful for your self-improvement" "It will be beneficial for your adulthood"	20.5	7.1	3.6	2.2	10.5	4.5
3. Desensitization to pain "You will come to feel nothing" "Once passed, it will become a pleasant memory" "The habit will become\part of your personality"	10.3	16.7	8.9	6.5	9.5	11.4
4. Achievement "You can achieve anything" "You can certainly succeed"	5.1	14.3	8.9	13.0	7.4	13.6

| | 5.1 | 2.4 | 7.1 | 4.3 | 6.3 | 3.4 |

5. Metaphorical outcome "Some day it will blossom" "It will bear fruit" "The fruit will be sweet"	5.1	2.4	7.1	4.3	6.3	3.4
6. Social result "You will receive cooperation" "You will be recognized" "Every problem will be solved harmoniously"	5.1	0.0	1.8	2.2	3.2	1.1
7. Other specific outcome	0.0	0.0	1.8	0.0	1.1	0.0
8. Unspecific outcome "Something good will come" "You will be rewarded" "The result will be good" "There will be a good time" "There is something you can gain"	30.8	45.2	42.9	50.0	37.9	47.7
TOTAL (N)	39	42	56	46	95	88

Table 2. Compensation for Suffering

S2: Perhaps because I experienced suffering when I was young . . .

R2	Male		Female		Total	
	A	Y	A	Y	A	Y
1. Natural, physiological outcome "I am gray-haired" "My body aches"	5.4	27.9	6.0	15.9	5.7	21.8
2. Economic, occupational outcome "I can now live an easy life" "I have become president of a big company"	10.8	2.3	16.0	6.8	13.8	4.6
3. Personal gratification						
(3a) Relaxation "I am happy now"	32.4 (10.8)	27.9 (7.0)	44.0 (22.0)	45.5 (4.5)	39.1 (17.2)	36.8 (5.7)
(3b) Maturation "I have come to understand what life is" "I have developed good judgment in appraising people"	(18.9)	(20.9)	(20.0)	(31.8)	(19.5)	(26.4)
(3c) Social gratification "People trust me" "I am old and happy, being well taken care of by my children"	(2.7)	(0.0)	(2.0)	(9.1)	(2.3)	(4.6)
4. Desensitization to suffering "Suffering no longer affects me" "I don't feel suffering as suffering"	10.8	16.3	10.0	13.6	10.3	14.9

5. Concern for others' suffering	21.6	16.3	18.0	6.8	19.5	11.5
(5a) Sensitization to others' suffering	(13.5)	(7.0)	(16.0)	(4.5)	(14.9)	(5.7)
"I cannot help offering help when someone is in trouble"						
"I do not want my children to suffer"						
(5b) Concern for fair share of suffering]	(8.1)	(9.3)	(2.0)	(2.3)	(4.6)	(5.7)
"I find today's children spoiled"						
"I am strict with children"						
6. Negative psychological outcome	8.1	7.0	4.0	6.8	5.7	6.9
"My mind is warped"						
"I cannot trust people"						
7. Other	10.8	2.3	2.0	4.5	5.7	3.4
TOTAL (N)	37	43	50	44	87	87

Table 3. Compensation for Kindness

S3: If you are kind to others . . .

	Male		Female		Total	
R3	A	Y	A	Y	A	Y
1. Reciprocal return of kindness "You will be treated kindly by others"	7.5	11.1	8.5	13.0	8.1	12.1
2. Reciprocal return in other forms "You will be helped when in trouble" "You will be rewarded" "You will be thanked"	30.0	35.6	30.5	28.3	30.3	31.9
3. Circulatory return "It will turn around and around and eventually come back to you"	12.5	0.0	8.5	0.0	10.1	0.0
4. Autistic satisfaction "You will feel better" "Your feelings will be enriched"	35.0	28.9	33.9	39.1	34.3	34.1
5. Societal gratification "The world will be at peace" "Society will become easier to live in"	7.5	2.2	11.9	4.3	10.1	3.3
6. Negative result "You will only lose" "It will be returned with viciousness" "You should not expect to be reciprocated"	0.0	20.0	1.7	10.9	1.0	15.4
7. Other	7.5	2.2	5.1	4.3	6.1	3.3
TOTAL (N)	40	45	59	46	99	91

Table 4. Compensation for Filial Piety

S4: If you carry out obligations of filial piety...

R4	Male		Female		Total	
	A	Y	A	Y	A	Y
1. Autistic satisfaction "You will not regret" "You will feel at peace"	27.0	17.1	21.1	38.9	23.4	27.3
2. Gratifying result from child "You, too, will be the receiver of filial piety" "Your child will emulate you"	32.4	0.0	45.6	2.8	40.4	1.3
3. Parental satisfaction "Your parents will be pleased"	5.4	22.0	1.8	30.6	3.2	26.0
4. Other gratification	8.1	39.0	14.0	11.1	11.7	26.0
(4a) Gratifying result from parents "You will receive more allowance"	(0.0)	(4.9)	(0.0)	(2.8)	(0.0)	(3.6)
(4b) Social approval "Neighbors will praise you"	(5.4)	(14.6)	(1.8)	(2.8)	(3.2)	(9.1)
(4c) Societal gratification "Through family harmony, human relations will carry on smoothly and everyone will be happy"	(0.0)	(4.9)	(8.8)	(0.0)	(5.3)	(2.6)
(4d) Gratification of both Ego and others "Both parents and yourself feel good"	(2.7)	(14.6)	(3.5)	(5.6)	(3.2)	(10.4)
5. Naturalness of filial piety "It will be only natural"	13.5	7.3	8.8	11.1	10.6	9.1
6. Negative result or appraisal "Nothing will come out" "Can you go to heaven?"	0.0	7.3	1.8	2.8	1.1	5.2
7. Other	13.5	7.3	7.0	2.8	9.6	5.2
TOTAL (N)	37	41	57	36	94	77

Table 5. Social Indebtedness for a Happy Life

S5: That we can live as happily as we do ...

R5	Male A	Male Y	Female A	Female Y	Total A	Total Y
1. Japanese, nation "Is because Japan has become a great country"	28.2	31.7	20.7	15.2	23.7	24.3
2. The deceased	15.4	2.4	27.6	0.0	22.7	1.4
(2a) Ancestors "Is thanks to the heritage from our ancestors"	(12.8)	(2.4)	(20.7)	(0.0)	(17.5)	(1.4)
(2b) Forerunners and other deceased "Is thanks to those who fought for the country and were killed"	(2.6)	(0.0)	(6.9)	(0.0)	(5.2)	(0.0)
3. Parents "Is thanks to our parents"	7.7	24.4	1.7	39.4	4.1	31.1
4. Other people "Is because of sacrifices made by so many people" "Is thanks to you, everyone"	17.9	7.3	13.8	9.1	15.5	8.1
5. Creditors not mentioned "Is a product of industriousness" "The country has its center, the family has its center"	23.1	29.3	31.0	30.3	27.8	29.7
6. Other	7.7	4.9	5.2	6.1	6.2	5.4
TOTAL (N)	39	41	58	33	97	74

Table 6. Attitude toward *On* Benefactor

S6: Because I once received <u>on</u> from that person ...

R6	Male		Female		Total	
	A	Y	A	Y	A	Y
1. Obligation to repay "I must repay him some time"	15.0	22.9	7.0	15.2	10.3	19.1
2. Willingness to repay "I want to help him" "I will do my best to return the *on*"	57.5	37.5	59.6	52.2	58.8	44.7
3. Inhibition, constraint "I must be patient with him" "I cannot talk back to him"	5.0	25.0	3.5	21.7	4.1	23.4
4. Acknowledgment, unforgetfulness "I must not forget that under any circumstances" "I am grateful"	17.5	4.2	21.1	4.3	19.6	4.3
5. Other	5.0	10.4	8.8	6.5	7.2	8.5
TOTAL (N)	40	48	57	46	97	94

Table 7. Resources for Investment in Home Life

S7: In order to build an ideal home life . . .

R7	Male A	Male Y	Female A	Female Y	Total A	Total Y
1. Energy expenditure "I will work hard" "I make every effort"	14.6	42.2	22.0	23.9	19.0	33.0
2. Moral resolution "I shall live faithfully" "Self-discipline is necessary"	43.9	13.3	27.1	15.2	34.0	14.3
3. Rationality, planning ability "First plan, and then act"	4.9	8.9	1.7	6.5	3.0	7.7
4. Cooperation, communication "Let us better understand each other" "All family members must cooperate"	29.3	28.9	44.1	47.8	38.0	38.5
5. Other	7.3	6.7	5.1	6.5	6.0	6.6
TOTAL (N)	41	45	59	46	100	91

Table 8. Causation or Reason for Success

S8: That he has achieved success . . .

R8	Male		Female		Total	
	A	Y	A	Y	A	Y
1. Energy expenditure, diligence "Is because of his diligence and effort" "Is because he never failed in endurance and effort"	75.0	65.9	68.6	79.6	71.4	73.3
2. Moral virtue "Is thanks to his virtue" "Is because of his sincerity"	7.5	7.3	5.9	2.0	6.6	4.4
3. Rationality, ability "Is because he managed well" "Is because he was farsighted"	0.0	2.4	2.0	0.0	1.1	1.1
4. Social attitude or relationships "Is because he respected others" "Is because of others' help"	2.5	9.8	7.8	6.1	5.5	7.8
5. Undesirable quality "Is a result of his trickery, manipulation, and cruelty" "Is due to his native talent and ugly ambition"	0.0	9.8	0.0	2.0	0.0	5.6
6. Combination of above "Is because of his effort, parents' power, good luck, and mastery over how to get along"	12.5	0.0	11.8	10.2	12.1	5.6
7. Other	2.5	4.8	3.9	0.0	3.3	2.2
TOTAL (N)	40	41	51	49	91	90

Bibliography

Abegglen, James C.
   1958. The Japanese Factory: Aspects of Its Social Organization. Glencoe: The Free Press.
Aida, Yuji
   1970. Nihonjin no ishiki kōzō [The structure of consciousness among the Japanese]. Tokyo: Kōdansha.
Aizawa, Shizuo, et al.
   1968. Morita ryōhō ni okeru shomondai—chiryōsha no kihon-teki taido o chūshin to shite [Problems of Morita therapy: the basic attitude of the therapist]. Seishin igaku [Clinical psychiatry] 10(10):811-815.
Ariga, Kizaemon
   1967. Hōken isei to kindaika [The vestiges of feudalism and modernization]. In Ariga Kizaemon Chosakushū [Collected works of Kizaemon Ariga], edited by T. Nakano, K. Kakizaki, and M. Yoneji, vol. 4. Tokyo: Miraisha.
Asahi Shimbun Special Correspondents
   1972. Guam ni ikita nijūhachinen [Twenty-eight years of life on Guam]. Tokyo: Asahi Shimbunsha.
Bateson, Gregory
   1935. Culture Contact and Schizmogenesis. Man 35:178-183.
   1967. Cybernetic Explanation. American Behavioral Scientist 10(8):29-32.
   1971. The Cybernetics of "Self": A Theory of Alcoholism. Psychiatry 34:1-18.
   1972. Steps to an Ecology of Mind. New York: Ballantine Books.
Beall, Lynnette
   1968. The Psychopathology of Suicide in Japan. The International Journal of Social Psychiatry 14:213-225.
Befu, Harumi
   1966-1967. Gift-giving and Social Reciprocity in Japan. France-Asie/Asia 188:161-177.
   1968. Gift-giving in a Modernizing Japan. Monumenta Nipponica 23:445-456. Reprinted in Lebra and Lebra 1974.

1971. Japan: An Anthropological Introduction. San Francisco: Chandler.

Bellah, Robert N.
1957. Tokugawa Religion. Glencoe: The Free Press.

BenDasan, Isaiah
1970. Nihonjin to yudayajin [Japanese and Jews]. Tokyo: Yamamoto Shoten.

Benedict, Ruth
1946. The Chrysanthemum and the Sword: Patterns of Japanese Culture. Boston: Houghton Mifflin.

Bennett, John W., and Ishino, Iwao
1963. Paternalism in the Japanese Economy: Anthropological Studies of *Oyabun-Kobun* Patterns. Minneapolis: University of Minnesota Press.

Bidney, David
1967. Theoretical Anthropology. New York: Schocken Books.

Blane, Howard T., and Yamamoto, Kazuo
1970. Sexual Role Identity among Japanese and Japanese-American High School Students. *Journal of Cross-Cultural Psychology* 1:345-354.

Blau, Peter M.
1964. Exchange and Power in Social Life. New York: John Wiley and Sons.

Borden, Mikako
1973. Morita Therapy. Manuscript.

Boutflower, Cecil H.
1939. The Individual Versus Society in Japan. Japan Society of London, *Proceedings* 36:1-18.

Bunkachō [National cultural agency]
1970. Shūkyō Nenkan [Yearbook of religion].

Caudill, William
1961. Around the Clock Patient Care in Japanese Psychiatric Hospitals: The Role of the *Tsukisoi*. American Sociological Review 26:204-214.
1962. Patterns of Emotion in Modern Japan. *In* Japanese Culture: Its Development and Characteristics, edited by R. J. Smith and R. K. Beardsley. Chicago: Aldine.

Caudill, William, and Plath, David
1966. Who Sleeps by Whom? Parent-Child Involvement in Urban Japanese Families. *Psychiatry* 29(4):344-366. Reprinted in Lebra and Lebra 1974.

Caudill, William, and Scarr, Harry A.
1962. Japanese Value Orientations and Culture Change. *Ethnology* 1:53-91. Reprinted in Lebra and Lebra 1974.

Caudill, William, and Schooler, Carmi
1969. Symptom Patterns and Background Characteristics of Japanese Psychiatric Patients. *In* Mental Health Research in Asia and the Pacific, vol. 1, edited by W. Caudill and T. Y. Lin. Honolulu: East-West Center Press.

Caudill, William, and Weinstein, Helen
1969. Maternal Care and Infant Behavior in Japan and America. *Psychiatry* 32:12-43. Reprinted in Lebra and Lebra 1974.

Chamberlain, Basil Hall
1971. Japanese Things. Rutland, Vt., and Tokyo: Charles E. Tuttle.

Cooley, Charles H.
1902. Human Nature and the Social Order. New York: Scribner.

DeVos, George A.
1960. The Relation of Guilt toward Parents to Achievement and Arranged Marriage among the Japanese. *Psychiatry* 23:287-301. Reprinted in Lebra and Lebra 1974.
1968. Suicide in Cross-Cultural Perspective. *In* Suicidal Behaviors: Diagnosis and Management, edited by H. L. P. Resnik. Boston: Little, Brown.
1973. Socialization for Achievement: Essays on the Cultural Psychology of the Japanese. Berkeley: University of California Press.
n.d. Role Narcissism and the Etiology of Japanese Suicide. Mimeographed. For a revised version of this paper, see DeVos 1973, chap. 17.
DeVos, George, and Wagatsuma, Hiroshi
1959. Psycho-Cultural Significance of Concern over Death and Illness among Rural Japanese. *International Journal of Social Psychiatry* 5:5-19.
Doi, L. Takeo
1962. "Amae": A Key Concept for Understanding Japanese Personality Structure. *In* Japanese Culture: Its Development and Characteristics, edited by R. J. Smith and R. K. Beardsley. Chicago: Aldine. Reprinted in Lebra and Lebra 1974.
1966. *Giri-ninjō*: An Interpretation. *Psychologia* 9:7-11.
1971. Amae no kōzō [The structure of *amae*]. Tokyo: Kobundo.
1972. The Japanese Patterns of Communication and the Concept of *Amae*. Mimeographed.
Dore, R. P.
1958. City Life in Japan. Berkeley and Los Angeles: University of California Press.
1967. Mobility, Equality, and Individuation in Modern Japan. *In* Aspects of Social Change in Modern Japan, edited by R. P. Dore. Princeton, N.J.: Princeton University Press.
Durckheim, Karlfried Graf von
1960. The Japanese Cult of Tranquility. London: Rider.
1962. *Hara*: The Vital Centre of Man. Translated from the German by Sylvia-Monica von Kospoth. London: George Allen and Unwin.
Durkheim, Emile
1951. Suicide. Translated by J. A. Spaulding and G. Simpson. Glencoe: The Free Press.
1961. The Elementary Forms of the Religious Life. Translated by J. W. Swain. New York: Collier Books.
Endo, Shusaku
1972. Gūtara ningengaku [Essays on a sluggard's way of life]. Tokyo: Kōdansha.
Erikson, Erik H., ed.
1965. The Challenge of Youth. Garden City, N.Y.: Doubleday.
Eto, Jun
1969. Amerika to watakushi [America and I]. Tokyo: Kōdansha.
Feuer, Lewis S.
1969. The Conflict of Generations. New York: Basic Books.
Fischer, John L., and Yoshida, Teigo
1968. The Nature of Speech according to Japanese Proverbs. *Journal of American Folklore* 81:34-44.
Fujita, Chihiro
1968. Nihon ni okeru shūdan seishin ryōhō—Morita ryōhō-teki tachiba kara no kentō [Group psychotherapy in Japan from the point of view of

Morita therapy]. *Seishin igaku* [Clinical psychiatry] 10(7):525-529.
1969. Morita ryōhō de iwareru fumon no imi [On the meaning of *fumon*—disregard of symptoms]. *Seishin ryōhō kenkyū* [Practice and theory of psychotherapy] 1(1):68-70.

Furukawa, Gen
1972. Kyōiku kenkyū hōkōki IV [Ambles in educational research IV]. *Sōbun* 107(April):18-21.

Genji, Keita
1961. Santō jūyaku [The third-rate executive]. Tokyo: Shinchōsha.

Goffman, Erving
1959. The Presentation of Self in Everyday Life. Garden City, N.Y.: Doubleday.
1967. Interaction Ritual. Garden City, N.Y.: Doubleday.

Goldberg, Philip A.
1965. A Review of Sentence Completion Methods in Personality Assessment. *In* Handbook of Projective Techniques, edited by Bernard I. Murstein. New York: Basic Books.

Goodenough, Ward H.
1963. Cooperation in Change. New York: Russell Sage Foundation.
1965. Rethinking "Status" and "Role" toward a General Model of the Cultural Organization of Social Relationships. *In* The Relevance of Models for Social Anthropology, edited by M. Banton. London: Tavistock Publications; New York: Frederick A. Praeger.
1968. Description and Comparison in Cultural Anthropology. Chicago: Aldine.

Gorer, Geoffrey
1962. Themes in Japanese Culture. *In* Japanese Character and Culture, edited by Bernard S. Silberman. Tucson: University of Arizona Press.

Gouldner, Alvin W.
1960. The Norms of Reciprocity: A Preliminary Statement. *American Sociological Review* 25:161-178.

Gross, Neal; Mason, Ward S.; and McEachern, Alexander
1958. Exploration in Role Analysis: Studies of the School Superintendency Role. New York: John Wiley and Sons.

Haga, Yaichi
1968. Kokuminsei jūron [Ten attributes of Japanese national character]. *In* Meiji bungaku zenshū [Collected literature of the Meiji era], vol. 44, edited by Sen'ichi Hisamatsu. Tokyo: Chikuma Shobō.

Hamaguchi, Esyun
1966. "Jōkyōteki" kōi no genri [On the principle of "situational" orientation—An analytical view of the national character of the Japanese]. *Shakaigaku hyōron* [Japanese Sociological Review] 16(3):51-74.
1970. Nihonjin no moraru shisutemu [The Japanese moral system]. *In* Hendōki no shakai to kyōiku [Society and education in our changing times], edited by Toshiaki Shigematsu. Tokyo: Reimei Shobō.

Hammond, Peter B.
1971. An Introduction to Cultural and Social Anthropology. New York: Macmillan.

Haring, Douglas G.
1967. Japanese Character in the Twentieth Century. *The Annals of the American Academy of Political and Social Science* 370:133-142.

Hasegawa, Nyozekan
    1966. The Japanese Character: A Cultural Profile. Translated by J. Bester. Tokyo: Kōdansha International Ltd.
Hatano, Isoko
    1954. Shōnenki [Boyhood]. Tokyo: Kōdansha.
Hayashi, Chikio; Nishihira, Shigeki; and Suzuki, Tatsuzo
    1965. Zusetsu Nihonjin no kokuminsei [Japanese national character illustrated]. Tokyo: Shiseidō.
Hearn, Lafcadio
    1904. Japan: An Attempt at Interpretation. New York: Grosset and Dunlap.
Herskovits, Melville J.
    1950. Man and His Works: The Science of Cultural Anthropology. New York: Alfred A. Knopf.
Hibbet, Howard
    1966. Tradition and Trauma in the Contemporary Japanese Novel. *Daedalus* 95(4):925-940.
Higa, Masanori
    1972. The Use of the Imperative Mood in Postwar Japan. *In* Transcultural Research in Mental Health, vol. 2 of Mental Health Research in Asia and the Pacific, edited by W. P. Lebra. Honolulu: The University Press of Hawaii.
Hinsie, Leland E., and Campbell, Robert J., eds.
    1960. Psychiatric Dictionary. New York: Oxford University Press.
Hirschmeier, Johannes
    1970. The Japanese Spirit of Enterprise, 1867-1970. *Business History Review* 44:13-38.
Holloway, Ralph L., Jr.
    1969. Culture: A Human Domain. *Current Anthropology* 10(4):395-412.
Homans, George Caspar
    1958. Social Behavior as Exchange. *American Journal of Sociology* 63:597-606.
Hoshino, Kanehiro
    1970. Bōryokudan no fukuji bunka: oyabun-kobun kankei [The subculture of the violent gang: Leader-follower relationships]. *Kagaku keisatsu kenkyūjo hōkoku: bōhan shōnen hen* [Reports of the national research institute of police science: Research on prevention of crime and delinquency] 11(1):19-32.
Hoshino, Makoto
    1969. Amae no shinri [The psychology of *amae*]. *Gendai no Esupuri* [L'Esprit d'Aujourd'hui] 38(July):144-156.
Hsu, F. L. K.
    1949. Suppression Versus Repression: A Limited Psychological Interpretation of Four Cultures. *Psychiatry* 12:223-242.
    1971. Hikaku bunmei shakai ron: kuran, kasuto, kurabu, iemoto [A comparative study of civilized societies: Clan, caste, club, and *iemoto*], translated by K. Sakuda and E. Hamaguchi. Tokyo: Baifukan.
Hsu, Jing, and Tseng, Wen-Shing
    n.d. Family Relations in Classic Chinese Opera. Mimeographed.
Hulse, Frederick S.
    1962. Convention and Reality in Japanese Culture. *In* Japanese Character and Culture, edited by Bernard S. Silberman. Tucson: University of Arizona Press.

276   *Bibliography*

Iga, Mamoru
      1961. Cultural Factors in Suicide of Japanese Youth with Focus on
      Personality. *Sociology and Social Research* 46(1):75-90.
      1966. Relation of Suicide Attempt and Social Structure in Kamakura.
      International Journal of Social Psychiatry 12:221-232.
      1967. Japanese Adolescent Suicide and Social Structure. *In* Essays in
      Self-Destruction, edited by E. S. Schneidman. New York: Science
      House.
Iga, Mamoru, and Ohara, Kenshiro
      1967. Suicide Attempts of Japanese Youth and Durkheim's Concept of
      Anomie: An Interpretation. *Human Organization* 26:59-68.
Ikeda, Kazuyoshi
      1969. Morita ryōhō to rogoserapi [Morita therapy and logotherapy].
      Kyushu shinkei seishin igaku [The Kyushu neuro-psychiatry] 15(2):160-
      163.
Ikemi, Torajiro
      1972. Naikanhō to shinshin igaku [The Naikan method and
      psychosomatic Medicine]. *In* Zen-teki ryōhō, Naikanhō [Zen-based
      therapy and the Naikan method], edited by Koji Sato. Tokyo: Bun-
      kodo.
Ishida, Eiichiro
      1961. The Culture of Love and Hate. *Japan Quarterly* 8:394-402. Re-
      printed in Lebra and Lebra 1974.
Ishida, Eiichiro, et al.
      1971. Nihonjin no kōkishin to enerugii no gensen [The sources of
      curiosity and energy among Japanese]. Roundtable discussion. *In* Ron-
      shū Nihon bunka [Essays on Japanese culture], special issue of *Enerugii*
      [Energy], edited by T. Umezao and M. Tada, pp. 7-19.
Ishida, Rokuro
      1968. Naikan bunseki ryōhō [Naikan analysis]. *Seishin igaku* [Clinical
      psychiatry] 10:478-484.
      1969. Naikan-Analysis. *Psychologia* 12:81-92.
Ishino, Iwao
      1953. The Oyabun-Kobun: A Japanese Ritual Kinship Institution.
      American Anthropologist 55(5):695-705.
Iwai, Hiroaki
      1963. Byōri shūdan no kōzō [The structure of pathological groups].
      Tokyo: Seishin Shobō.
      1966. Delinquent Groups and Organized Crime. *Sociological Review
      Monograph* 10:199-212. Reprinted in Lebra and Lebra 1974.
Iwai, Hiroshi
      1967. "Shikari" no igi ni tsuite no ni-san no hanron [Opinions on the
      significance of "scolding" in Morita therapy]. *Shinkeishitsu* 7(1/2):18-20.
      1969. Gaikokujin no mita Morita ryōhō—sono hihan no kentō [Exami-
      nation of foreign critiques of Morita therapy]. *Seishin ryōhō kenkyū* [Prac-
      tice and theory of psychotherapy] 1(1):22-31.
Jacobson, Avrohm, and Berenberg, Albert N.
      1952. Japanese Psychiatry and Psychotherapy. *The American Journal of
      Psychiatry* 109:321-329.
Kambe, Tadao
      1972. Nihon ni okeru seinen no jisatsu [Suicide among Japanese adoles-
      cents]. *Kyoto Furitsu Daigaku gakujutsu hōkoku: jinbun* [Scientific reports
      of Kyoto Prefectural University: The humanities] 24:41-46.

Kaplan, Bert, ed.
 1961. Studying Personality Cross-Culturally. New York: Harper and Row.

Kardiner, Abram
 1939. The Individual and His Society. New York: Columbia University Press.

Kardiner, Abram, et al.
 1945. The Psychological Frontiers of Society. New York: Columbia University Press.

Kasahara, Yomishi
 1969. Hitomishiri—seishi (shisen) kyōfushō ni tsuite no rinshō-teki kōsatsu [Hitomishiri—The fear of eye-to-eye confrontation]. *Seishin bunseki kenkyū* [The Japanese journal of psychoanalysis] 15(2):30-33.
 1970. Fear of Eye-to-Eye Confrontation among Neurotic Patients in Japan. Honolulu: Culture and Mental Health Program, Social Science Research Institute, University of Hawaii. Reprinted in Lebra and Lebra 1974.

Kasuga, Shojiro
 1961. Nihon Kyōsantō wa dare no monoka? [To whom does the Japanese Communist Party belong?]. *Bungei shunjū* [Literature year in and year out] (August):74-80.

Kato, Hidetoshi
 1972. Weltanschauung. *Japan Quarterly* 19(1):36-40.

Kato, Hidetoshi, ed.
 1966. Nihon bunka ron [Essays on Japanese Culture]. Tokyo: Tokuma Shoten.

Kato, Hidetoshi, et al.
 1971. Mura no sahō, toshi no sahō [Manners in villages, manners in cities]. Roundtable discussion. *In* Ronshu Nihon bunka [Essays on Japanese culture], special issue of *Enerugii* [Energy], edited by T. Umezao and M. Tada, pp. 121-132.

Kato, Masaaki
 1959. Report on Psychotherapy in Japan. *International Journal of Social Psychiatry* 5:56-60.
 1969. Self-Destruction in Japan: A Cross-Cultural, Epidemiological Analysis of Suicide. *Folia Psychiatrica et Neurologica Japonica* 23:291-307. Reprinted in Lebra and Lebra 1974.

Kawai, Hayao
 1972. Nihon to seiō no jigakōzō no hikaku [A comparative study of the Japanese and Western ego structure]. *In* Gendaijin no byōri [Pathology of modern man], vol. 1, edited by Masaaki Kato, et al. Tokyo: Seishin Shobō.

Kawai, Hiroshi, and Kondo, Kyoichi
 1960. Discussion on Morita Therapy. *Psychologia* 3:92-99.

Kawakita, Michiaki
 1961. The World of *Shibui. Japan Quarterly* 8:33-42.

Kawasaki, Ichiro
 1965. The Japanese Are Like That. Rutland, Vt., and Tokyo: Charles E. Tuttle.
 1969. Japan Unmasked. Rutland, Vt., and Tokyo: Charles E. Tuttle.

Kawashima, Takeyoshi
 1949. Hyōka to hihan [Evaluation and criticism]. *Minzokugaku kenkyū* [Japanese journal of ethnology] 14(4):1-8, 263-270.

278   *Bibliography*

1951a. On no ishiki no jittai [The actual state of *on* consciousness]. *Chūō kōron* [Central review] 66(March):119-129.

1951b. *Giri* [Obligation]. *Shisō* [Thought] (September):759-766.

1957. Ideorogii to shite no kazoku seido [The institutional system of the family as an ideology]. Tokyo: Iwanami.

1967. Nihonjin no hō ishiki [The Japanese consciousness of law]. Tokyo: Iwanami.

Keesing, Roger M., and Keesing, Felix M.
1971. New Perspectives in Cultural Anthropology. New York: Holt, Rinehart, and Winston.

Keisatsuchō Keijikyoku [Detective Bureau, (National) Police Agency]
1970. Shōwa 45 nen no hanzai jōsei [Crime trends in 1970]. Mimeographed.

Kerlinger, Fred N.
1950. Decision-making in Japan. *Social Forces* 30:36-41.

Kiefer, Christie W.
1970. The Psychological Interdependence of Family, School, and Bureaucracy in Japan. *American Anthropologist* 72:66-75. Reprinted in Lebra and Lebra 1974.

Kirkup, James
1970. A Sense of Occasion. *Japan Quarterly* 17(3):272-275.

Kitsuse, John I.
1962. A Method of Reform in Japanese Prisons. *Orient/West* 7(11):17-22.

1965. Moral Treatment and Reformation of Inmates in Japanese Prisons. *Psychologia* 8:9-23.

Kluckhohn, Florence R., and Strodtbeck, Fred L.
1961. Variations in Value Orientations. Evanston, Ill.: Row, Peterson.

Koestler, Arthur
1960. The Lotus and the Robot. New York: Harper and Row.

Kogi, Sadataka
1969. Yakuza jukeisha no kenkyū [Study of imprisoned *yakuza*]. *Hanzaigaku zasshi* [Acta Criminologiae et Medicinae Legalis Japonica] 35(1):34-42.

Koike, Kazuo, et al.
1969. Symposium: Nihonjin wa naze yoku hatarakuka? [Why do Japanese work hard?]. *Gendai no esupuri* [L'Esprit d'Aujourd'hui] 38:211-244.

Kondo, Akihisa
1953. Morita Therapy: A Japanese Therapy for Neurosis. *American Journal of Psychoanalysis* 13:31-37.

1962. Seishin ryōhō ni okeru akuseputansu (ukeire) no igi ni tsuite [Acceptance: Its meaning in psychotherapy]. *Shinkeishitsu* 3(1):13-18.

1966. Morita ryōhō [Morita therapy]. *Seishin igaku* [Clinical psychiatry] 8(9):707-715.

Kora, Takehisa
1964. Morita ryōhō [Morita therapy]. *Shinkeishitsu* 5(1):1-16.

1965. Morita Therapy. *International Journal of Psychiatry* 1:611-645.

Kora, Takehisa, and Sato, Koji
1958. Morita Therapy—A Psychotherapy in the Way of Zen. *Psychologia* 1:219-225.

Kroeber, Alfred L., and Kluckhohn, Clyde
1952. Culture: A Critical Review of Concepts and Definitions. Cam-

bridge, Mass.: Peabody Museum of American Archaeology and Ethnology, Harvard University.

Kroeber, Alfred L., and Parsons, Talcott
1958. The Concepts of Culture and Social System. *American Sociological Review* 23:582-583.

La Barre, Weston
1954. The Human Animal. Chicago: University of Chicago Press.
1962. Some Observations on Character Structure in the Orient. *In* Japanese Character and Culture, edited by Bernard S. Silberman. Tucson: University of Arizona Press.

Lanham, Betty B.
1956. Aspects of Child Care in Japan: Preliminary Report. *In* Personal Character and Cultural Milieu, edited by D. G. Haring. Syracuse, N.Y.: Syracuse University Press.
1966. The Psychological Orientation of the Mother-Child Relationship. *Monumenta Nipponica* 21(3-4):322-333.

Lasswell, Harold D., and Kaplan, Abraham
1950. Power and Society. New Haven, Conn.: Yale University Press.

Lebra, Takie Sugiyama
1969. Reciprocity and the Asymmetric Principle: An Analytical Reappraisal of the Japanese Concept of *On*. *Psychologia* 12:129-138. Reprinted in Lebra and Lebra 1974.
1969-1970. Logic of Salvation: The Case of a Japanese Sect in Hawaii. *International Journal of Social Psychiatry* 16:45-53.
1970. Religious Conversion as a Breakthrough in Transculturation: A Japanese Sect in Hawaii. *Journal for the Scientific Study of Religion* 9:181-196.
1971*a*. The Social Mechanism of Guilt and Shame: The Japanese Case. *Anthropological Quarterly* 44:241-255.
1971*b*. Intergenerational Continuity and Discontinuity in Moral Values among Japanese. Paper presented at the Conference on Culture and Mental Health in Asia and the Pacific, Honolulu, March 15-19, 1971. *In* Youth, Socialization, and Mental Health, vol. 3 of Mental Health Research in Asia and the Pacific, edited by W. P. Lebra. Honolulu: The University Press of Hawaii, 1974. Also reprinted in Lebra and Lebra 1974.
1972*a*. Acculturation Dilemma: The Function of Japanese Moral Values for Americanization. *Council on Anthropology and Education Newsletter* 3(1):6-13.
1972*b*. Reciprocity-based Moral Sanctions and Messianic Salvation. *American Anthropologist* 74:391-407.
1972*c*. Religious Conversion and Elimination of the Sick Role. *In* Transcultural Research in Mental Health, vol. 2 of Mental Health Research in Asia and the Pacific, edited by W. P. Lebra. Honolulu: The University Press of Hawaii.
1973*a*. Shakaijinruigaku-teki ni mita Nihonjin no kokoro to kōdō [A social-anthropological view of Japanese mind and behavior]. *Kokoro to shakai* [Mind and society] 4:35-46.
1973*b*. Ancestral Influence on the Suffering of Descendants in a Japanese Cult. Paper presented at the Ninth International Congress of Anthropological and Ethnological Sciences, Chicago, Aug. 28- Sept. 8, 1973. To be published in *Ancestors*, edited by William H. Newell (The Hague: Mouton).

1974. The Interactional Perspective of Suffering and Curing in a Japanese Cult. *The International Journal of Social Psychiatry*, 23:281-286.

Lebra, Takie S., and Lebra, William P., eds.
1974. Japanese Culture and Behavior: Selected Readings. Honolulu: The University Press of Hawaii.

Lee, Kwang-Kyu, and Harvey, Youngsook K.
1973. Teknonymy and Geononymy in Korean Kinship Terminology. *Ethnology* 12:31-46.

Lifton, Robert Jay
1962. Youth and History: Individual Change in Postwar Japan. *Daedalus* 91:172-197.

Linton, Ralph
1936. The Study of Man: An Introduction. New York and London: Appleton-Century.
1945. The Cultural Background of Personality. New York: Appleton-Century-Crofts.

Maeda, Shigeharu
1969. Hitomishiri [Stranger anxiety]. *Seishin bunseki kenkyū* [The Japanese journal of psychoanalysis] 15(2):16-19.

Malinowski, Bronislaw
1959. Crime and Custom in Savage Society. Paterson, N. J.: Littlefield.

Maruyama, Magoroh
1963. The Second Cybernetics: Deviation-Amplifying Mutual Causal Processes. *American Scientist* 51:164-179.

Maruyama, Masao
1956. Gendai seiji no shisō to kōdō [Ideology and action in contemporary politics], vol. 1. Tokyo: Miraisha.
1972. Rekishi ishiki no kosō [The ancient layer of historical consciousness]. *In* Nihon no shisō [Japanese ideology], vol. 6, edited by Masao Maruyama. Tokyo: Chikuma Shobō.

Matsuda, Michio
1964. Nihon-shiki ikuji-hō [The Japanese method of child-rearing]. Tokyo: Kōdansha.

Matsumoto, Y. Scott
1970. Social Stress and Coronary Disease in Japan: A Hypothesis. *Milbank Memorial Fund Quarterly* 48:9-36.

Mead, George H.
1967. Mind, Self, and Society. Chicago: University of Chicago Press.

Miller, George A.; Galanter, Eugene; and Pribram, Karl H.
1960. Plans and the Structure of Behavior. New York: Holt, Rinehart, and Winston.

Minami, Hiroshi
1949. Shakai shinrigaku no tachiba kara [From the standpoint of a social psychologist]. *Minzokugaku kenkyū* [Japanese journal of ethnology] 14(4):271-274.
1953. Nihonjin no shinri [The psychology of the Japanese]. Tokyo: Iwanami.
1954. Human Relations in Japanese Society. *Annals of Hitotsubashi Academy* 4:148-162.

Minamoto, Ryoen
1969. Giri to ninjō [Obligation and human feelings]. Tokyo: Chūō Kōronsha.

Miura, Momoshige, and Usa, Shinichi
  1970. A Psychotherapy of Neurosis, Morita Therapy. *Yonago Acta Medica* 14:1-17. Reprinted in Lebra and Lebra 1974.
Morita Ryōhō [Morita Therapy]
  1966. Dai sankai seishin igaku konwakai [Morita therapy: Third psychiatric conference]. *Seishin igaku* [Clinical psychiatry] 8(9):716-738.
Morita, Shoma
  1953. Shinkei suijaku to kyōhakukannen no konjihō [The fundamental therapy for neural fatigue and obsessive ideas]. Tokyo: Hakuyōsha.
  1960. Shinkeishitsu no hontai to ryōhō [The essential characteristics and therapy of shinkeishitsu]. Tokyo: Hakuyōsha.
Morris, Charles W.
  1964. Signification and Significance. Cambridge, Mass.: M.I.T. Press.
Morris, Ivan
  1970. Mind Your Language. *Japan Quarterly* 17(4):453-456.
Mugishima, Fumio; Hoshino, Kanehiro; and Kiyonaga, Kenji
  1971. Bōryoku dan'in no danshi to shisei: bōryokudan no dentō-teki fukuji bunka no kenkyū [Tattooing and finger chopping among criminals—A study of the traditional subcultures of organized criminal gangs]. *Kagaku keisatsu kenkyūjo hōkoku: bōhan shōnen hen* [Reports of the national research institute of police science, research on prevention of crime and delinquency] 12(2):131-140.
Murase, Takao
  1971. Naikan Therapy. Honolulu: Culture and Mental Health Program, Social Science Research Institute, University of Hawaii. Reprinted in Lebra and Lebra 1974.
Nadel, S. F.
  1957. The Theory of Social Structure. London: Cohen and West.
Nakamura, Hajime
  1964. Ways of Thinking of Eastern Peoples: India, China, Tibet, Japan. Edited by Philip P. Wiener. Honolulu: East-West Center Press.
Nakamura, Hajime, comp.
  1962. Shin bukkyō jiten [New dictionary of Buddhism]. Tokyo: Seishin Shobō.
Nakane, Chie
  1967. Tate shakai no ningen kankei [Human relations in a vertical society]. Tokyo: Kōdansha.
  1970. Japanese Society. Berkeley and Los Angeles: University of California Press.
Nakao, Hiroyuki
  1969. Kōdō shugi yori mita Morita ryōhō. [Morita therapy from the viewpoint of behaviorism]. *Kyushu shinkei seishin igaku* [The Kyushu neuropsychiatry] 15(2):157-160.
Nakasato, Yoshimasa
  1970. Bōryoku dan'in no kachikan ni kansuru kenkyū, dai nihō—bōryoku dan'in ga kitai suru oyabunzō [Value systems of members of violent gangs, II: Expected traits of gang leaders]. *Kagaku keisatsu kenkyū hōkoku: bōhan shōnen hen* [Reports of the national research institute of police science, research on prevention of crime and delinquency] 11(1):33-37.
Nitobe, Inazo
  1969. Bushido: The Soul of Japan. Rutland, Vt., and Tokyo: Charles E. Tuttle.

Niyekawa, Agnes M.
1966. Authoritarianism in an Authoritarian Culture: The Case of Japan. *International Journal of Social Psychiatry* 12:283-288.

Noguchi, Takehiko, et al.
1968. Anpo to Haneda to no rakusa [The difference between the fight against the Japan-U.S. mutual security pact and the fight at Haneda airport]. Roundtable discussion. *Asahi jaanaru* [Asahi journal] (January 7):126-133.

Nomura, Akichika
1962a. Kokusai-teki ni mita Morita ryōhō zakkan [Morita therapy viewed in an international perspective]. *Shinkeishitsu* 3(1):1-18.
1962b. Psychotherapy in Japan—Morita's Psychotherapy. *Shinkeishitsu* 3(1):25-30.

Noonan, J. Robert
1969. A Note on an Eastern Counterpart of Frankl's Paradoxical Intention. *Psychologia* 12:147-149.

Norbeck, Edward, and DeVos, George
1961. Japan. *In* Psychological Anthropology, edited by F. L. K. Hsu. Homewood, Ill.: The Dorsey Press.

Norbeck, Edward, and Norbeck, Margaret
1956. Child Training in a Japanese Fishing Community. *In* Personal Character and Cultural Milieu, edited by D. G. Haring. Syracuse, N.Y.: Syracuse University Press.

Ogino, Koichi
1968. Amae riron (Doi) o megutte [On Doi's *amae* theory]. *Seishin bunseki kenkyū* [Japanese journal of psychoanalysis] 14(3):5-9.

Ohara, Kenshiro
1965. Nihon no jisatsu: kodoku to fuan no kaimei [Japanese suicide: An interpretation of loneliness and anxiety]. Tokyo: Seishin Shobō.
1970. Jisatsuron: seinen ni okeru sei to shi no ronri [On suicide: The logic of youth on life and death]. Tokyo: Torami Shobō.

Ohara, Kenshiro, and Reynolds, David
1968. Changing Methods in Morita Psychotherapy. *International Journal of Social Psychiatry* 14:305-310.

Okakura, Kakuzo
1923. The Book of Tea. New York: Duffield.

Okumura, Nikichi; Sato, Koji; and Yamamoto, Haruo, eds.
1972. Naikan ryōhō [Naikan therapy]. Tokyo: Igaku Shoin.

Parsons, Talcott
1937. The Structure of Social Action. New York and London: McGraw-Hill.
1951. The Social System. Glencoe: The Free Press.
1954. A Revised Analytical Approach to the Theory of Social Stratification. *In* Essays in Sociological Theory. Glencoe: The Free Press.

Parsons, Talcott, and Shils, Edward A., eds.
1951. Toward a General Theory of Action. Cambridge, Mass.: Harvard University Press.

Pelzel, John C.
1970. Human Nature in the Japanese Myths. *In* Personality in Japanese History, edited by Albert M. Craig and Donald H. Shively. Berkeley and Los Angeles: University of California Press. Reprinted in Lebra and Lebra 1974.

Piers, Gerhart, and Singer, Milton B.
    1953. Shame and Guilt. Springfield, Ill.: Charles C. Thomas.
Plath, David W.
    1964. The After Hours: Modern Japan and the Search for Enjoyment.
    Berkeley and Los Angeles: University of California Press.
    1966. Japan and the Ethics of Fatalism. *Anthropological Quarterly*
    39:161-170.
Reischauer, Edwin O.
    1965. The United States and Japan. 3rd ed. New York: The Viking
    Press.
Richie, Donald
    1971. Japanese Cinema. Garden City, N.Y.: Doubleday.
Riesman, David
    1955. The Lonely Crowd. Garden City, N.Y.: Doubleday.
    1964. Japanese Intellectuals—and Americans. *The American Scholar*
    34(1):51-66.
Rin, Hsien
    1972. Ajia taiheiyō chiiki ni okeru seishin igaku to seishin iryō no kako,
    genzai, mirai [Past, present, and future of psychiatric discipline and
    treatment in Asia and the Pacific]. Roundtable discussion chaired by
    Masaaki Kato. *Seishin igaku* [Clinical psychiatry] 14:980-1001.
Rohlen, Thomas P.
    1971. *Seishin kyōiku* in a Japanese Bank: A Description of Methods and
    Consideration of Some Underlying Concepts. *Council on Anthropology
    and Education Newsletter* 2(1):3-8.
Ryu, Shintaro
    1971. Nakute nanakuse [No people are without bad habits]. Tokyo:
    Kurashi no Techōsha.
Sahlins, Marshall D.
    1965. On the Sociology of Primitive Exchange. *In* The Relevance of
    Models for Social Anthropology, edited by M. Banton. New York:
    Frederick A. Praeger.
Sakaguchi, Minoru
    1967. Morita ryōhō ni okeru shikari no igi [The meaning of scolding in
    Morita therapy]. *Shinkeishitsu* 7(1/2):14-17.
Sakamoto, Masaru
    1963. Dakuryū ni kōshite [Against the polluted current]. *Bungei shunjū*
    [Literature year in and year out] (June):92-100.
Sakuda, Keiichi
    1967. Haji no bunka saikō [Reconsideration of shame culture]. Tokyo:
    Chikuma Shobō.
Sakurai, Shotaro
    1961. On to giri [*On* and *giri*]. Tokyo: Asahisha.
Sato, Koji
    1959. The Concept of "On" in Ruth Benedict and D. T. Suzuki.
    Psychologia 2:243-245.
    1965. I. Yoshimoto: Forty Years of Naikan. *Psychologia* 8:23-24.
Sato, Koji, ed.
    1972. Zen-teki ryōhō, Naikanhō [Zen-based therapy and the Naikan
    method]. Tokyo: Bunkōdō.
Seibu Nippon [Western Japan]. Daily.
Seidensticker, E. G.
    1970a. The Pulverizers. *Encounter* 34:81-87.

284　*Bibliography*

1970*b*. Kazan [The volcano]. Chūō Kōron [Central review] (December):405-406.
Seishin Bunseki Kenkyū [Japanese journal of psychoanalysis]
    1969. [Special issue on *Hitomishiri* (stranger anxiety)]. 15 (2).
Setouchi, Harumi
    1968. Kanojo no ottotachi [Her husbands]. Appeared in a serial from Jan. 21, 1967 to Mar. 19, 1968 in the *Hawaii Hōchi* [Hawaii news] (Japanese language daily). Honolulu: Hawaii Hōchi.
Seward, Jack
    1968. *Hara-Kiri*: Japanese Ritual Suicide. Rutland, Vt., and Tokyo: Charles E. Tuttle.
Sheridan, M. B.
    1970. Symbolist Aspects of the *Nō. Japan Quarterly* 17(4):456-462.
Shimizu, Ikutaro
    1968. Nihon-teki naru mono [Things Japanese]. Tokyo: Ushio Shuppansha.
Silberman, Bernard S., ed.
    1962. Japanese Character and Culture. Tucson: University of Arizona Press.
Slater, Philip E.
    1963. On Social Regression. *American Sociological Review* 28:339-364.
Smith, Robert J., and Beardsley, Richard K., eds.
    1962. Japanese Culture: Its Development and Characteristics. Chicago: Aldine.
Sofue, Takao
    1972. Nihonjin no ningen keisei to sei [Personality development and sex for Japanese]. *Sōgō kyōiku gijutsu* [Techniques for integrative education] 27(1):98-104.
Spiro, Melford E.
    1951. Culture and Personality: The Natural History of a False Dichotomy. *Psychiatry* 14:19-46.
    1961. Social Systems, Personality, and Functional Analysis. *In* Studying Personality Cross-Culturally, edited by B. Kaplan. New York: Harper and Row.
Sugano, Ken
    1972. Hōsō de tsukau keigo no seikaku [Respect words used in broadcasting]. *Bunken geppō* (monthly bulletin of NHK, the national public broadcasting network) Dec.:1-10.
Sugihara, Yoshie, and Plath, David W.
    1969. *Sensei* and His People. Berkeley and Los Angeles: University of California Press.
Sumiya, Mikio
    1966. Dainippon Teikoku no shiren [The great empire of Japan under test]. *In* Nihon no rekishi [The history of Japan], edited by M. Inoue, et al., vol. 12. Tokyo: Chūō Kōronsha.
Suwaki, Hiroshi; Yokoyama, Shigeo; and Takezaki, Haruhiko
    1969. Naikan ryōhō no kenkyū [On Naikan psychotherapy]. *Seishin igaku* [Clinical psychiatry] 11(9):707-711.
Suzuki, Daisetsu
    1960. Zen ni yoru seikatsu [Living by Zen]. Tokyo: Shunjūsha.
Suzuki, Tomonori
    1970. Noirōze no seikatsu shidō [Life guidance for neurotics]. Tokyo: Seishin Shobō.

Tada, Michitaro
1958. Haji to taimen [Shame and face]. *In* Gendai rinri [Contemporary ethics], vol. 6. Tokyo: Chikuma Shobō.

Takeda, Ryoji
1972. Naikanhō [Naikan method]. *In* Zen-teki ryōhō, Naikanhō. [Zen-based therapy and the Naikan method], edited by Koji Sato. Tokyo: Bunkōdō.

Takeuchi, Katashi
1965. On Naikan Method. *Psychologia* 8:2-8.

Takiuchi, Taizo
1972. Oyako shinjū to Nihonjin no kodomokan [Parent-child double suicide and Japanese view of children]. *Kyoto Furitsu Daigaku gakujutsu hōkoku: jinbun* [Scientific reports of Kyoto Prefectural University: The humanities] 24:47-60.

Takizawa, Kiyoto
1972. Gendai bunka to Nihonjin no ijōsei [Current culture and Japanese abnormality]. *In* Gendaijin no byōri [Pathology of modern man], vol. 1, edited by Masaaki Kato, et al. Tokyo: Seishin Shobō.

Tanaka, Sen'o
1971. Aesthetic Background to the Tea Ceremony. *Japan Quarterly* 18(4):414-429.

Tanaka, Yasumasa
1971. Gendai Nihonjin no ishiki [The consciousness of contemporary Japanese]. Tokyo: Chūō Kōronsha.

Tashiro, Saburo
1970. Kōkōsei [High school students]. Tokyo: Iwanami.

Togawa, Yukio, et al., eds.
1953. TAT Nihon-ban shian 1, kaiga tōkaku kensa zuhan [The tentative Japanese version of the thematic apperception test, No. 1]. Tokyo: Kaneko Shobō.

Tōkei Sūri Kenkyūjo Kokuminsei Chōsa Iinkai [Research committee on Japanese national character, The institute of statistical mathematics].
1961. Nihonjin no kokuminsei [A study of Japanese national character]. Tokyo: Shiseidō.
1970. Daini Nihonjin no kokuminsei [The Japanese national character: Second study]. Tokyo: Shiseidō.

Ushijima, Yoshitomo
1961. Seiō to Nihon no ningen keisei [Personality development in the West and Japan]. Tokyo: Kaneko Shobō.

Veith, Ilza
1971. On the "Principle of the Heart" and the Psychiatric Insights of Zen. *The New England Journal of Medicine* 285:1458-1460.

Vogel, Ezra F.
1962. Entrance Examinations and Emotional Disturbances in Japan's "New Middle Class." *In* Japanese Culture: Its Development and Characteristics, edited by Robert J. Smith and Richard K. Beardsley. Chicago: Aldine.
1963. Japan's New Middle Class: The Salary Man and His Family in a Tokyo Suburb. Berkeley and Los Angeles: University of California Press.

Vogel, Ezra F., and Vogel, Suzanne H.
1961. Family Security, Personal Immaturity and Emotional Health in a Japanese Sample. *Marriage and Family Living* 23:161-166.

Wagatsuma, Hiroshi
  1967. The Social Perception of Skin Color in Japan. *Daedalus* 96(2):407-443.
Wallace, Anthony F. C.
  1970. Culture and Personality. 2nd edition. New York: Random House.
Wallace, W. L., ed.
  1969. Sociological Theory: An Introduction. Chicago: Aldine.
Watsuji, Tetsuro
  1962. Rinrigaku [Ethics]. Part 1 of Watsuji Tetsuro zenshū [Collected works of Watsuji Tetsuro], edited by Y. Abe, vol. 10. Tokyo: Iwanami.
Watzlawick, Paul; Beavin, J. H.; and Jackson, D. D.
  1967. Pragmatics of Human Communication: A Study of Interactional Patterns, Pathologies, and Paradoxes. New York: Norton.
Weber, Max
  1947. The Theory of Social and Economic Organization. Translated by A. M. Henderson and T. Parsons. New York: Oxford University Press.
  1958. The Protestant Ethic and the Spirit of Capitalism. Translated by T. Parsons. New York: The Scribner Library.
  1963. The Sociology of Religion. Translated by Ephraim Fischoff. Boston: Beacon Press.
White, Leslie A.
  1949. The Science of Culture: A Study of Man and Civilization. New York: Farrar, Straus.
Wilkins, Leslie T.
  1965. Social Deviance. Englewood Cliffs, N.J.: Prentice-Hall.
Wolff, Kurt H., ed.
  1950. The Sociology of Georg Simmel. New York: The Free Press of Glencoe.
Yamada, Minoru
  1971. Vowa anāru. *In* Ronshū nihon bunka [Essays on Japanese culture], special issue of *Enerugii* [Energy], edited by T. Umezao and M. Tada, pp. 103-106.
Yamamoto, Shichihei
  1972. Okamoto Kozo o unda "Nihongun naimuhan" ["The internal affairs corps of the Japanese army" that produced an Okamoto Kozo]. *Shokun* [You, folks] (August):96-114.
Yamamura, Kozo
  1968. A Re-examination of Entrepreneurship in Meiji Japan (1868-1912). *The Economic History Review* 21:144-158.
Yamamura, Yoshiaki
  1971. Nihonjin to haha [The Japanese and mother]. Tokyo: Tōyōkan Shuppansha.
Yamazaki, Toyoko
  1965. Shiroi Kyotō [The gigantic white tower]. Tokyo: Shinchōsha.
Yap, Pow-Meng
  1960. The Possession Syndrome. *Journal of Mental Science* 106:151-156.
Yoshida, Masaaki; Fujii, Kazuko; and Awata, Junko
  1966. Nihonjin no on-ishiki no kōzō [Structure of the moral concept "on" in the Japanese mind]. *Shinrigaku kenkyū* [Japanese journal of psychology] 37(2):74-85; 37(4):195-203.
Yoshida, Teigo
  1967. Mystical Retribution, Spirit Possession, and Social Structure in a Japanese Village. *Ethnology* 6:237-262.

1972. Nihon no tsukimono: shakai jinruigaku-teki kōsatsu [Possession in Japan: A social-anthropological examination]. Tokyo: Chūō Kōronsha.

Yoshimoto, Inobu
1965. Naikan yonjūnen [Forty years of Naikan]. Tokyo: Shunjūsha.

Index

abandonment, 151, 214
Abegglen, 31
ability principle, 180
achievement, 44, 75, 76, 155, 165, 199, 252, 256
age, 148
aged, the, 64-65, 79, 142
aggression, 257
Aida, 40, 47, 48
ainoko, 24, 25
Aizawa et al., 226, 230
akirame, 165, 167, 188, 254
amae, 54, 55, 64, 256
amaeru and *amayakasu*, 54, 55, 58, 64, 240
American-Japanese comparison, 26, 32, 35, 40, 46, 56, 57, 60, 76, 110-111, 125, 126, 127, 130, 133, 139-140, 143, 144, 145, 147, 150, 151, 166, 192
ancestor, 236, 237, 238, 239, 242, 243, 244
Anglo-American, 11
aniki and *otōto-bun*, 173, 178, 179
animal spirit, 237, 242; fox, 237, 238, 242, 243, 244; snake 239
anomic behavior, 131-133
anonymity, 131-132
anxiety, 198-199, 213, 217
appeasement, 142-144
arrogance, 128, 132, 180, 182, 207, 213
arugamama, 223-225

assassination, 194
attendance, 52
authority, 14-16, 123, 149
autonomy, 39, 43, 156, 158, 163, 257. *See also* independence

ba, 22
bachi, 13
bakuto, 170, 171, 174
Bateson, xviii, 77, 233, 256
batsu, 78
Befu, 97, 100, 142, 106
belly, 159, 186
belongingness, 22-37, 150, 158, 184, 195, 251, 252, 253, 255
BenDasan, 6, 16, 30, 136
Benedict, xviii, 1, 12, 13, 14, 69, 79, 91, 93, 133, 139, 142, 143, 151, 192, 255
Bennett and Ishino, 51
Blau, 101
boasting, 127, 245
body, 176, 184, 186; contact, 138-142, 143; and spirit, 164
bōnasu-būmu, 98
bōnenkai, 118, 119
bontai, 235-246
Borden, 215
Boutflower, 26
breast-feeding, 138-139
bribery, 95
Buddhism, 10, 17, 102, 234, 243; Shin sect, 202; Zen, 216

Buddhist: doctrine, 165, 167; idea of reincarnation, 196; ideal, 224
bun, 51, 67-69, 82, 179, 199
bunke, 174
bushido, 190
butsudan, 27

Caudill, 63, 64
Caudill and Plath, 140
Caudill and Scarr, 156, 158, 159
Caudill and Weinstein, 139, 143, 144
Chamberlain, 193
child training, 145-153
Chinese-Japanese comparison, 6, 9, 10, 12, 33, 42, 43, 60, 130, 150
chōnin, 161
chū, 105, 108
chūgen, 98, 99
chūkaisha, 235, 236, 240, 241, 245
co-bathing, 119, 139, 148
collectivism, 25-28, 35-37, 257
comedian, 72, 130, 131
commitment, 150; role, 82, 85, 251; total, 31-32
communication, 152, 192, 195, 226, 245, 229; anticipatory, 251; body, 139; eye to eye, 48; intercultural, 252; mediated, 122; meta-, 158; nonverbal, 28, 46, 47, 252-253; refracted, 122; self-, 123; signs of, 236; subtle, 61, 246; triadic, 122; unity of, 115, 118
compensation: nonreciprocal, 107-109; three-generational, 108; rank-ordered, 108
complementarity, 77, 103, 233, 240, 241, 242, 243-244, 245, 246, 248-249, 252
conformism, 28-31, 73
conformity, 39, 41, 201, 252, 253, 254; role, 149
Confucianism, 6-9, 18
consensus, 28, 38, 125
contentment, 162-163, 168, 192, 254, 256; the child contented, 143
co-sleeping, 119, 140-141, 148
cosmology, 9-11
courtesy, 182
cram school, 75, 77
cross-situational behavior, 133-136

death, cultural investment in, 190; of mother, 188

co-dying, 197
the dead, 27, 44, 65
departed kin, 237
the dying, 61
the imagined state of being dead, 192, 212
dependency, 50-66, 144-145, 200, 207, 208, 214, 251, 253, 254, 256. *See also* interdependence
deshi. See sensei and *deshi*
deviancy, 169, 171, 190; underworld, 169-189
DeVos, 12, 13, 82, 83, 102, 155, 192, 194, 198
DeVos and Wagatsuma, 155
diary, 123, 229
discipline, 214, 231, 244
dōhai, 72
Doi, 13, 40, 46, 54, 92, 156, 226
donchan sawagi, 118
Dore, 27, 33, 34, 37, 66, 120, 140
doryoku, 75
dōzoku, 88
Durkheim, 9, 159

echo, social, 44-46
emotion, 16-19
emotional anarchism, 160-161, 255
emotionalism, 161
empathy, 38-49, 93, 122, 251, 252, 253, 257; appeal for, 56-57, 153
empathetic: forgiveness, 246; guilt, 195; kindness, 158; role, 238
emperor, 14-15, 52, 82, 123, 174, 200
employment, 31-32
en, 165, 166
Endo, 160
energy, 163, 213
enkai, 126, 135
enryo, 29, 41, 44, 125, 252
entrance examination, 32, 60, 187, 199, 256
ephemerality, 166
equality, 119, 120, 256, 257
equalitarianism, 28, 29, 78
equals in interpersonal relations, 222
esthetic sensibility, 19-21
Eto, 26
exclusiveness, 184

face, 42, 124, 132, 208, 219, 220, 221; aggressive, 126-128; mechanisms for

defending, 122-126; orientation, 231, 253; sensitivity to, 182-183
factionalism, 78
faddism, 29, 73, 74
fatalism, 165-166, 256
fear of eye-to-eye confrontation, 218-223
Feuer, 86
filial piety, 102, 176
finger-chopping, 186, 194
Fischer and Yoshida, 159
Forty-Seven Samurai, 129, 177
Fujita, 217, 228
furo, 139
Furukawa, 56
fushō-fuzui, 60

gekokujō, 16, 109
generosity, 126-127, 255
Genji, 119
German-Japanese comparison, 15
gift-exchange, 96-101; occasions for, 97-98
gimu, 93 n.; *chūshin*, 106
giri, 46, 91, 92, 93, 94, 95, 107, 158, 178, 192, 254
gisei, 189, 253
Goffman, xviii, 121, 122
Goodenough, 68
Gorer, 59
Gouldner, 91
gratitude, 92, 94, 102, 208, 209, 211, 241, 252, 255, 256
group egotism, 35
guilt, 12-13, 36-37, 48-49, 59, 83, 92, 94, 102, 152, 154, 193, 194, 209, 242, 252, 253, 256
gurentai, 170, 171

Haga, 3, 9, 10, 17, 18
Hamaguchi, 13, 70
Hammond, 137
hara, 159, 160, 163, 164, 186, 191
harakiri, 129, 190
Hasegawa, 19, 83
Hatano, 124
Hayashi, Nishihara, and Suzuki, 64
Hearn, 193
heart, 159
hesokuri, 61
Hibbet, 160
hierarchical: frame of reference, 72; orientation, 251, 252

Higa, 72
Hinsie and Campbell, 216
Hirschmeier, 34
hito, 2
hitomishiri, 222, 223
homicide, 196
honke, 157, 174
honne, 136
Hoshino, K., 175, 178
hospitality, 40
hotoke, 10
Hsu, F. L. K., 6, 88
Hsu, J., and Tseng, W., 60
Hulse, 134
humanism, 5
humility, 125, 127, 128, 180, 213-214, 246, 255
husband and wife, 40, 52-53, 60-61, 62
hypochondriac temperament, 217, 224, 226

identity, establishment of, 23-25
ie, 35, 64, 87, 172, 173
iemoto, 88
Iga, 192, 198
Iga and Ohara, 192
iki, 20, 21
ikka, 172, 173, 174, 176, 177, 178, 181, 182, 184
illness: neurosis, 216-223; the sick, 63-64, 199
independence, 65-66
individuality, 43, 156, 158, 257
indulgence, 54-55, 154, 208
infanticide-suicide, 196-197
innen, 13, 165
intellectualism, 225
interactional relativism, 6
interdependence, 138, 257
intimacy, 230, 253
intimate interaction, 114-120, 251, 254
introspection, 159-160, 204, 214, 257
introspective convolution, 218
ippondachi, 65, 66
Ishida, E., 16, 17, 87
Ishida, E. et al., 10
Ishida, R., 202, 213
ishin denshin, 115
Ishino, 51
ittaikan, 25, 46, 88, 115, 142, 197
Iwai, Hiroaki, 170, 177, 179, 180, 182, 185

Jacobson and Berenberg, 215
Japanese-Americans, 25
Jews-Japanese comparison, 16, 30
jibun, 2, 67, 156, 159, 204
jijitsu principle, 226, 228, 229
jikkan, 160
jiman, 127, 128
jingi, 181, 183, 184
joretsu ishiki, 69
junjō, 161, 162
junshi, 195, 200

kaishain, 23
Kambe, 194
kami, 234, 236, 243, 244
kamikaze pilot, 164, 191
kao, 182, 183
Kardiner, 250
Kasahara, 218, 219, 220, 221, 222
Kasuga, 31
Kato, H., 13, 74
Kato, H. et al., 22
Kato, M., 191, 192, 228
Kawai, Hayao, 19
Kawai and Kondo, 217
kawaisō, 48
Kawakita, 20
Kawasaki, 33, 36
Kawashima, xviii, 93, 106
keigo, 71
keijime, 136
kenri chūshin, 106
Kerlinger, 29
Keyerling, 17
ki, 161
Kiefer, 33
kin-tract, 88
Kirkup, 111
Kitsuse, 202, 212
Kluckhohn and Strodtbeck, 156
ko, 105, 107, 108
kobun. See *oyabun* and *kobun*
kōden, 99
kohai. See *sempai* and *kohai*
Koike, 83
kokata. See *oyakata* and *kokata*
Kojiki, 9
kokoro, 38, 159, 161, 195
Kondo, 215, 216, 217, 223, 226, 227, 228
Kora, 215, 216, 224, 227
Kora and Sato, 216, 217, 224

Korean-Japanese comparison, 6, 150
kuchi, 159
kuizome, 146
kurō, 75, 102, 103
kuyō, 239, 240, 243, 244
kyōdai, 179
kyoiku-mama, 60

Lanham, 145, 146, 147, 148, 149
Lebra, xi, 9, 45, 79, 80, 91, 257
Lee and Harvey, 85
Linton, 68, 250

Maeda, 222
magokoro, 45, 62, 162, 186, 195, 252, 253
Malinowski, 91
Maruyama, Masao, 15, 16, 109
masculinity, 58-59, 182, 185
masochism, 44, 193; moral, 189, 253
masochistic: behavior, 200; version of reverberation, 45; self-denial, 255
maternal: figure, 214; nurturance, 62, 102; role, 239
Matsuda, 138, 143
Matsumoto, 119
mature character, 164
maturity, 41, 136, 142, 167
Mead, xviii, 233, 249
meddlesomeness, 41, 158, 254
meiwaku, 41, 199, 207, 208, 209
migawari, 88, 176
military, 170; the Japanese, 109; life of prewar Japan, 51; regimentation, 84; Japanese soldiers, 56, 166
Miller, Galanter, and Pribram, xvii
mimai, 98, 99
Minami, 51, 52
Miura and Usa, 215, 216
mizukusai, 116
mobility: status, 76, 166; promotion, 177
moral: degeneration, 148; integrity, 159; rehabilitation, 201; significance, 163
morality, 11-14, 101-107, 162, 201
moratorium, social, 158-159
Morita, S., 215, 216, 218, 224, 225, 227
Morita therapy, 215-216, 223-231
Morris, I., 73
mother and child, 57-60, 124, 138, 141, 143, 144, 145, 151, 152, 153, 187,

206, 207, 209, 253. *See also* maternal
mother-in-law and daughter-in-law,
47, 62-63, 108, 109, 122, 209, 241
mouth, 159, 252
moxacautery, 150
muen, 238, 243
muga, 162, 192
Mugishima et al., 185, 186
muko yōshi, 87, 89
mura hachibu, 36
Murase, 202
mutism, 145, 258

Nadel, 68, 69
Naikan, 201-214, 227, 231, 253
Nakamura, 165
Nakane, 22, 23, 28, 34, 61, 69, 114, 116
Nakao, 215, 227
nationalism, 163, 170, 255; dedication
to the nation, 60; patriotic zeal, 187
naturalism, 21, 231
nawabari, 184, 185
Nihongi, 9
nijikai, 135
ningensei, 6
ninjō, 46, 93, 107, 161, 178, 179; *ninjō
kachō*, 64
Nitobe, 191
Niyekawa, 29
Nogi, Maresuke, 62, 195, 200
Noguchi et al., 161
Noh drama, 20, 48
Nomura, 215
Noonan, 215
Norbeck and Norbeck, 143, 146, 148
nudity, social, 116-117, 119, 121, 131,
254
nurturance, 239, 240, 243, 251

Ogino, 55
Ohara, 191, 196, 198, 199
Ohara and Reynolds, 227
okaeshi, 93, 207, 208, 211
Okakura, 20
Okamura et al., 202
omoiyari, 38-49, 102, 123, 126, 131, 158,
208, 254
omote. See ura and *omote*
on, 90-96, 101-108, 158, 177, 195, 208,
240, 251, 252, 254, 255, 267
onbu, 141
ongaeshi, 91, 94, 103, 104, 105

onjin, 91, 96, 102, 103
osekkai, 41
otōto-bun. See aniki and *otō-bun*
oya, 51, 52, 176
oyabun and *kobun*, 51, 65, 77, 110, 181,
187, 251
oyakata and *kokata*, 51
owabi, 239, 240, 243, 244
ozendate, 40

Parsons, xvi, 3, 68
Parsons and Shils, xvi, 3
parthenogenesis, 66, 77
patronage, 50-52, 53
Pelzel, 9, 10, 11, 12, 17
phobia of interpersonal relations,
218-223
pollution, 161, 162, 238, 239
pride, 36, 80
propriety, status, 78-79
psychic interaction, 218, 224, 226
psychotherapy, 124, 213. *See* Morita
therapy; Naikan
pure self, 168
purity, 161-163, 166, 191, 253, 255

rancor, 44, 193, 242
rashii, 78; *kodomo rashiku*, 78; *onna
rashii*, 78; *otoko rashii*, 78
reciprocity, 90-109, 240-241, 243, 254;
generalized, 101-107; matrix, 211;
transitive, 96, 251
regimentation, 120
Reischauer, 19, 21
repayability, 99-100, 208
repayment, 103, 208, 241, 253, 254,
255
resignation, 165-168, 166, 167, 188,
224, 254, 256
reversal, role, 61, 65; status, 96, 241,
257
reward and punishment, 150-153
Richie, 48
Riesman, 3, 74
ritual interaction, 120-131, 220, 251,
254
ritualism, 125-126, 135
Rohlen, 33
role: name, 84-85; narcissism, 83, 85,
198; versability, 85-87, 254; vicariism, 87-89, 198, 251
role-cluster personality, 250

romantic relationship, 61
rōnin, 75, 158
Ryu, 27

Sakaguchi, 226, 231
sake-cup ceremony, 175, 186
Sakurai, 91, 105
Sato, K., 202, 216
seating arrangement, 180; taking a
    seat, 181
secret language, 172
seibo, 98, 99
Seichō no Ie, 45
Seidensticker, 39
seishin kōgosayō, 218
self, 156-168, 207, 231; acceptance,
    228; consciousness, 217, 219, 228;
    reconceptualization, 211; reflection,
    203, 206, 254; repulsion, 221, 227
sempai and *kōhai*, 34, 51, 70, 72, 77, 81,
    87, 105, 181, 251
sensei and *deshi*, 51, 74, 77
seppuku, 190, 191, 193, 194
Setouchi, 62
sewa, 102, 103, 207, 211; *nyōbō*, 62
Seward, 190, 193, 194
sex, 61-63, 78, 149; sex-related spirit,
    237; sexual promiscuity, 244; sex-
    uality, 87, 119, 140; virility, 164
shame, 1, 36, 79-80, 153, 182, 199, 200,
    221
shatei, 173, 179
Shimizu, 3, 4, 48
shimpai, 102, 103, 207, 208, 209
shinda tsumori, 192, 212
shinjū, 195, 196, 197
shinkeishitsu, 215-231; disposition, 218;
    etiology, 217-218; symptoms, 216-
    217
Shin sect. *See* Buddhism
Shinto, 163, 186, 234
shinyō, 14
shugendō, 234
shugyō, 244, 245
shūshin, 57, 102
Simmel, xviii, 171
simulated kinship, 51-52, 172-176
sin, 238, 244
sincerity, 162, 194, 239, 245, 252; sin-
    cere repentance, 186
situational interaction, 110-136
situationalism, 13-14, 111; sensitive to
    situational variation, 219

skinship, 138
socialization, 137-155, 220
social preoccupation, 2-6
Sofue, xviii, 18
Sōka Gakkai, 45
Soto. See uchi and *soto*
spontaneity, 115-117; suppression of,
    121
status: commitment, 198-199; display,
    73-75, 243-245, 255; elevation,
    75-77, 89, 103, 245, 252, 254, 255;
    mobility, 76
    dichotomization of behavior,
    70-73
    hierarchical orientation, 179-180
    rank order, 69-70, 79
    vertical alliance, 77-78, 158
stranger anxiety, 222-223, 230
strategic manipulability of *amae*, 55
strategy, 43, 80; the creditor's expecta-
    tion and, 95-96; status as a, 80-82;
    shared belongingness as a, 33-34
student revolt, *taishūdankō*, 76
substitutive role, 87
Sugano, 70
suicide, 130, 190-200, 212, 237, 238; an
    aged person's, 199; cohesive, 197;
    double, 18, 192, 195-196; mass, 191;
    remonstration, 193; Squad, the, 51;
    vicarious, 197-198
Suisen-Sansei-Iganashi System, 30
sumanai, 92, 94, 209, 214
Sumiya, 200
sunao, 149
supernatural, 232-249, 236, 237; god,
    44, 65, 144; spirit, 239, 240
supplication, 237-240, 243, 244, 251
Suwaki et al., 202, 204
Suzuki, T., 216, 227, 231

taiatari, 164, 186
taijin-kyōfu-shō, 218
taitoku, 225, 226, 228
Takada, 196
Takeda, 203, 207, 213
Takiuchi, 196, 197
Takizawa, 41, 42
Taoism, 234
Tashiro, 76
tatemae, 136
tateshakai, 69
teasing, 152
tattooing, 185

tekiya, 171, 174
temper tantrum, 143, 150
therapy, 43, 54, 232; group, 230; folk, 150; social, 43; work, 228-229; therapeutic community, 229-231
togetherness, 26-27, 145, 195, 254
toilet training, 146
traveling gangster, 28, 158; itinerant *yakuza*, 184
trustful, 143
trustworthiness, 45
trustfulness, 148
tsukisoi, 64
tsumi, 238, 239, 244

uchi and *soto*, 112, 113
un, 165, 166
uniforms, 24, 119
ura and *omote*, 112, 113
urami, 44
Ushijima, 149

Veith, 215
vicarious: achiever, 251; *deshi*, 74; experience, 36, 38; kinship, 88; role, 252; satisfaction, 89; sharing, 153. *See also* role: vicariism
Vogel, 32, 40
Vogel and Vogel, 142, 143, 144, 145, 151
vulnerability, 43-44

Wallace, A. F. C., 248, 249
Wallace, W. L., 210
war prisoner, 13, 86, 133
Watsuji, 12, 47, 162
Watzlawick et al., 158, 233
weaning, 138, 139, 146
Weber, 86
wet-rice agriculture, 17, 83
work ethic, 83

xenophilia, 74, 255, 256

yakuza, 5, 169, 189
Yamada, 160
Yamamoto, 109, 133
Yamato *damashii*, 163
Yamato race, 24, 163
Yamamura, K., 35
Yamamura, Y., 62, 63, 154, 155
Yamazaki, 81, 89
Yap, 233
yokubō shizenshugi, 18, 117
Yoshida, M. et al., 91
Yoshida, T., 222
Yoshimoto, 202, 203, 204, 206, 207, 210, 213, 214

zakone, 120
zange, 92
Zen. *See* Buddhism
Zengakuren, 86

About the Author

Takie Sugiyama Lebra is well qualified to comment on Japanese behavior. Reared and educated in Japan (B.A. Gakushuin University, Tokyo), she completed her M.A. and Ph.D. at the University of Pittsburgh. Professor Lebra has made frequent field trips to Japan in recent years, and from this research has published articles on Japanese religion, moral values, healing, and women. The conclusions in this book are based on her personal experiences as a "native" and as a critical observer, and on her extensive reading of Japanese as well as Western literature relevant to this subject. She is professor of anthropology at the University of Hawaii, and is the editor (with William P. Lebra) of *Japanese Culture and Behavior: Selected Readings.*

Of related interest—

Brandon's Guide to Theater in Asia
by James R. Brandon

The living theater of Asia offers the traveler a unique cultural experience rich in exotic colors, sights, and sounds. This complete guide by a noted authority solves the problem of how to find it in 14 Asian countries. Describes the many theatrical forms, seasons, and environments. Lists theater addresses, hours and days of performances, best seats, when and where to buy tickets, prices in local currencies—and many other useful facts.
192 pages, illustrated, 1976, ISBN 0-8248-0369-8, paper

The Kabuki Theatre
by Earle Ernst

"This is the best book on Kabuki in a Western language and is likely to remain so for a very long time" (*Times Literary Supplement*). Every aspect of Kabuki— from historical development, through details of production, to attitudes of the Japanese audience—spiced with references to actors, roles, and plays, and illustrated with 58 excellent photographs.
AN EAST-WEST CENTER BOOK 東西
368 pages, 1974, ISBN 0-8248-0319-1, paper

Unsui: A Diary of Zen Monastic Life
by Giei Satō

Text by Eshin Nishimura, edited by Bardwell L. Smith
Daily life in the monastery is portrayed here in 97 delicate watercolor sketches drawn by Giei Satō, recollecting with humor and steadfast warmth his days as an *unsui*, an apprentice monk. Each of the charming, cartoonlike drawings is enhanced by a brief description of the event depicted, a touch of Zen teaching, or a note on monastic life. "Satō's art is a total refreshment . . . handlettered, rich with pastel colors, the book is appealing as well as enlightening" (*Publisher's Weekly*).
AN EAST-WEST CENTER BOOK 東西
142 pages, 6-7/8" x 9-7/8", 1973, ISBN 0-8248-0277-2, cloth
ISBN 0-8248-0272-1, paper

The Japanese Mind: Essentials of Japanese Philosophy and Culture
edited by Charles A. Moore

"This is a great book, extremely useful for a comprehensive approach to Japanese culture" (*Journal of Asian Studies*).
AN EAST-WEST CENTER BOOK 東西
384 pages, 1967, ISBN 0-8248-0077-X, paper

Available at your bookseller, or write for prices and ordering information to:
THE UNIVERSITY PRESS OF HAWAII
2840 Kolowalu St.
Honolulu, Hawaii 96822

Anthropology/Travel – Japan   ISBN 0-8248-0460-0

JAPANESE PATTERNS OF BEHAVIOR

"This volume should establish Takie Lebra among the first-rank inter-
preters of Japanese culture. . . . what I find particularly excellent in this
volume is Lebra's capacity to integrate not only a personal point of view,
but an appreciation of what others have written. . . . To sum up, Lebra's
volume takes us well beyond the chrysanthemum and the sword."

—George A. DeVos, in *American Anthropologist*

"The best introduction to the dynamics of Japanese interpersonal relations
that has yet come to hand. It is truly indispensable reading for all who have
any involvement with Japan or the Japanese."   —*Choice*

"A highly useful source recommended to all those interested in the
behavior and personality of Japanese and not contented with heretofore
available sources. It will remain a standard reference for a long time to
come, both for novices and specialists."   —*Monumenta Nipponica*

TAKIE SUGIYAMA LEBRA is well qualified to comment on Japanese
behavior. Reared and educated in Japan, she completed her doctorate in
the United States, and now lives and teaches in Hawaii. Professor Lebra
has made frequent field trips to Japan in recent years, and from her
research has published articles on Japanese religion, moral values, healing,
and women. Her conclusions in this book are based on these personal experiences as a "native" and as a critical observer, and also on extensive
Japanese as well as Western literature relevant to this subject. A professor
of anthropology at the University of Hawaii, she is editor (with William P.
Lebra) of *Japanese Culture and Behavior: Selected Readings*.

AN EAST-WEST CENTER BOOK 叐
The University Press of Hawaii
Honolulu, Hawaii 96822   *Cover design by A. O. K. Hammond*